STUDIA MISSIONALIA

Publication of the Faculty of Missiology, Gregorian University.

Publication de la Faculté de Missiologie de l'Université Grégorienne.

MARIASUSAI DHAVAMONY, S.J., *Director*.

MISSION AND HUMAN PROGRESS

MISSION ET PROGRÈS HUMAIN

EDITRICE PONTIFICIA UNIVERSITÀ GREGORIANA
ROMA 1998

IMPRIMI POTEST

P. GIUSEPPE PITTAU, S.I.
Rector Universitatis
Romae, die 19 aprilis 1998

IMPRIMATUR

Dal Vicariato di Roma, 23 aprile 1998
Sac. LUIGI MORETTI
Segretario Generale

ISBN 88-7652-787-7
© E.P.U.G. - ROMA - 1998

EDITRICE PONTIFICIA UNIVERSITÀ GREGORIANA
Piazza della Pilotta, 35 - 00187 Roma, Italia

CONTENTS — SOMMAIRE

Mission and Human Progress
Mission et Progrès Humain

ROLAND MEYNET, Solidarité humaine dans l'Epître aux Galates 1

GERALD O'COLLINS, Jesus Christ the Liberator: in the Context of Human Progress 21

MARIASUSAI DHAVAMONY, Christian Theology of Plenary Humanism 37

PIERO GHEDDO, Annuncio e Progresso Umano 57

SERGIO BERNAL, Chiesa e Progresso Umano 81

JOSEPH JOBLIN, Promotion humaine dans Populorum Progressio 103

JOHANNES SCHASCHING, Die Soziallehre der Kirche und der Fortschritt der Völker 119

PETER K. SARPONG, Justice and Peace and the Integrity of Creation 133

CEAM, Promotion Humaine et Mission Evangelisatrice 145

MUHIB O. OPELOYE, Religious Humanism among the Yoruba of Nigeria 161

PAUL JACKSON, Christian-Muslim Collaboration in Human Development 177

FABC-FEISA, Christian-Muslim Dialogue for Justice and Solidarity 193

PETER C. PHAN, Human Development and Evangelization 205

SWAMI RAMA, A Hindu Call to Humanism 229

MADAN DEVANAYAKAM, The Ultimate Objectives of Nehru's Socialism 237

ALEX WAYMAN, Human Progress according to Buddhism 251

YVES RAGUIN, Le Bouddhisme et le Bien-Être des Autres 269

FABC, Alla ricerca della giustizia: La Chiesa in dialogo con la società in Sud-Est Asia 279

CONTRIBUTORS — COLLABORATEURS

SERGIO BERNAL, Professor of Sociology and the Social Doctrine of the Church, Gregorian University, Rome.

MADAN DEVANAYAKAM, Professor of Sociology, Government College, Coimbatore, India.

MARIASUSAI DHAVAMONY, Professor of Theology and Phenomenology of Religions, Gregorian University, Rome.

PIERO GHEDDO, Missiologist, PIME, Milano.

PAUL JACKSON, Director of Christian-Muslim Dialogue Centre, Patna, India.

JOSEPH JOBLIN, Segretario, Commissione: «Storia dei Movimenti sociali e delle strutture sociali», Rome.

ROLAND MEYNET, Professor of New Testament Exegesis, Gregorian University, Rome.

GERALD O'COLLINS, Professor of Dogmatic Theology, Gregorian University, Rome.

MUHIB O. OPELOYE, Associate Professor of Islamic Studies, Lagos State University, Nigeria.

PETER C. PHAN, Professor of Theology, The Catholic University of America, Washington D.C. USA.

YVES RAGUIN, Ricci Institute, Taipei, Taiwan.

PETER C. SARPONG, Bishop of Kumasi, Anthropologist and Theologian, Ghana.

JOHANNES SCHASCHING, Professor of the Social Doctrine of the Church, Wien.

CONTRIBUTORS — COLLABORATEURS

SWAMI RAMA, The Himalayan Institute, Honesdale, USA.

ALEX WAYMAN, Professor of Sanskrit and Buddhist Studies, Columbia University, New York.

Solidarité humaine dans l'Épître aux Galates

ROLAND MEYNET

On sait que l'un des sujets majeurs, sinon le sujet central, de l'Épître aux Galates est le rapport entre la loi et la foi. Le problème que Paul est amené à traiter est de savoir si les disciples de Jésus issus du paganisme doivent être soumis aux prescriptions de la Loi de Moïse ou si la foi au Christ suffit au salut, sans les oeuvres de la Loi. Faut-il, en d'autres termes, devenir juif pour être chrétien? Doit-on, en particulier, se faire circoncire, pour entrer avec Abraham dans l'alliance avec Dieu et dans la communion totale avec les disciples juifs de Jésus? Pour ne pas sortir des conduites les plus concrètes, un juif chrétien peut-il prendre ses repas avec ceux qui partagent la même foi au Christ ressuscité mais qui ne sont pas circoncis et ne pratiquent pas les mêmes prescriptions alimentaires que lui? Dans quelle mesure donc et de quelle manière les «judéo-chrétiens» et les «pagano-chrétiens» (ou «ethnico-chrétiens») sont-ils véritablement unis? La solidarité est ainsi au coeur du débat.

Pierre, le premier des Douze, avait été affronté très tôt à cette question: allait-il, oui ou non, partager la nourriture du centurion romain Corneille? Les Actes racontent combien il avait résisté à une telle perspective et qu'il n'avait pas fallu moins d'une triple révélation divine pour qu'il se laisse enfin persuader d'entrer dans la maison de ce païen (Ac 10). Plus tard, à Antioche (selon Ga 2,11-14; voir la planche, p. 5)[1], le

---

[1] Voir R. MEYNET, «Composition et genre littéraire de la première section de l'Épître aux Galates», *Paul de Tarse. Congrès de l'ACFEB (Strasbourg, 1995)*, ed. J. Schlosser, LeDiv 165, Paris 1996, 51-64. Malheureusement, les mises en page du texte de Paul n'ont pas été imprimées dans cet article comme il avait été prévu; c'est pourquoi elles sont reproduites ici, pour aider la lecture.

même problème se posera à lui: certes, il n'éprouvait plus de difficulté à partager le repas des pagano-chrétiens de cette ville. Mais, quand des émissaires de la communauté de Jérusalem arrivèrent, il cessa de manger avec les chrétiens non juifs et entraîna même son compagnon juif Barnabé dans son hypocrisie (2,13). C'est qu'il craignait qu'on lui reprochât d'avoir adopté une conduite qui rompait nettement avec les prescriptions de la Loi de Moïse. Les chrétiens juifs de Jérusalem en effet étaient restés attachés aux règles strictes de la Loi qui interdisaient de frayer avec les païens, fussent-ils disciples de Jésus, partageant pourtant la même foi au Christ. La solidarité humaine la plus élémentaire, celle qui consiste à accepter de manger avec l'autre, était ainsi gravement bafouée.

Et pourtant, quelque temps auparavant (Ga 2,1-10; voir la planche, p. 4), un accord était intervenu sur ces questions entre Paul et les autorités de Jérusalem. Tite, le compagnon ethnico-chrétien de Paul n'avait pas été contraint de se soumettre à la circoncision (Ga 2,3); la position de ce verset, en plein centre de la première partie, souligne l'importance de la décision, malgré les contestations des adversaires de Paul qui les qualifie de «faux frères» (Ga 2,4-5). L'attitude des notables de Jérusalem envers Tite est ainsi en contraste frappant avec celle de Képhas telle qu'elle est stigmatisée en position parallèle, au centre de la partie correspondante (2,13; voir la planche, p. 5): alors que Tite, le compagnon païen de Paul, n'est pas contraint de se faire circoncire pour être en communion avec les Juifs chrétiens de Jérusalem, à Antioche au contraire, Barnabé, le compagnon juif de Pierre, est entraîné à se séparer des païens chrétiens avec lesquels ils avaient coutume de manger!

Une fois réglé le problème personnel de Tite, l'accord de Jérusalem prévoit la répartition des tâches entre Paul et Pierre (2,7-9): tandis que ce dernier annoncera l'Évangile aux circoncis, Paul se consacrera à l'évangélisation des incirconcis. Encadrant cela, est énoncée la seule loi qui devra régler les rapports entre les deux composantes de l'Eglise, et c'est justement celle de la solidarité: les notables de Jérusalem n'imposent à Paul et aux incirconcis «rien de plus» (2,6) sinon «seulement de se souvenir des pauvres» (2,10). La solidarité économique entre chrétiens, qu'ils soient juifs ou qu'ils soient d'origine païenne, est l'unique loi à laquelle ils seront soumis. Toute la conduite chrétienne se résume dans cette unique exigence du partage des biens. Et Paul de signaler en terminant qu'il a bien eu soin de s'y tenir.

C'est surtout dans la troisième section de l'Épître (5,2-6,18), qualifiée de «parénétique», c'est-à-dire «morale», que le lecteur s'attend à trouver énoncés et explicités les conseils que l'apôtre donne à ses destinataires pour les aider à régler leur conduite. La première section (1–2) en effet est appelée habituellement, bien qu'improprement[2], «autobiographique» et la deuxième section (3,1–5,1) est dite «doctrinale». Il fallait cependant commencer par relever comment, dans l'histoire du débat, et des conflits, entre judéo-chrétiens et ethnico-chrétiens, la question de la solidarité s'était imposée comme la seule loi qui devait régir leurs rapports.

Les commentateurs ont souvent tendance à accorder moins de place et donc de poids à la dernière section qu'à la première et surtout à la seconde. Et pourtant, elle représente en quelque sorte le point d'aboutissement de toute l'Épître. S'il est capital en effet de connaître son histoire et plus encore sans doute de réfléchir sur sa foi, il n'en est pas moins important de savoir ce qu'il faut faire. L'objet de cette enquête requiert donc que l'on s'attarde davantage sur cette dernière section. Il n'est pas question de fournir ici une analyse rhétorique détaillée de la section; il sera cependant utile de s'appuyer sur les résultats d'une telle analyse pour traiter du thème de la solidarité, qui, on le verra, ne se limite pas aux relations entre chrétiens, mais qui commande aussi leurs rapports avec tous les hommes.

La troisième section de l'Épître comprend trois séquences: deux séquences relativement brèves (5,2-12 et 6,11-18) encadrent une séquence nettement plus développée, puisqu'elle est formée de trois passages (5,13-18; 5,19-26; 6,1-10)[3].

---

[2] Voir la discussion sur le «genre littéraire» de cette section dans l'article cite a la note précédente.

[3] Pour la définition précise des termes «passage», «séquence» et «section» voir R. MEYNET, *L'Analyse rhétorique, une nouvelle méthode pour comprendre la Bible. Textes fondateurs et exposé systématique*, «Initiations», Les Éditions du Cerf, Paris 1989.

L'ACCORD DE JÉRUSALEM
(Ga 2,1-10)

¹ Ensuite, après quatorze ans,   de nouveau je montai à   *Jérusalem*,
avec **BARNABÉ**,   en prenant aussi avec moi   ***Tite***.
. ² Je montai à la suite d'une révélation.
Je leur exposai **L'ÉVANGILE**   que je proclame chez   ***les Nations***
mais en privé aux **notables**   pour éviter de courir ou d'avoir couru en vain.

> ³ Or pas même Tite mon compagnon, qui était   ***grec***,
> ne fut contraint de se faire   *circoncire*.

⁴ (C'était) à cause des faux-frères infiltrés qui s'étaient introduits
pour espionner notre liberté   que nous avons dans le Christ Jésus
. afin de nous réduire en esclavage,
⁵ auxquels pas même une heure   nous acceptâmes de nous soumettre
afin que la vérité de **L'ÉVANGILE**   demeure   pour   ***vous***.

> ⁶ Mais de la part de ceux qui passaient pour des **notables**,
>   (ce qu'alors ils pouvaient être peu m'importe,
>   Dieu ne regarde pas la personne de l'homme)
> à moi les **notables** n'imposèrent *rien de plus*.
> ---
> ⁷ Mais voyant au contraire
>   - que m'avait été confiée   **L'ÉVANGILE** *du Prépuce*
>   . comme à Pierre   *de la Circoncision*
>   . ⁸ car Celui qui suscita Pierre   pour l'apostolat   *de la Circoncision*
>   - m'a suscité moi aussi   pour   ***les Nations***.
>   ---
>   . ⁹ et connaissant la grâce qui m'avait été donnée,
>   ---
> Jacques, Képhas et Jean, les **notables** qui sont les colonnes,
> me donnèrent la droite ainsi qu'à **BARNABÉ** en signe de communion:
>   - nous devions être nous   pour   ***les Nations***
>   . eux   pour   *la Circoncision*.
> ---
> ¹⁰ *Seulement* des pauvres **nous devions** nous souvenir.
> Et cela j'ai eu à coeur de le faire.

Le conflit d'Antioche
(Ga 2,11-21)

¹¹ Quand vint Képhas à Antioche,
je lui résistai en face car **IL ÉTAIT BLÂMABLE**:
    + ¹² Car avant que ne viennent certains d'auprès de Jacques
        IL MANGEAIT AVEC LES NATIONS;
    – mais quand ils vinrent,
        IL SE DÉROBA ET SE TINT À L'ÉCART,   craignant ceux de la circoncision.

    ¹³ Et le suivirent-dans-**L'HYPOCRISIE**   le reste des Juifs,
    de sorte que même Barnabé   fut entraîné par son **HYPOCRISIE**.

¹⁴ Mais quand je vis qu'**IL NE MARCHAIT PAS DROIT**
selon **la vérité de l'Évangile**, je dis à Képhas devant tous:
    + «Si toi qui es   *Juif*, tu vis comme les Nations et non comme les Juifs,
    – comment veux-tu contraindre les **Nations** à judaïser?

¹⁵ Nous, nous sommes *Juifs* de naissance
et non pas de ces **PÉCHEURS**   des   **Nations**.
    ¹⁶ Mais sachant que n'est justifié aucun homme par les oeuvres de la Loi
        sinon par **la Foi en Jésus Christ,**
            nous aussi dans le Christ Jésus nous avons cru
        afin d'être justifiés par **la Foi en Christ**
    et non par les oeuvres de la Loi,
car par les oeuvres de la Loi "n'est justifiée aucune chair".
• ¹⁷ Mais si, cherchant à être justifiés dans le Christ,
    nous aussi sommes trouvés **PÉCHEURS**,
= alors le Christ est serviteur du péché. Certes pas!
    ----
        ¹⁸ Car si JE REBÂTIS ce que J'AI ABATTU,
        je me démontre moi-même **TRANSGRESSEUR**.
    ----
¹⁹ Moi en effet, par la Loi, à la Loi j'ai été mis à mort;
afin de vivre pour Dieu,   avec le Christ je suis crucifié.
    ²⁰ Je vis non plus moi,   mais vit en moi le Christ.
Ce que maintenant je vis dans la chair, je le vis dans **la foi au Fils de Dieu**
    lui qui m'a aimé et s'est livré lui-même pour moi.
²¹ Je ne rejette pas **la grâce de Dieu**;
• Car si c'était par la Loi que venait la justification,
= alors le Christ serait mort pour rien.»

Les séquences extrême de la troisième section

Les séquences extrêmes se correspondent (voir p. 7). Paul y revient sur le problème de la circoncision que ses adversaires judaïsants veulent imposer aux Galates ethnico-chrétiens. Cette question particulière peut paraître secondaire au lecteur moderne; elle est en revanche emblématique du rapport à la Loi toute entière. C'est en effet par la circoncision que le prosélyte devient juif et par conséquent qu'il est soumis à toutes les autres prescriptions de la loi de Moïse; c'est donc bien la question morale qui est abordée ici, puisqu'il s'agit de savoir ce qu'il faut faire ou ne pas faire. Et ce faire n'est pas un simple détail, anatomique ou liturgique, puisqu'il engage toute la conduite morale de ses destinataires: «un peu de ferment fait fermenter toute la pâte» (5,9).

Chacune de ces deux séquences se trouve focalisée sur une affirmation extrêmement claire et forte qui dénie toute valeur aussi bien à la circoncision qu'à l'incirconcision et qui oppose à cette alternative d'une part «la foi opérant par l'amour» (5,6d) et d'autre part «la nouvelle création» (6,15d). Le verbe «opérer» de 5,6d marque nettement que, si elle s'oppose à «la loi», «la foi» n'en implique pas moins un faire. La première séquence joue donc le rôle d'introduction de la section parénétique de l'Épître. Quant à la séquence symétrique (6,11-18), écrite de la main même de l'Apôtre (6,11), elle signe et authentifie toute la lettre; cependant, sa fonction première n'en est pas moins de conclure la troisième section, faisant inclusion avec la première séquence (5,2-12). Cette dernière séquence fait donc partie de la section proprement parénétique de l'Épître: preuve en est qu'elle énonce la «règle» de conduite (6,16) que suivront l'ensemble des disciples du Christ. La solidarité — mieux, l'unité — de ceux que Paul appelle en finale «frères» (18b) ne sera pas assurée par la marque physique de la circoncision, mais par «les marques de Jésus» (17c), c'est-à-dire par sa Croix (12e.14b). Cette nouvelle marque, opposée à celle de la circoncision et de son contraire, est tellement radicale qu'elle est qualifiée, au centre de la séquence, de «nouvelle création» (15d); c'est elle qui constitue «l'Israël de Dieu» (16c).

Première séquence (Ga 5,2-12)	Dernière séquence (Ga 6,11-18)
² VOICI, **moi**, Paul, JE VOUS DIS: si vous vous faites *circoncire*, Christ ne vous servira de rien. ³ Je l'atteste de nouveau à tout homme qui se fait *circoncire*: il se doit de faire toute LA LOI.	¹¹ VOYEZ avec quelles grosses lettres JE VOUS ÉCRIS de ma propre main: ¹² Tous ceux qui veulent faire bonne figure dans LA CHAIR ce sont ceux qui imposent que vous soyez *circoncis* uniquement afin de n'être pas *persécutés* pour LA CROIX du Christ; ¹³ car les *circoncis*, eux-mêmes n'observent pas LA LOI mais ils veulent que vous soyez *circoncis* afin de se vanter dans votre CHAIR.
⁴ Vous êtes retranchés du Christ, vous qui dans LA LOI vous justifiez; de LA GRÂCE vous êtes déchus. ⁵ Pour nous, en effet, c'est par l'Esprit, de LA FOI que nous attendons l'espérance de la justification.	¹⁴ Pour **moi**, puissé-je ne pas me vanter sinon dans LA CROIX de notre Seigneur Jésus Christ par qui le monde est crucifié pour **moi** et **moi** pour le monde.

⁶ Dans le Christ Jésus,
ni la *circoncision*   n'a de valeur,
ni le prépuce,
    mais LA FOI opérant par l'amour.
	¹⁵ Car
	ni la *circoncision* n'est quelque chose ni le prépuce,
	    mais LA NOUVELLE CRÉATION.

⁷ Vous couriez bien! Qui vous a coupés d'obéir à la vérité? ⁸ Cette conviction ne vient pas de Celui qui vous appelle. ⁹ Un peu de ferment fait fermenter toute la pâte.	¹⁶ Et tous ceux qui suivront cette règle, la paix soit sur eux et la miséricorde et sur l'Israël de Dieu.
¹⁰ **Moi**, je suis convaincu pour vous dans le Seigneur que vous ne penserez pas autrement. Quant à celui qui vous trouble, il en portera la peine, quel qu'il soit.	¹⁷ Désormais, que personne ne me cause des ennuis, car **moi**, je porte dans mon corps les marques de Jésus!
¹¹ Pour **moi**, FRÈRES, si je prêche encore la *circoncision*, pourquoi suis-je encore *persécuté*? Il est donc retranché, le scandale de LA CROIX! ¹² Ils devraient être coupés, ceux qui vous bouleversent!	¹⁸ LA GRÂCE de notre Seigneur Jésus Christ soit avec votre *esprit*, FRÈRES. Amen!

Ce qui se trouve ainsi posé dans les deux séquences extrême, et spécialement en leur coeur, sera déployé à loisir dans la longue séquence centrale.

La séquence centrale de la troisième section

Premier passage (Ga 5,13-18)

¹³ Vous, en effet, c'est à la liberté que vous avez été appelés, frères.

– Seulement pas la liberté comme prétexte à **la chair**,
+ mais par *L'AMOUR* servez-vous *les uns les autres.*

= ¹⁴ *En effet* toute **LA LOI** s'accomplit en une seule parole:
= «*TU AIMERAS* ton prochain *comme toi-même.*»

: ¹⁵ *Mais si* vous vous mordez et déchirez *les uns les autres*
: regardez de ne pas être détruits *les uns par les autres.*

. ¹⁶ Or je dis:
+ Marchez selon *L'ESPRIT*
– et vous ne satisferez pas la convoitise de **la chair**.

= ¹⁷ *En effet* **la chair** convoite contre *L'ESPRIT*
= et *L'ESPRIT* contre **la chair**;
= en effet ils s'opposent *l'un à l'autre*
= afin que vous ne fassiez pas *ce que vous voulez.*

: ¹⁸ *Mais si* vous êtes conduits par *L'ESPRIT*,
: vous n'êtes pas sous **LA LOI**.

Ce passage comprend deux parties construites en parallèle. — Le premier segment de la première partie (13) précise la nature de la liberté chrétienne, de manière négative (13b) puis positive: de manière paradoxale, la «liberté» consiste dans le «service», ou, sans doute mieux, «l'asservissement» mutuel (13c). Le premier segment de la deuxième partie (16) est de composition analogue, puisque, après le membre introductif[4], il reprend, en ordre inverse, un membre positif, à l'impératif (16b qui correspond à 13c) et un membre négatif

---

[4] «Paul use souvent des mots *legô de* = «je dis donc», pour annoncer qu'il reprend une idée déjà exprimée en lui donnant un nouveau développement (3,17; 4,1; 5,2, etc.)» (P. BONNARD, *L'Épître de saint Paul aux Galates*, CNT [N] Neuchâtel-Paris, 1972², p. 112).

(16c qui correspond à 13b); «la chair» qui était opposée à «l'amour» (13bc) est maintenant opposée à «l'Esprit» (16bc). — Les morceaux centraux (14 et 17) commencent également par «en effet» et donnent donc la raison du commandement donné précédemment. — Enfin, les derniers segments (15 et 18) qui commencent tous deux par «mais si vous» s'opposent à ce qui les précède; comme dans les premiers segments (13 et 16), se retrouve dans les deux membres de ces segments finaux l'opposition entre une affirmation (conditionnelle: 15a.18a) et une négation (15b. 18b).

«La Loi» se retrouve au centre de la première partie (14a) et à la fin de la deuxième (18b)[5]; la première fois elle est présentée de manière positive comme un équivalent de «l'amour», la deuxième fois de manière négative, puisqu'elle est opposée à «l'Esprit» et mise en équivalence avec «la chair». La chute du passage ne laisse pas de surprendre[6].

L'idée de solidarité est fortement soulignée dans la première partie avec «les uns les autres», en termes finaux des morceaux extrêmes (13c.15ab), mais aussi en finale du morceau central avec «comme toi-même» (14b); cette solidarité joue dans l'amour (13c.14), mais peut jouer aussi dans le mal (15a) et aboutir à la mort (15b). La reprise de «l'un à l'autre» dans la deuxième partie (17c) indique au contraire le combat entre la chair et l'Esprit qui est au coeur de chacun Ainsi, deux lois s'opposent, au centre de chacune des deux parties: la loi de l'amour qui doit régler les rapports entre les hommes et ce que Paul appellera ailleurs «la loi du péché»[7] ou de la «convoitise» qui empêche l'homme de faire ce que pourtant il désire profondément, qui l'empêche de répondre à la vocation à laquelle il a été appelé, «la liberté» (13a). Le paradoxe, ou le mystère de la liberté est qu'elle ne saurait s'exercer et se réaliser que dans le service mutuel (13c.14b); le paradoxe, ou le mystère de la Loi est que l'on ne peut en être libéré (18b) qu'en s'y soumettant, qu'en l'accomplissant (14).

---

[5] Selon la loi n° 4 de Lund (voir R. MEYNET, *L'Analyse rhétorique*, p. 147).
[6] «Après le verset 16 on aurait attendu une conclusion du paragraphe qui aurait dit: Si vous êtes guidés par l'Esprit, vous n'êtes plus sous le pouvoir de la chair» (B. CORSANI, *Lettera ai Galati*, CSANT, Genova 1990, p. 356).
[7] Rm 7,23-25; 8,2.

La vie est à ce prix, car, si la solidarité ne joue pas dans le service mutuel entre les hommes, ce sera l'animalité qui l'emportera (15a) et qui portera à la mort (15b).

Le fondement de la solidarité est indiqué par le qualificatif que Paul utilise pour s'adresser à ses destinataires, dès le début: c'est parce que, comme Cain et Abel, ils sont «frères» (13) que les hommes sont tentés par la «convoitise de la chair» (16c), mais aussi qu'ils «sont appelés» (13a) à «se servir les uns les autres par l'amour» (13c). Il est enfin bien évident que le terme de «frères» implique la filiation divine: Dieu n'est pas nommé une seule fois dans le passage, mais il est présent dès le début, puisque c'est lui le sujet réel du premier verbe, «vous avez été appelés», qui est un passif théologique. Répondant à celui de la première phrase, le verbe de la dernière phrase, «vous êtes conduits» a un complément d'agent: c'est «l'Esprit» de Dieu (18a).

Deuxième passage (Ga 5,19-26)

Comme le premier, ce passage est formé de deux parties construites en parallèle. Les premières sous-parties (19-21b et 22-23a) sont introduites par deux segments (19a et 22a) qui s'opposent en tous points: les «oeuvres» désignent ce que l'homme produit, le «fruit» au contraire ce qui lui est donné et qu'il cueille; les «oeuvres» sont au pluriel et elles divisent, le «fruit» au singulier est unifié et unifiant. La multiplicité des «oeuvres de la chair» se répercute dans une longue liste de quinze vices qui, d'ailleurs, ne s'achève pas, puisqu'elle se disperse sur «et choses semblables» (19b-21b); inversement, la liste des vertus (22b-23a) est plus courte et fermée sur un chiffre qui indique souvent la totalité.

Il n'est pas question ici de traiter la question difficile et très discutée de l'organisation interne des deux listes et de leurs rapports mutuels. Qu'il suffise de noter que, à part «idolâtrie et sorcellerie» (20a) qui regardent le rapport à Dieu, pratiquement tous les autres termes des deux listes concernent la relation avec les hommes. Même la «tempérance» à la fin de la liste des vertus (23a) engage le prochain, dans la mesure où elle s'oppose à «beuveries et ripailles» de la fin de la liste des vices (21b): en effet, l'expérience commune montre que c'est souvent là que naissent ou éclatent les conflits; on peut sans doute en dire autant pour les trois premiers termes de la liste des vices (19b).

[19] Elles sont manifestes	LES OEUVRES	DE *LA CHAIR*, lesquelles sont:
- fornication,	impureté,	débauche,
- [20] idolâtrie,	sorcellerie,	
- inimitiés,	discorde,	jalousie, **emportements**,
- disputes,	dissensions,	scissions, [21] *envies*,
- beuveries,	ripailles	et choses semblables.

: Je vous dis cela comme j'ai déjà dit:

— ceux qui pratiquent *ces choses*
— n'hériteront pas du royaume de Dieu.

[22] Mais	LE FRUIT	DE L'ESPRIT, c'est:
+ amour,	joie,	paix,
+ patience,	bienveillance,	bonté,
+ confiance, [23]	douceur,	tempérance.

: Contre de *telles choses* il n'est pas de Loi.

:: [24] Mais ceux qui sont au Christ ont crucifié *LA CHAIR*
— avec *les passions* et *les convoitises*.
[25] Si nous vivons par L'ESPRIT, alignons-nous sur L'ESPRIT.
:: [26] Ne cherchons pas *la vaine gloire*,
— nous *provoquant* les uns les autres, nous *enviant* les uns les autres.

Les deuxièmes sous-parties (21cde et 23b-26) concluent chacune des deux parties, mais de manière surprenante: on aurait pu s'attendre en effet à ce que les versets 24-26 qui reviennent sur «passions» et «convoitises» (24b) ainsi que provocation et envie mutuelles (26b) soient placés en finale de la première partie, en opposition directe et contiguë avec la liste des vices[8]; d'autre part «hériter le royaume de Dieu» de 21e

---

[8] «Convoitises» de 24b (*epithumíais*) est de même racine que «emportements» de 20b (*thumoí*) et le participe «nous enviant» de 26b renvoie à «envies» de 21a.

désigne ce que recevront ceux qui cueillent le fruit de l'Esprit et on le verrait donc mieux, au positif, après le déploiement du fruit de l'Esprit. Mais, par un jeu subtil de négations (spécialement en 21e et 26a), les deux sous-parties sont, pour ainsi dire, interverties. Ce qui a pour effet, d'une part de mettre en valeur, au milieu du passage, la filiation divine niée (21e) et, en finale (26b) une ultime mise en garde contre la négation de la fraternité entre les hommes. Encore une fois, c'est la solidarité humaine qui est en question. Le ton demeure ainsi menaçant, à la fin de chacune des deux parties du passage, ce qui souligne sans doute l'importance capitale de ce qui est en jeu: les manquements à la fraternité mettent gravement en péril la filiation divine.

Dernier passage (Ga 6,1-10)

Ce passage est formé de deux parties (1-5 et 6-10); étant donné les difficultés et l'importance du texte pour le thème de la solidarité humaine, chacune de ses deux parties mérite d'être analysée d'abord en elle-même, avant d'être lues ensemble.

La première partie comprend trois morceaux: deux morceaux développés (1-2a et 3-5) encadrent un morceau très court (2b). Les conditionnelles par lesquelles commencent les morceaux extrêmes (1a et 3a) jouent le rôle de termes initiaux, tandis que les unimembres avec lesquels ils s'achèvent (2a et 5; où est repris le même verbe «porter», où «fardeaux» est synonyme de «charge» et où «chacun» s'oppose à «les uns des autres») remplissent la fonction de termes finaux. Ces deux morceaux envisagent deux situations complémentaires, ou deux aspects complémentaires de la même situation, celle des rapports entre les membres de la communauté: en effet, d'un morceau (1-2a) à l'autre (3-5), la même opposition «soi-même – les autres» se retrouve («un homme» et «le» en 1ab – «toi-même» et «toi aussi» en 1cd; «sa propre oeuvre» et «en soi seulement» – «non pas en un autre» en 4). Le premier morceau recommande la correction fraternelle (1ab) avec l'humilité nécessaire à cet exercice (1cd). Ce dernier segment est ambigu et a été interprété de manières diverses: ou bien en effet celui qui redresse son frère doit savoir qu'il est menacé, lui aussi, de tomber dans la même faute, ou bien il peut être tenté d'orgueil en comparant sa propre conduite avec celle de celui qu'il corrige.

```
+ ¹ Frères,              même SI est pris  UN HOMME       en quelque faute,
+ vous les spirituels,   redressez -       LE             en esprit de douceur,

      : veillant à       TOI-MÊME
      : à ne pas         TOI AUSSI être tenté.

              = ² LES UNS DES AUTRES    portez      les fardeaux!
```

| ET AINSI VOUS ACCOMPLIREZ LA LOI DU CHRIST. |

```
+ ³ Car SI quelqu'un pense  être          quelque chose,
    alors qu'il             n'est         rien,          il se leurre lui-même;

  - ⁴ mais              SA PROPRE OEUVRE       que chacun l'examine,
      : et alors        EN SOI SEULEMENT       il aura de quoi se vanter
      : et              NON PAS EN UN AUTRE.

              = ⁵ CHACUN en effet       portera       sa propre charge!
```

Si l'on tient que cette partie forme un tout fortement unifié, et si l'on considère que le morceau symétrique (3-5) du premier (1-2a) commence par «car», il semble préférable de penser que le dernier morceau est un complément du premier. Les finales (2a et 5) paraissent donner la clé, qui opposent «les uns des autres» et «chacun»: s'il faut corriger les autres en pensant aussi à soi-même, il faut s'examiner soi-même sans se comparer aux autres. Ainsi, les conclusions des deux morceaux, qui peuvent sembler contradictoires au premier regard, sont en réalité complémentaires.

Ces conseils, qui pourraient paraître de simple sagesse humaine, sont appelés par le morceau central (2b) «loi du Christ». Le génitif, «du Christ», peut être compris en deux sens qui ne s'excluent pas l'un l'autre: la loi à laquelle le Christ a obéi lui-même, celle qu'il a donnée à ses disciples.

```
+  ⁶ Que CELUI QUI EST INSTRUIT DE LA PAROLE   fasse participer
+  à tous          SES BIENS                       CELUI QUI L'INSTRUIT.

                  : ⁷ Ne vous y trompez pas,
                  : on ne se moque pas de Dieu.

= En effet    ce    qu'aura   semé          un homme,
= c'est       cela  qu'il     moissonnera.

      = ⁸ Car    celui qui   sème          dans SA CHAIR
        : de     la chair    moissonnera   la perdition;
      = mais     celui qui   sème          dans L'ESPRIT
        : de     l'Esprit    moissonnera   la vie éternelle.

= ⁹ De faire    le bon      ne nous décourageons pas:
= car en son temps nous     moissonnerons,
                  : si nous ne nous relâchons pas.

                  : ¹⁰ Ainsi donc, tandis que nous avons le temps,
+  oeuvrons      LE BIEN       envers      tous,
+  et surtout                  envers      NOS COMPAGNONS DE FOI.
```

La seconde partie comprend trois morceaux: deux morceaux qui comprennent six membres (6-7 et 9-10) encadrent un morceau plus court qui compte quatre membres (8).

Le premier morceau (6-7) est formé de trois segments bimembres: le premier segment (6ab) est construit de manière concentrique[9], le dernier (7cd) de façon parallèle. Le morceau est organisé de manière concentrique: le troisième segment (7cd), qui commence avec «en effet», se rapporte au premier segment qu'il explique par une sorte de loi générale: le sujet de 7cd, «un homme» renvoie au sujet de 6, «celui qui est instruit de la Parole»; «ce» et «cela» de 7cd renvoient à

---

[9] En suivant l'ordre du grec:

   QU'IL FASSE PARTICIPER
                        celui qui est instruit de
                                            la Parole
                        celui qui l'instruit
   À TOUS SES BIENS.

avec verbe et nom régi aux extrémités, sujet et bénéficiaire ensuite, «Parole» enfin au centre qui est en relation avec les extrémités, en particulier «tous ses biens».

«tous ses biens» de 6b. Ainsi le partage des «biens» est présenté non comme une perte, mais comme une sorte d'investissement qui portera du fruit. Il est aussi possible de comprendre que la loi générale de la fin du morceau (7cd) s'applique non seulement à celui qui fait participer à tous ses biens celui qui l'instruit, mais aux deux personnages: aussi bien à celui qui instruit de la «parole» qu'à celui qui le «fait participer à tous ses biens». Au centre (7ab), intervient un troisième personnage, «Dieu»: c'est lui qui donnera la moisson (comme le dira explicitement la fin du morceau central: 8d) comme c'est lui dont la «Parole» est transmise et qui, à travers le prédicateur, est le donateur ultime la Parole.

Le morceau central (8) est construit de manière tout à fait parallèle et oppose «sa chair» à «l'Esprit», «la perdition» à «la vie éternelle».

Le troisième morceau (9-10) comprend deux trimembres qui commencent de manière semblable: les premiers membres sont à l'impératif, «faire le bon» (*to kalón*) est synonyme de «opérer le bien» (*to agathón*). Les membres centraux (9c et 10a) insistent sur les conditions temporelles de persévérance et d'urgence du commandement.

Les segments qui encadrent le morceau central (7cd et 9) ont en commun de reprendre l'image des semailles et de la moisson, comme dans le morceau central («semer» – «moissonner» en 7cd, 8ab, 8cd, «faire le bon» – «moissonner» en 9ab). Dans les segments extrêmes (6 et 10) «biens» de 6b est repris au singulier en 10b; «celui qui est instruit de la Parole» et «celui qui l'instruit» de 6 sont tous deux «compagnons de Foi» (10c). A noter que «tous» est repris en position symétrique: au début du second membre (6b) et à la fin de l'avant-dernier membre (10b).

Partant d'un exemple concret de solidarité (entre l'évangélisateur et l'évangélisé), Paul élargit l'application de cette règle de manière absolue: «faire le bon» (9a), «oeuvrer le bien» (10b); il l'élargit aussi en notant en finale que, si la solidarité doit régir les relations entre chrétiens, «les compagnons de foi» (10c), cela n'est qu'un cas particulier, même s'il est privilégié, d'une règle qui s'applique à «tous» (10b).

+ ¹ **Frères**, même si *un homme est pris en quelque faute*,
+ **vous** *LES SPIRITUELS*, REDRESSEZ-le en esprit de douceur,
　　　: veillant à **toi**-même
　　　- à ne pas **toi** aussi être tenté.
+ ² Portez les fardeaux les uns des autres.

> Et ainsi vous accomplirez la Loi du Christ.

　　= ³ Car si *quelqu'un* pense être quelque chose, n'étant rien,
　　= *il* se leurre lui-même;
　　　　: ⁴ mais que *chacun* examine sa propre oeuvre,
　　　　: et alors en soi seulement il aura de quoi se vanter
　　　　- et non pas en un autre.
　　= ⁵ Car *chacun* portera sa propre charge.

+ ⁶ Que *CELUI QUI EST INSTRUIT* de la parole FASSE-PARTICIPER
+ de tous ses biens *celui qui l'instruit*.

　　　　: ⁷ Ne vous y trompez pas,
　　　　: on ne se moque pas de Dieu.
+ En effet ce qu'aura semé un homme,
+ c'est cela qu'*il* moissonnera.

> ⁸ Car celui qui sème dans sa chair à lui
> 　de　　la chair　　　moissonnera　la perdition;
> mais celui qui sème　dans l'Esprit
> 　de l'Esprit　　moissonnera　la vie éternelle.

　　= ⁹ De faire　le bien ne **nous** décourageons pas:
　　= car en son temps **nous** moissonnerons,
　　　　　: si nous ne nous relâchons pas.

　　　　　: ¹⁰ Ainsi donc, tandis que **nous** avons le temps,
　　= 　oeuvrons le bon envers tous,
　　= et surtout envers les **compagnons de foi**.

Les deux parties du passage sont complémentaires. Leurs débuts marquent bien les deux catégories de personnes visées: la première partie s'adresse aux «spirituels», chargés de «redresser» celui qui pèche (1), la seconde est adressée à «l'enseigné» qui doit partager ses biens avec «celui qui l'enseigne» (6). Les deux verbes employés ont des connotations semblables[10]; on peut donc penser que les «spirituels» sont les responsables de la communauté, dont la fonction est de veiller à son unité. Quant au verbe par lequel commence la deuxième partie, *koinō-néō* («faire-participer»), il est de la même famille que *koinō-nía*, «le partage», «la communion»: c'est encore l'unité de la communauté qui est visée, sa solidarité, mais cette fois-ci, non plus du côté des responsables, mais des disciples. Ainsi, la première partie veut régler les relations du maître avec son disciple, la deuxième du disciple avec son maître.

La première partie est centrée sur la loi du Christ (2b) qui est, si l'on peut dire, l'origine ou la cause de la conduite des disciples, tandis que la deuxième partie est centrée sur la conséquence de cette conduite (8), à savoir la sanction qui sera appliquée par «Dieu» (nommé en 7b).

À noter enfin que, tandis que la fin de la première partie (3-5) et le début de la deuxième (6-8) sont toutes deux à la troisième personne, en revanche le début de la première partie (1-2) est à la deuxième personne («vous» puis «tu») et la fin de la dernière partie (9-10) est à la première personne du pluriel: Paul finit donc par s'intégrer à la communauté à laquelle il s'adresse au début, réalisant ainsi la communion à laquelle il appelle tous ses destinataires; l'élargissement est souligné par l'emploi de «tous» (10b). Cette composition concentrique est confortée par l'inclusion formée par «frères» au tout début (1a) et par «compagnons de foi» tout à la fin (10c; surtout si l'on se rappelle que le mot traduit par «compagnons» peut signifier aussi «parents»)[11].

---

[10] Le verbe *katartízō* (6,1b) signifie d'une part «mettre en ordre», c'est-à-dire «arranger», «former un tout», «gouverner» ou «diriger», d'autre part «remettre en ordre», c'est-à-dire «mettre en état», «former un tout de divers éléments» (BAILLY, *Dictionnaire Grec-Français*); c'est pourquoi il a été traduit par «redresser».

[11] Il pourrait donc être tentant de traduire la dernière expression par «frères dans la foi», comme le fait la *Bible de Jérusalem*.

L'ensemble de la deuxième séquence (Ga 5,16–6,10)

5,¹³ VOUS en effet, c'est à la liberté que vous avez été appelés, FRÈRES. Seulement, que la liberté ne serve pas de prétexte pour la chair, mais par *L'AMOUR* asservissez-vous *LES UNS AUX AUTRES*.

¹⁴ Car toute la **LOI s'accomplit** en une seule parole:
«Tu *AIMERAS* ton prochain comme toi-même.»

¹⁵ Mais si vous vous mordez et vous déchirez les uns les autres, prenez garde de ne pas être détruits les uns par les autres.

¹⁶ Je le dis: marchez selon *l'Esprit*, et vous ne satisferez pas la convoitise de *la chair*.

¹⁷ Car *la chair* convoite contre *l'Esprit* et *l'Esprit* contre *la chair*:
Car ils s'opposent l'un à l'autre afin que vous ne *fassiez* pas ce que vous voulez.

¹⁸ Mais si vous êtes conduits par *l'Esprit*, vous n'êtes pas sous la **LOI**.

¹⁹ Or les oeuvres de *la chair* sont manifestes; ce sont fornication, impureté, débauche, ²⁰ idolâtrie, sorcellerie, haines, querelle, jalousie, fureurs, disputes, dissensions, scissions, ²¹ envies, beuveries, ripailles et choses semblables.
Je vous préviens, comme je vous en ai déjà prévenus:
ceux qui *pratiquent* ces choses n'hériteront pas du ROYAUME DE DIEU.

²² Mais le fruit de *l'Esprit* c'est
AMOUR, joie, paix, patience, bienveillance, bonté, confiance, ²³ *DOUCEUR*, tempérance.
Contre de telles choses il n'y a point de **LOI**. ²⁴ Ceux qui sont au Christ Jésus ont crucifié *la chair* avec ses passions et ses convoitises. ²⁵ Si nous vivons par *l'Esprit*, conformons-nous à *l'Esprit*. ²⁶ Ne cherchons pas la vaine gloire, nous provoquant les uns les autres, nous enviant les uns les autres.

6,¹ FRÈRES, même si quelqu'un est pris en faute, VOUS les spirituels, redressez-le en esprit de *DOUCEUR*, veillant toi-même à ne pas être tenté, toi aussi. ² Portez les fardeaux *LES UNS DES AUTRES*!

Ainsi vous **accomplirez** la **LOI** du Christ.

³ Car si quelqu'un se croit quelque chose alors qu'il n'est rien, il se leurre. ⁴ Que chacun examine sa propre *oeuvre*, et alors il aura de quoi se vanter pour lui seul, et non pour autrui. ⁵ Car chacun portera son propre fardeau.

⁶ Que celui qui est instruit de la Parole fasse participer à tous ses biens celui qui l'instruit. ⁷ Ne vous y trompez pas: on ne se moque pas de Dieu. Quoi qu'un homme sème, il le moissonnera.

⁸ Car celui qui sème dans *sa chair* moissonnera, de *la chair*, la corruption;
celui qui sème dans *l'Esprit* moissonnera, de *l'Esprit*, LA VIE ÉTERNELLE.

⁹ Ne nous décourageons pas de *faire* le bien; au temps voulu, nous moissonnerons, si nous ne nous relâchons pas. ¹⁰ Ainsi donc, tandis que nous en avons le temps, *oeuvrons* le bien envers tous, mais surtout envers nos compagnons de foi.

Les passages extrêmes (5,13-18 et 6,1-10) sont parallèles entre eux:

— ils commencent avec l'apostrophe «frères», accompagnée de «vous» (5,13 et 6,1); ce sont les seuls endroits de la séquence où cette apostrophe apparaisse;

— les premières parties sont centrées sur une mention de la «loi», chaque fois «accomplie» (5,14 et 6,2b); ces morceaux centraux sont précédés du même «les uns les autres» (5,13c et 6,2a);

— les secondes parties des passages extrêmes (5,16-18 et 6,6-10) sont centrées sur des morceaux où se retrouve la même opposition entre «la chair» et «l'Esprit».

C'est sur cette opposition qu'est construit le passage central de la séquence (5,19-26). La «Loi» se retrouve au centre des premières parties des passages extrêmes (5,14 et 6,2b), à la fin du premier passage (5,18) et au coeur de la deuxième partie du passage central (5,23). «Toute la Loi» s'accomplit dans «l'amour» (5,14): ce mot se retrouve au début du premier passage (5,13) et au début de la liste du «fruit de l'Esprit»; il ne se retrouvera pas dans le dernier passage, mais «douceur», l'avant-dernier terme de la liste du fruit de l'Esprit (5,23) sera repris au début du dernier passage (6,1)

L'opposition entre «oeuvres» et «fruit» au début de chacune des deux parties du passage central (5,19a et 22a) retentit dans l'ensemble de la séquence:

— les mots appartenant au champ sémantique du «faire» se retrouvent dans les trois parties: «faire» (*poiéō*) en 5,17b et 6,9a, «oeuvre(s)» (*érgon*) en 5,19a et 6,4b, «oeuvrer» (*ergázomai*) en 6,10a, enfin «pratiquer» (*prássō*) en 5,21c.

— «fruit» de 5,22a appartient au même champ sémantique que «moissonner» de 6,7-9 (quatre fois). Le premier fruit de l'Esprit est «l'amour» (5,22a), ce que l'on moissonnera de l'Esprit est «la vie éternelle» (6,8b); «le Royaume de Dieu» (5,21d) entre dans la même série («hériter» de 6,21d comme «moissonner» de 8ab sont au futur).

Le schéma suivant tente de synthétiser l'ensemble de la section.

Seule compte la Foi opérant par		L'AMOUR	5,2-12

La Loi	s'accomplit dans	L'AMOUR	5,13-18
	Les OEUVRES	de la chair	
	-------	-------	5,19-26
	Le FRUIT	de l'Esprit	
L'amour	s'accomplit en	VIE ÉTERNELLE	6,1-10

Seule compte	la	CRÉATION NOUVELLE	6,11-18

Ainsi la section toute entière entend énoncer la seule loi à laquelle sont soumis tous les disciples de Jésus, d'où qu'ils viennent, aussi bien les judéo-chrétiens que les ethnico-chrétiens. Cette loi n'abolit pas la loi de Moïse, elle «l'accomplit» (5,14). C'est «la loi du Christ» (6,2) que, comme leur maître, les chrétiens doivent «accomplir». Telle que Paul la présente, cette loi ne prévoit guère ce qu'on a coutume d'appeler «les devoirs envers Dieu». Elle est toute orientée à la régulation des rapports entre les hommes. Non pas seulement des chrétiens entre eux, mais avec tous. Il faut bien noter en effet que, si la séquence centrale est sans aucun doute de construction concentrique, cela n'empêche aucunement qu'elle culmine en quelque sorte sur le dernier verset (6,10): même si le devoir de solidarité des chrétiens «envers leurs compagnons de foi» est naturellement prioritaire, c'est l'exigence de faire le bien envers «tous» qui y est énoncée comme la règle de base.

Jesus Christ the Liberator:
in the Context of Human Progress

GERALD O'COLLINS

Two terms, "the Liberator" and "Human Progress", obviously demand some separate reflection before we can reasonably face the central question implied by the title given to me for this article: what does Jesus' liberating work have to do with human progress? What then should be said about these two terms? Let us look first at "Jesus Christ the Liberator".

In his *De Spiritu Sancto* of 375 A.D. St Basil of Caesarea highlighted the functional thrust of Jesus' titles:

> Because of the many ways grace is given to us poor human beings by him whose goodness and wisdom are manifold, he is described by innumerable other titles: Shepherd, King, Physician, Bridegroom, Way, Door, Fountain, Bread, Axe, and Rock. These titles do not describe his nature, but...are concerned with his manifold energies, by which he satisfies the needs of each (8.17).

In what ways do the "manifold" goodness, wisdom and energies of the Liberator satisfy our needs and give us grace? How can this title be expounded, justified and so take its place with the "innumerable other" christological titles?

To say that "Jesus Christ" is "the Liberator" is close to uttering a tautology. After all the theophoric name of "Jesus" or *Yehosua* in Hebrew means "God saves" or "God is salvation". While the Hebrew Scriptures extend the title of "Saviour" to some human figures, the New Testament calls only God (8 times) and Jesus (16 times) "Saviour". The anointing of kings (e.g. 1 Sam 16:12-13) or of prophets (e.g. Isa 61:1-9) made some figures a "Messiah" or "Christos" with a mission to lead and deliver people who were suffering from various needs. In the case of Jesus the link between anointing and such a liberating function emerges clearly when St Luke summarizes the public ministry: "God anointed Jesus of Nazareth with the Holy Spirit and with power...he went about doing good and healing all who were oppressed by the devil" (Acts 10:38). The divine power exercised by the anointed One prevailed over any satanic power to deliver those who had fallen under the control of the devil.

Naming Jesus "the Liberator" is almost synonymous with naming him not only "Saviour" but also "Redeemer". Despite the long-standing vogue of the latter title in public liturgy and popular piety, the New Testament never applies it as such to Jesus. Only Moses is called *lutrōtes* (Acts 7:35) — that is to say, "redeemer" (New Jerusalem Bible) or "liberator" (New English Bible, New Revised Standard Version and Revised English Bible). The New Testament yields here a range of related verbs such as *lutroō* ("redeem, set free, liberate"), *agorazō* ("buy, redeem, ransom"), *exagorazō* ("set free"), *eleutheroō* ("set free"), *nikaō* ("conquer, overcome"), *ruomai* ("save, rescue, deliver") and *sōzō* ("save, rescue, deliver"), and related nouns such as *lutron* ("means of release, means of redeeming") and *apolutrōsis* ("setting free, deliverance, release, liberation") and *eleutheria* ("freedom, liberty"). The rare *eleutherōtes* ("liberator") came into some marginal usage only after the first-century A.D.; *eleutherōsis* ("setting free"), while present in classical Greek, is not used by the New Testament. The Lord's Prayer acknowledges God (the Father) to be the One who "delivers" (Matt 6:13; *ruomai*). Perhaps "the Deliverer" (*ho ruomenos*) of Rom 11:26 is also the Father, but more likely Paul refers the title to Christ[1]. Elsewhere in the Pauline corpus Jesus is said to have freed or liberated (*eleutheroō*) us (Gal 5:1) and to be our *apolutrōsis* or "redemption" (1 Cor 1:30). This language justifies setting the christological titles of "Redeemer", "Liberator" and

---

[1] On the probability that *ho ruomenos* is christological rather than theological — that is to say, refers to Christ rather than to God (the Father) — see J.A. FITZMYER, *Romans*, The Anchor Bible 33 (New York: Doubleday, 1993), pp. 619-20, 624-25. The NEB, NRSV and REB all translate *ho ruomenos* as "the Deliverer", whereas the NJB prefers "the Redeemer".

"Deliverer" alongside a title that the New Testament frequently assigns to Jesus: the "Saviour".

Here it is interesting to remark on the linguistic choices made by the *Catechism of the Catholic Church*. Apropos of Christ's "work", the nouns "redemption" ("rédemption" in the original French edition[2]), "salvation" ("salut"), and "liberation" ("libération") occur, and in that order as regards their frequency. The same order of frequency holds true with the verbs "redeem" ("rédimer"), "save" ("sauver"), and "liberate" ("libérer"). The *Catechism* calls Jesus "Redeemer" ("Rédempteur", as well as the adjective in such phrases as "l'amour rédempteur" and "le sacrifice rédempteur"), "Saviour" ("Sauveur"), and only twice "Liberator" ("Libérateur"; nn. 457, 633)[3].

Having paid some attention to the biblical background for the christological title of "the Liberator", let us look at the other key term in the title of this article: "human progress". What is it and how do we evaluate it? Does it simply converge with social and political progress: with universal education and involvement in government; with proper food, housing, medical care and employment opportunities for all; with full respect for children, women, minorities, native peoples, the handicapped and the aged; with a wide-ranging and effective care for the environment; with the promotion of all the basic human rights and responsibilities — in short, with the full implementation of justice and consequently of peace? Details could be filled out here by drawing on papal and conciliar documents such as John XXIII's *Pacem in Terris* (1963), the Second Vatican Council's *Gaudium et Spes* (1965), Paul VI's *Populorum Progressio* (1967), John Paul II's *Sollicitudo Rei Socialis* (1987) and *Centesimus Annus* (1991). In their vision of human progress, Christian believers include, of course, the movement of the Holy Spirit in leading all men and women towards the consummation of Christ's rule and God's kingdom. In the light of the incarnation, life, death and resurrection of Jesus, together with the mission of the Holy

---

[2] Paris: Mame/Plon, 1992.
[3] The English version of the *Catechism* (Vatican City: Libreria Editrice Vaticana, 1994), unlike the French and other editions, does not list in its index the noun "liberation".

Spirit, true human progress entails necessarily a christological, pneumatological and eschatological dimension. This article takes the second term "human progress" in an integral sense that refuses to bracket off the eschatological work of Christ and his Spirit in leading all people towards an authentic social and political progress. Hence I understand "the context of human progress" to entail always and everywhere the liberating work of the crucified and risen Jesus. After these terminological preliminaries, let me focus the title of this article by putting two questions: how did the earthly Jesus' preaching of the kingdom concern human progress? What connection might be drawn now between the liberating work of Jesus and the final reign of God?

I

Beyond question, Jesus' message of the kingly power and rule of God was central to his proclamation of liberation. God ruled and would rule, because he had come and was coming with strength to save his people. Some insist that this message was totally "spiritual" and not "material"[4]. Thus Rudolf Schnackenburg wrote in his now classic *God's Rule and Kingdom*: "The salvation proclaimed and promised by Jesus in this reign and Kingdom of God is purely religious in character"[5]. Did Jesus take no stand on social and political issues? (In putting this question, one must insist that "political" is not to be reduced to national, even less nationalistic, issues. It refers to all matters of public and civic concern). Without going as far as Schnackenburg, John Meier assures his readers: "Jesus was not interested in and did not issue pronouncements about *concrete* social and political reforms, either for the world in general or for Israel in *particular*. He was not proclaiming the reform of the world; he was proclaiming the end of the world". Here Meier stresses a major

---

[4] A desire to correct a recurrent stereotype that salvation in the Old Testament was understood to be material or political and salvation in the New Testament was understood to be spiritual and other-worldly motivated me when writing the article "Salvation" for the *Anchor Bible Dictionary*, ed. D.N. FREEDMAN, vol. 5 (New York: Doubleday, 1992), pp. 907-14.

[5] *God's Rule and Kingdom* (London: Burns and Oates, 1968), p. 95.

difference between Jesus and such Old Testament prophets as Amos, Hosea, Isaiah, and Jeremiah:

> While prophesying judgment and salvation in the future, [they] were also passionately concerned about *particular* social and political ills of their day. To take but a few examples: Amos denounces the cruel treatment of prisoners of war (Amos 1:3-2:3) and selling the poor into slavery to pay a paltry debt (2:6-7). Hosea pronounces judgment on the dynasty of the Israelite King Jehu for Jehu's massacre of the previous royal house of Omri (Hos 1:4). The Books of Isaiah and Jeremiah are replete with *concrete* commands and warnings that the prophets give to kings and officials of Judah, even on *particular* matters of statecraft and international diplomacy[6].

Like an antiphon, "concrete" and "particular" chime through this passage and leave one with the questions: do pronouncements of a social and political character (about ills to be corrected and reforms to be introduced) always have to be "concrete" and "particular"? Can the agenda for social and political reform also be broad and general?

One should agree with Meier about the priority of the future kingdom in Jesus' proclamation and normal absence of quite specific pronouncements in that proclamation. However, Jesus' rejection of divorce by either partner (Mark 10:2-12 parr.), command to love one's enemies (Luke 6:27-28 par.), and foundation for men *and* women of a new egalitarian family based on obedience to the divine will (Mark 3:34-35 parr.) shows how he was *also* concerned with human progress in the social area. By extending the divine mercy to tax-collectors, who collaborated with Roman and Jewish rulers, by speaking out against hatred of foreigners in the parable of the Good Samaritan (Luke 10:30-37), and by prophetically electing the Twelve as a symbol of his desire to reform Israel, Jesus took stands that clearly touched political life of people, both nationally and internationally. His table

---

[6] J.P. MEIER, *A Marginal Jew. Rethinking the Historical Jesus*, vol. 2 (New York: Doubleday, 1994), p. 331; italics mine.

fellowship with impure outcasts (Mark 2:13-17; Matt 11:19; Luke 15:1; 19:7) and his attitude in welcoming women as disciples (e.g. Luke 8:1-3) showed Jesus leading the way in delivering people from bondage with a religious revolution with obvious social and political implications.

But let me pause for a moment to focus matters on Jesus' attitude towards religion and law and try to expand the case for his being a non-reformer. At first glance it looks as though Jesus did not aim at changing anything very much, but remained within the "special" structures prescribed by Israel's religion. He preached only to the chosen people. With hardly an exception (see Mark 7:24-30) his ministry did not extend to the gentiles. When he healed a leper, he urged the man to show himself "to the priest and offer the gift that Moses commanded" (Mark 1:43). The ten lepers whom he cured were likewise instructed to show themselves to the priests (Luke 17:14). Jesus observed the passover and other religious feasts. He not only worshipped in the Temple, but also courageously drove out those who defiled the sacred place by their mercenary activities (Mark 11:15-19). To sum up: it appears that Jesus respected the religious claims of the sacred law, the holy times and the sacred place of the Temple which worked to separate the chosen people from the rest of the human race.

Further, it can well seem that Jesus accepted the legal, economic and social structures of his time almost as if they were absolute and endorsed by God. When did he challenge the institution of slavery, seek any radical reconstruction of society or question the legal system of occupying military forces? A letter-writer to *Time* magazine (6 November, 1972) scorned some American clergy for countenancing civil disobedience, because that showed how they had "forgotten that *Jesus never interfered with Caesar's laws*" (italics mine). Surely it looks as if Jesus understood the public order of his world as an unchallengeable, even sacred, order of things?

These are serious reflections and lively objections. Let us take them up in turn. First, although Jesus did restrict his preaching to the chosen people, he called humanity as such to decision. He addressed his Jewish audiences as human beings. He invited them *qua* men and women to accept the good news, repent and be saved. He spoke to them in parables, the language of everyday, not the special religious language of some "holy" people. Jesus lived in one world, the world of all humankind. It was for both Jews and Gentiles (see Matt 8:11) that Jesus expected the future kingdom of God[7].

Second, he demanded a neighbourly love towards any other human beings in need. He expressed this teaching in the parable of the Good Samaritan (Luke 10:25-37) and also, if it goes back to his ministry, the account of the judgement by the Son of Man (Matt 25:31-46)[8]. For Jesus the responsibility of realistic love was supreme. When the need confronted him, he healed the handicapped on the sabbath — an action of mercy which his critics interpreted as violating sacred law (e.g. Mark 3:1-6; Luke 13:10-17)[9].

Third, he respected but refused to emphasize Temple sacrifice and other special offerings. By praising the poor widow for her tiny offering to the Temple treasury, he challenged common convictions about such offerings (Mark 12:41-44). Even if Jesus seems to have usually observed Jewish religious customs, he questioned or even abolished the accepted sacred/profane distinctions in the matter of food and eating (Mark 7:1-23). Although he risked physical injury and courted murderous hostility by driving out those who defiled the Temple, nevertheless, he attached no absolutely sacred value to the place. The Temple and its cult would soon be replaced by something better (Mark 14:57-58 parr.). In the material Matthew collected for the Sermon on the Mount (Matt 5-7) Jesus repeatedly laid claim to an authority above the sacred law of Moses.

Finally, Jesus refused to endorse as sacred the public order of his time. He broke open and changed the contemporary social structures by the ways he which he spoke and behaved. His new brotherhood and sisterhood deprived old family bonds of their sacrosanct value. "Whoever does the

---

[7] See J.P. MEIER, *A Marginal Jew*, vol. 2, pp. 309-17.
[8] See D.A. HAGNER, *Matthew 14-28*, Word Biblical Commentary (Dallas: Word Books, 1995), pp. 737-47.
[9] On these two healing stories see MEIER, *A Marginal Jew*, vol. 2, pp. 681-85.

will of God", he declared, "is my brother, sister and mother" (Mark 3:35; see Matt 8:21-22 par.). He associated with and found disciples among women, persons considered inferior in social and religious status. He represented a sufficiently real threat to Caesar's laws for his death to come at the hands of a Roman prefect.

In contrasting Jesus with the Old Testament prophets, Meier highlights the way Jesus proclaimed "the end of the world", whereas they were passionately concerned about "the social and political ills of *their day*" (italics mine). Here one should not forget that the prophets also announced the day of the Lord, that day when God was to intervene decisively in judgement against the wickedness of Israel (Jer 17:16-18; Amos 5:18-20; 8:9-10; Ezek 7:1-27), of Babylon (Isa. 13:6,9), or of Egypt (Ezek. 30:3). On this doomsday God would judge sinners and manifest the divine glory (Isa 2:11-12). Jeremiah (30:5-9) and later prophets came to fill the phrase with a somewhat more positive sense, which had not been totally lacking in earlier usage. "The day of the Lord" would bring Israel's restoration in a time of final conflict and final victory (Zech 14:1-21). This doomsday of judgement was to destroy evildoers and spare the good (Mal 3:13-4:3). In essence to talk of that day was to see God as the awesome future of history, not only for the chosen people but also for all nations. One should not ignore the way in which the prophets went beyond a here and now concern with particular social evils to announce the future and final action of God in putting an end to bad situations. Their message of doomsday and the end of the world was not totally different from Jesus' proclamation of the end of the world and what it would bring, the final kingdom.

To be fair to Meier, in commenting on the "poor" and the beatitudes he not only relates Jesus' message of the divine kingdom with that of the prophets and the psalms but also opposes any sharp contrast between a purely socioeconomic meaning and purely religious one:

> In the background of the beatitudes stands the whole OT picture of God as the truly just king of the covenant community of Israel, the king who does what Israel's

human kings often failed to do: defend widows and orphans, secure the rights of the oppressed, and in general see justice done (so, e.g., Ps 146:5-10). It is not by accident that the first of the core beatitudes has as its promise the kingdom of God [Matt 5:3 par.]. What human kings have not done and apparently will never do in Israel, God the king will do on the last day. (This, by the way, is why one should not play off a "purely" socioeconomic sense of "the poor" against a "purely" religious sense; given the OT background in the Prophets and Psalms, the first sense implies the second). The core beatitudes indeed declare a revolution, but it is a revolution wrought by God alone as this present world comes to an end[10].

It is the last sentence that bothers me. Of course, it will take God "on the last day" to bring about this revolution in its fullness. But here and now Jesus calls on those who hear him to anticipate this full revolution by accepting new attitudes towards the poor, moral outcasts, marriage partners, women, children, collaborators, and foreigners. The prayer he passes on to his disciples includes a revolutionary attitude towards those who have offended and harmed us: forgiving others now is a condition for receiving God's definitive forgiveness on the last day (Matt 6:12 = Luke 11:4). When proclaiming the beatitudes and the rest of his message, does Jesus expect no progress to be made within human history towards implementing his call to establish a new religious order that *also* entails new social, economic and political responsibilities? Is nothing of the future kingdom to be implemented within this word before it all comes to an end as God's final kingdom arrives? Would Jesus disagree with John Paul II's call to realize now something of that future kingdom by trying to liberate people from evil? In the encyclical letter *Redemptoris Missio* (7 December 1990) the Pope writes: "Working for the Kingdom means acknowledging and promoting God's activity, which is present in human his-

---

[10] Ibid.

tory and transforms it. Building the Kingdom means working for liberation from evil in all its forms" (nr. 15).

Meier certainly does not want to endorse a dualistic worldview that would deny any relevance of the kingdom preaching to innerworldly realities, as if redemption were simply a kind of Platonic or even Gnostic flight to a better, spiritual world. But, being convinced that for Jesus "the definitive arrival of God's kingly rule was imminent", he concludes that for Jesus "calls for social and political reform" were "beside the point"[11]. However, the more one stresses the imminent arrival of the final kingdom, the more puzzling it becomes to find Jesus inculcating new attitudes, which obviously affect lasting structures within society and between societies: towards marriage partners, women, children, those considered moral outcasts, foreigners, and enemies. It would seem "beside the point" to call for such revolutionary changes, if God's kingly rule was just about to be arrive.

Commenting on Luke 4:11-30, Jesus' programmatic sermon in the Nazareth synagogue, Meier notes how it affirms God's power to be at work in setting free the imprisoned and exiled. He rightly comments that this sermon may be "the result of Luke's creative redaction of Mark's story of Jesus in Nazareth in Mark 6:1-6"[12]. Nevertheless, that scene expresses at least Luke's view of what Jesus' proclamation aimed at: a new religious and social order that would bring liberation for those oppressed by various forms of evil.

To complete this sketch of elements of human progress entailed by Jesus' preaching of the kingdom, let us look at several sayings or blocks of sayings that stand a good chance of stemming from the earthly Jesus himself[13]. Evidently Jesus understood his ministry to involve both a struggle with Satan and demonic forces which had been controlling human affairs (e.g. Luke 10:18) and the establishment of God's kingly rule. He saw human existence as a kind of battlefield dominated by one or other invisible, otherworldly forces: either

---

[11] MEIER, *A Marginal Jew*, vol. 2, p. 332.
[12] *A Marginal Jew*, vol. 2, p. 492.
[13] For helpful comments on Luke 10:18, Mark 3:27, Luke 11:20, Luke 17:20-21 and Luke 10:23-24, see Meier, *A Marginal Jew*, vol. 2, pp. 492-93, 417-22, 404-23, 434-39 and 423-30, respectively.

God or Satan. Through his exorcising activity in particular, Jesus showed himself to be a kind of bandit who had begun to achieve the divine victory over the satanic forces (Mark 3:27). He summed up what was happening: "if it is by the finger of God that I cast out the demons, then the kingdom of God has come to you" (Luke 11:20 par.). This talk of "the finger of God" suggests the divine power working through a visible, human agent, and may well refer back to Moses and Aaron. Just as they were empowered by God to liberate a suffering people from slavery (Exod 8:15), so now Jesus enjoyed the same power to deliver those enslaved by demonic power. In another apparently authentic saying Jesus rejected signs for calculating the precise timing for the end of the age; he invited his hearers to open their eyes and see the kingdom already present in his ministry: "the kingdom of heaven is not coming with things that can be observed; nor will they say, 'Look, here it is!' or 'There it is!' For, in fact, the kingdom of God is among you" (Luke 17:20-21). Elsewhere we hear Jesus interpreting his ministry as fulfilling the divine promises of salvation: "Blessed are the eyes that see what you see! For I tell you many prophets and kings desired to see what you see, but did not see it, and to hear what you hear, but did not hear it" (Luke 10:23-24 par.). God's promise of integral salvation was being fulfilled by Jesus' words and deeds. Among other things he had been delivering those suffering from sickness and diabolic possession, accepting women as disciples, and extending God's mercy through table fellowship with tax collectors and other public sinners.

Finally, we might recall a Q-saying that illuminates Jesus' sense of his ministry for the kingdom: "the blind receive their sight, the lame walk, the lepers are cleansed, the deaf hear, the dead are raised, and the poor have good news brought to them" (Matt 11:5 par.)[14]. Five types of miracles and the preaching of the good news characterized Jesus' activity for the kingdom. At least in the early stages of his ministry, did Jesus' think of his proclamation of the good news and prophetic actions (both miraculous and otherwise) as en-

---

[14] For an excellent discussion of Matt 11:2-6, see MEIER, *A Marginal Jew*, vol. 2, pp. 131-37.

joying merely a last-minute value with the divine kingdom about to overtake the world? Did Jesus imagine that he would be alive on earth at the time of the kingdom's consummation? Or does the record of his ministry suggest rather some interim period in which the power of the divine rule already present might enable human beings to be freed from dehumanizing conditions to progress religiously in ways that would also radically affect their social and political living? It is significant that John Meier allows for a shift of scenario on the part of John the Baptist and Paul, a shift that enabled them to entertain an interim period[15]. Perhaps the forthcoming third volume of Meier's *magnum opus* will allow for such a shift on the part of Jesus, a shift that would be highly relevant to his liberating work for integral human progress.

In any case this third volume must surely discuss a question that helps to shape a balanced evaluation of the stands Jesus took during his ministry: the reasons for the decision taken by some religious authorities in Jerusalem to have Jesus removed from the scene. Many scholars have concluded that the Temple nobility, or at least some of them, had a vested interest in getting rid of Jesus as a troublemaker whose message threatened the current social and political order[16]. If Jesus' proclamation had been totally religious and eschatological and in no way seemed to challenge the situation of those in power, their motivation for sending him to death could only have been "merely religious" and would have had nothing to do with changes in social and economic arrangements — that is to say, nothing to do with social structures of sin and a call to integral human progress. But is such a one-sided view an accurate version of their motivation?

Whatever we conclude about the intentions of the earthly Jesus, everything is not saved or lost by our conclusions. We have the witness of the gospels, in particular the Synoptic Gospels. Mark and then Luke and Matthew, when remembering and interpreting Jesus for their communities of faith, acknowledged, or at least implied, that the offer of divine sal-

---

[15] See Meier, *A Marginal Jew*, vol. 2, p. 132.
[16] See e.g. E.P. SANDERS, *Jesus and Judaism* (Philadelphia: Fortress, 1985), pp. 305-06.

vation he made through his words and deeds *also* enjoyed massive social and political repercussions. The new attitudes towards and relationships with others that he encouraged must deeply shape human beings in their progress towards a new society, both here and hereafter.

II

In the post-New Testament world, as we move towards the final kingdom that will realize cosmically the saving divine self-communication already achieved in Christ, what is there to say about his liberating work and human progress? His incarnation, life, death and resurrection (with the gift of the Holy Spirit) had opened the road to the true future for all men and women, that absolute future which will complete and clarify the entire history of the cosmos and the human race. The *eschaton* will fully identify Jesus the Liberator with his cause, human progress in its integrity. Yet here and now as Word and Wisdom of God, the risen Christ is active through his Spirit, anticipating everywhere the final presence of God in the coming kingdom. How should we evaluate this interim-time in history — in terms of human progress and Christ's liberating work?

The modern dream of emancipation, through which free and intelligent human beings would everywhere become the active subjects of civilized progress rather than remain the passive objects of oppression, has collapsed. Along with the rational liberalism encouraged by the Enlightenment, Marxism now counts among the "gods who have failed". Auschwitz, Dresden, the Gulag Archipelago, Hiroshima, the Katyn Woods, Nanking, Pnom-Penh, Sarajevo, Verdun and so many other places of mass killing have signalled the death of proud hopes for a brave new world, a kingdom built by human hands alone.

In the post-modern situation we need to hear even more the call to accept the "Gospel values" (*Redemptoris Missio*, 20) as in hope we all journey together towards the final kingdom. In a special, but not exclusive way, Christ's liberating work continues through the Church, the sacrament of salvation for all human beings. Christ's community serves the kingdom by its preaching, by sharing new life in him, and by its "commitment to justice and peace, education and the care of the sick, and aid to the poor and children" (ibid.). The responsibility to which Christian hope for the final kingdom gives rise transcends mere "private" morality, if there could ever be such a thing. Christian believers should seek to alleviate and eliminate misery through working for a world situation in which individuals will be freed from all oppression. The bishops at Vatican II reflected on the manifold nature of this degradation: "Never before today have human beings been so keenly aware of fredom, yet at the same time, new forms of social and psychological slavery make their appearance" (*Gaudium et Spes*, 4). The old crimes of murder and brutality continue. The trenches of World War I symbolize the twentieth century's steady march into savagery. So far well over one hundred million men and women have been killed in this century.

Faith in Christ's liberating work inescapably implies an obligation to strive for progress towards peace in our world. That earthly life continues to be so brutal for so many is intolerable. Their faith in Jesus our Liberator should impel Christians to take up the cause of those who suffer economic injustice, cultural backwardness or any other form of human misery. Jesus' account of judgement sets our hope for the coming kingdom in just such a context of responsibility for the alleviation of physical and mental suffering" "I was hungry and you gave me food" (Matt 25:35). The sequence is not: "I was hungry and you preached patience to me". There is a hard particularity about the duty imposed by the hope for the coming kingdom.

The pressure behind responsible Christian service for a better world stems from a hope for the full redemption of human beings. Social and political action prove the truth of our belief in the climax of Christ's liberating work, the complete redemption to come for human beings and their world. Such action anticipates the final freeing of our bodies which now face death. To hope in a glorious bodily future for human beings and their world means placing oneself under the obligations shaped by that hope. It is hardly a coincidence that in 1 Corinthians St Paul repeatedly inculcates a full service of love that will contribute to the world's progress while also recalling the Christian hope for the resurrection of the body promised by the liberating work of the risen Jesus (Ch. 15). Here, if anywhere, the indicative of Christ's liberation involves the imperative of our responsible commitment to a better world.

Christian Theology of Plenary Humanism

MARIASUSAI DHAVAMONY

Introduction

In the first place the term hominization has in the scientific language the meaning of the conditions of the genesis of the human being, its place in the nature, and still more, the new turn which it impresses to the history of life. The problem is put by the naturalist who is attentive to the whole diversity, to the richness of the real, preoccupied as much to underline the biological originality of man as to establish his links with the organic world. Thus hominization is the introduction in the history of the life of the human phenomenon; it is not appearance of a new species but that of a new form of life. The human external form of the biosphere is of the same order of greatness as the biosphere itself. Humanity is not a part of life but the equivalent, the homologue of life. The two worlds are not foreign, but to pass from one to the other it is necessary to imagine, at the origin of the human sphere, of the sphere of reflection which is the continuation of the animal sphere, of the biosphere, a general phenomenon of transformation: the hominization[1].

Humanism signifies a complex of intellectual and philosophical tendencies which have for object the development of the essential qualities of man. It affronts more his spiritual problems than the material ones. Every philosophical orientation which places man at the centre of one's own interests and measures the themes and directions of one's research in terms of man is called humanism. Protagoras: man is the

---

[1] See the article of JEAN PIVETEAU, *L'hominisation*, in *Encyclopedia Universalis*, Paris 1986, under the word: "Homme".

measure of all things. Humanism also means interest for the classical Greco-roman culture, interest for the literary and philosophical studies with particular reference to the cultural movement develped in Italy in the 14th and 15th century[2].

In the common language the term "human" has many senses. It refers to what is proper to man in as much as a mortal and limited being both physically and psychologically and spiritually, in opposition to the eternal and the Absolute. It sometimes signifies what is conformable to the nature of man; what is natural in a human being; hence worthy of comprehension and compassion. It is human to err. It is human to yield to natural instincts. Then, it refers to one who has the sentiments of understanding, of compassion, of solidarity, of equity, of mercy towards others. Such and such a person is very human.

It appears that we have to admit a distinction between man and the human, between hominization and humanization, for man does not always act according to the standard and requirements of what is human. For example violence has been always present in the history of man but there has been also hope for peace, non-violence and self-sacrifice and self-dedication for the good of other men. Man does not always rise up to the ideal of the human. The progress in hominization reflects the natural dynamism of the human nature; this dynamism is of infinite capacity, and hence it can go on developping in the field of logico-scientific, technological dimension of man. But there need not be necessarily a simultaneous progress in the humanization, for the former can impede the latter or be an obstacle to the latter. Here perhaps the distinction between civilization and culture may throw some light. For culture is humanization in the spiritual sense while civilization is the betterment of this spiritualization in the material, rational, technological sense. One can for instance write with an ordinary tool or with the technologically developed tool. Besides humanization also brings out the dominance of man over hominization, over his unlimited dynamism for a better, more human, way of life.

---

[2] See the article of JEAN-CLAUDE MARGOLIN, *Humanisme*, in *Encyclopedia Universalis*, op. cit.

Paul VI in his homily at the closing of the Vatican Council II said: "All this doctrinal riches is aimed at the only one direction: to serve man. Man, we say, in all his condition, in all his infirmity, in all his necessity. The Church has in a certain sense declared itself to be the handmaid of humanity... All this and all that which we can say on the human value of the Council has perhaps deviated the mind of the Church in the Council in the anthropocentric direction of the modern culture? Deviated, no; turned to it, yes. But he who observes well this prevalent interest of the Council for the human and temporal values cannot deny that such an interest is due to the pastoral character which the Council has chosen as its programme and ought to recognize that such an interest is never disjoined from the more authentic religious interest, either on account of charity which uniquely inspires it (and where there is charity, there is God) or on account of the link, always affirmed and promoted by the Council, of the human and temporal values with those properly spiritual, religious and eternal: on man and on the earth it sets itself but to raise itself to the Kingdom of God... The Catholic religion and human life reaffirm themselves their alliance and their convergence in one only human reality: the Catholic religion is for humanity; in a certain sense it is the life of humanity... To know man, the true man, the integral man, it is necessary to know God"[3]. The Pope makes a solemn appeal to a concerted action for the integral development of man and for the common progress of humanity[4]. That is to say, he appeals for a new humanism, more rich and universal, called by the Pope plenary humanism which originates from man but which ought to find its fulfilment in God in order not to risk to render the world still more inhuman. "There is no true humanism if it is not open to the Absolute in the recognition of a vocation which offers the true idea of human life. Far from being the ultimate norm of values, man does not realize himself except by transcending himself. According to the just expression of Pascal: "Man surpasses infinitely man"[5].

---

[3] Cfr. *Enchiridion Vaticanum*, Vol. 1, Edizioni Dehoniane, Bologna, 1987, 2 ed. pp. 285ff.
[4] *Populorum Progressio* n. 5.
[5] *Populorum Progressio* n. 42.

Plenary humanism, open to the Absolute, can be of two kinds: one, founded on reason, nourished by moral virtues and expressed by human institutions: the other, Christian: "In manifesting Christ, the Church reveals to men their true situation and calling, since Christ is the head and exemplar of that renewed humanity, imbued with that brotherly love, sincerity and spirit of peace, to which all men aspire". (AG 8)

1) MAN AT THE TRANSCENDENTAL HORIZON OF LIFE

The word 'horizon' is here used not in the usual English sense of something which we may widen or expand or go beyond, but in the sense of a frame-work or viewpoint which provides the limits for certain activities performed within it. It is called 'transcendental' because it refers to the implicit depth-dimension of the human subject; i.e., man in his structure is a transcendental relation to the Absolute, to God. Every human experience presupposes a reference to the transcendent and every human experience is a self-transcendence in its depth-dimension. That is to say, the absolute and unique relation to the Absolute, to God is the fundamental and co-conscious horizon of, and in, our manifold conscious relations to the world. Such a pre-reflexive reference is an 'unthematic' experience which means that this experience and the reality which is experienced cannot be adequately expressed or 'objectified' in what we will call 'thematic' expression. The 'thematic' expression consists in the reflexive elucidation in concepts, images and historical realities of the primary depth experience.

Man in his existence in the world of persons and objects is a transcendental relation to God and his whole being is a participation of God. Hence the pre-reflexive self-consciousness of man, involving self-transcendence and the immanent presence and awareness of God evoked in the consciousness of the world and of other men is by its nature a religious consciousness. For to be present to oneself is to stand before God who is the ground of everything. One cannot conceive of a spiritual being except in its openness to the totality of being, to the Absolute. Only the Absolute Being fully corresponds to the total objective capacity of the spiritual subject.

Since a spiritual subject as such always reacts totally and indivisibly, in every particular act the human subject has to tend to its last end and to express its total capacity in some way. Thus we understand why St Thomas Aquinas says: "*Omnia cognoscentia cognoscunt implicite Deum in quolibet cognito. Sicut enim nihil habet rationem appetibilis nisi per similitudinem primae bonitatis, ita nihil est cognoscibile nisi per similitudinem primae veritatis*"[6]. Tending to the last end, the human subject necessarily assimilates and apprehends finite objects because they are the participations of the Absolute.

In the order of tendency and desire, only an existing last end can give true signification to a tendential action. All particular ends derive their value because they participate existentially in the Absolute Act of existing.

The human subject having a spiritual form is perfect according to its natural act of existing; it can increase still in perfection by intentional assimilation of being and thus can tend to full possession of being. A spiritual subject attains God not only by way of assimilation like material beings but by way of operation. The attainment of God by way of natural knowledge is possible for the human intellect by means of its own powers. Besides this, there is a natural desire for the immediate vision of God in the human subject. Knowing the existence of the cause, the human subject tends to know the essence of the cause itself; knowing the existence of God, it desires to know the essence of God in himself. This is the very dynamism of the spiritual subject considered as spiritual act of existing; namely, to be open to the totality of being. In the historical order in which we live there is an exigency of God in us calling us for the immediate vision of God, consequent on our being ordained to the supernatural end as our only last end.

The Church cannot remain neutral and indifferent to atheistic humanism, for it does not see itself as an extrinsic foreign imposition on man but an embodiment of God's call to man which transforms man in his authentically human and free being in the highest sense. The Church's mission is religious and by this very fact supremely human in character. (GS 11)

---

[6] *De Veritate* 22.2.1m.

Precisely by Christian faith in God, true humanism, i.e., man's full development as man is attained. The problem of God is approached in the mirror of the idea of full human development. Hence atheism for the sake of man to keep his liberty is meaningless. "Modern man is in a process of fuller personality development and of a growing discovery and affirmation of his own rights. But the Church is entrusted with the task of opening up to man the mystery of God, who is the last end of man; in doing so it opens up to him the meaning of his own existence, the innermost truth about himself. The Church knows well that God alone, whom it serves, can satisfy the deepest cravings of the human heart, for the world and what it has to offer can never fully content it. It also realizes that man is continually being aroused by the Spirit of God and that he will never be utterly indifferent to religion... For man will be ever anxious to know, if only in a vague way, what is the meaning of his life, his activity, and his death... The most perfect answer to these questionings is to be found in God alone who created man in his own image and redeemed him from sin". (GS 41)

Henri de Lubac has affronted the problem of establishing a lasting basis for humanism and has concluded to the necessity of theism as a first principle for true humanism[7]. True humanism requires God for its basis; to be lasting it requires Christ. According to Marx, religion is born of the dualism between the idea and reality; between the idea which man forms of himself and his concrete existence. Religion will have place as long as this hiatus exists. Marx's aim was to put an end to that sense of insufficiency and lack of adaptation by realizing a world where man would feel really at home[8].

One cannot uproot the idea of God because it is essentially the Presence of God in man. One cannot get rid of this Presence. There is no man without values. There are no values which establish the value of man absolutely without an Absolute. Man is of absolute value because he is illumined by a ray of light from the face of God. His development in

---

[7] *The Drama of Atheist Humanism*, Sheed and Ward, New York, 1950; also DE LUBAC, *The Unmarxian Socialist*, Sheed and Ward, New York, 1948.

[8] Cfr. HENRI NIEL, *Atheisme et Marxisme*, in *Lumiere et Vie*, 1955, p. 75.

history implies an eternity[9]. "Man surpasses man". Even the humanists of the exclusive type are prepared to admit it. They require a movement towards transcendence at the very heart of immanence. But this movement will be efficacious only if there is a Beyond which is both transcendent and immanent at the same time[10].

2) MAN AT THE THEOLOGICAL HORIZON

The word 'theologal' refers to the communion with the living God. This communion surpasses the 'natural' capacities of man, and is possible only through the gratuitous self-communication of God. As we have seen, transcendental horizon reveals that man is by nature a religious quest, open to God's self-communication. This new horizon is based on the active and universal saving Will of God who offers himself in Jesus Christ. Unhesitatingly they grant that God gives each man sufficient grace for salvation. This theologal life is expressed thematically in and through man's religious life in various ways; and explicitly and more clearly does it find expression, under God's special intervention, in and through the Judeo-Christian salvation history. The theologal is clarified in and through categorial realities; i.e., realities which exist in history. The categorial thus becomes the visibile form which interpretes the mystery of God.

The 'Heilsgeschichte' means both 'saving history' and 'history of salvation' and is nowadays widely used to refer to those saving acts of God in human history which are recorded in the Scriptures of the Old and New Testament. The central facts are the events of the life, work, death and resurrection of Jesus Christ, and the experience of his presence and continuing work within the fellowship of his disciples. Although Jewish and Hellenistic speculations and myths influenced the development and expression of the early Church's Christology, but all such elements were subordinated to a Christological structure which received its character not

---

[9] HENRI DE LUBAC, *The Discovery of God*, Henry Regnery Company, Chicago, 1967, pp. 180ff.
[10] Ibidem p. 184.

from syncretism, not from Hellenism, not from mythology, but from the Salvation History. For Judaism, time has a beginning and will have an end. The idea of cyclic time is no more followed. Jahweh no longer manifests himself in cosmic time (like the gods of other religions) but in a historical, irreversible time. Each new manifestation of Yahweh in history is not reducible to an earlier manifestation. His gestures are personal interventions in history and reveal their deep meaning for his people. Hence the historical event acquires a new dimension and becomes a theophany. Christianity goes further in valorizing history. Since God was incarnated, i.e., since he took on a historically conditioned human existence, history acquires the possibility of being sanctified. A clearly defined historical time was sanctified by the presence and work of Christ. When a Christian participates in the liturgical time, there is no longer the repetition of the mythical time but the re-enactment of what took place in historical time in which Christ lived, suffered, and rose again. God's intervention in history, and above all his incarnation in the historical person of Jesus Christ, have a transhistorical purpose; namely, the salvation of all men. For Christianity time is real because it has a meaning — the redemption. The meaning of the sacred history is unique, because the incarnation is a unique fact. Christ died for our sins once only, once for all[11]; it is not an event subject to repetition, which can be reproduced several times. The development of history is thus governed and oriented by the unique fact of Christ and his redemptive work.

A basic component of religious involvement among Christians is God's gift of his love[12]. We have to love God with our whole heart and whole soul, with our whole mind and with our whole strength[13]. God's love floods our hearts through the Holy Spirit given to us[14]. It grounds the conviction of St Paul that "there is nothing in death or life, in the realm of spirits or superhuman powers, in the world as it is

---

[11] Hebrews ch. 8; 1 Peter 3.18.
[12] In this section I have been inspired by Bernard Lonergan's manuscript under the title *Faith and Beliefs*, 1969.
[13] Mk 12.30.
[14] Rom. 5.5.

or the world as it shall be, in the forces of the universe — nothing in all creation that can separate us from the love of God in Christ Jesus our Lord"[15]. There is a profound difference between particular acts of loving and the dynamic state to which we refer when we say that someone is in love or falls in love with someone. The dynamic state of being in love is a first principle in one's life; while it has its causes, conditions, occasions, still as long as it lasts it forms a basic principle of one's thinking and acting. Being-in-love with God is supremely the first principle of man's thoughts and feelings, hopes and fears, joys and sorrows. There exists in man a capacity for holiness, a capacity for love that, in its immediacy, does not regard the transient shape of the world but the mysterious reality, immanent and transcendent, that we name God.

But being in love is not found only in Christianity. God gives all men sufficient grace for salvation. Nor is his grace without fruit. Heiler's points of radical unity of religions, also refer to being in love with God. A basic component of religious involvement among Christians is God's gift of his love. Now, this is true also of the basic component of religious involvement in world religions.

To be in love in an unrestricted manner is to be in love with someone transcendent. When someone transcendent is my beloved, the one to whom my being belongs, he is in my heart, real to me from within me. When that love is the fulfillment of my unrestricted thrust to the intelligible, the true, the real, the good, then the one that fulfills that thrust must be supreme in intelligence, truth, goodness. Since my loving him is my transcending of myself, it also is a denial of the self that is transcended. Since loving him means loving attention to him, it is prayer, meditation and contemplation. Since love of him is fruitful, it overflows into love of all those he loves. Finally, from an experience of love focussed on mystery, there wells forth a longing for knowledge, while love itself is a longing for union; so for the lover of the unknown beloved, bliss is knowledge of him and union with him, however they may be achieved.

---

[15] Rom. 8.38f.

This is the theological horizon in which the meeting of the world religions can take place. I call this universalist theologal life, for it is common to all religious people who respond to God's gift of his love. The knowledge that results from God's gift of his love contitutes the universalist faith; it is a knowledge that consists in one's response to the values and disvalues. Fr Lonergan describes this universalist faith as the "transvaluation of values that results from God's gift of his love"[16]. The values that are transvalued may be different but the process of transvaluation has its constant ground in God's gift of his love.

Values that are transvalued may be different. Similar religious experiences become thematized and objectified differently, depending on culture, values, particular horizons in various stages of human development. Besides, the human self-transcendence itself ever being precarious, involves a tension between the self that is transcended and the self that transcends. The history of religions is a witness to different kinds of self-transcendence; enough to take a glance at the notion of the supreme Being in various religions. The balance between the transcendence and immanence of the supreme being is not always correctly struck; if transcendence is over-emphasized, then God becomes remote, irrelevant and almost forgotten; if immanence is over-stressed, then the loss of reference to the transcendent will empty religious symbols, rituals, ceremonies of their true meaning and leave them as idols, magic, and myth.

Thus the common theologal life is expressed and objectified thematically in diverse ways, giving rise to different beliefs, cults, symbols in world religions. The expression has its origin both from God's direct intervention in history and from man's experience of God's gift of his love. The theologal life finds its concrete expression in and through the historical realities of God's salvific plan. These realities become the visible forms which manifest and interpret the mystery of God and of his plan of salvation. In Christianity this finds expression in and through the salvation history of what God has done for us in Jesus Christ. What distinguishes the

---

[16] See his above-mentioned manuscript, p. 8.

Christian, then, is not God's grace which he shares with men of other religions, but the mediation of God's grace through Jesus Christ our Lord.

Christianity is related to the theologal life in a way analogous to that in which the sacramental word and grace are related to the salvation history of the individual. Grace and sacrament have an inner cohesion, but they are not identical; they can precede one another in the temporal order of history; grace may already be given where the sacrament is not yet given; a valid sacrament may yet need to find fulfillment in that very grace which the sacrament signifies. It Christianity *is* Christ, the absolute action of God for man, in which God gives his very self, then Christianity — the Church — cannot renounce its claim to absolute character and universal mission. The Church and the Christian must recognize that the Church as salvific reality (and not merely as a benevolent and experienced partner in dialogue) now has an actual and positive relationship to the non-Christian world. This is how we understand the Second Vatican's statement that the Church is the sacrament of world's salvation[17].

3) Man at the Christological horizon

The Second Vatican Council outlines the role of the Church in the modern world by focusing its attention on the fundamental problem of the modern man, namely how to make man succeed as man. It believes that "it can contribute much to humanizing the family of man and its history through each of its members and its community as a whole". (GS 40)

It explicitly acknowledges the birth of a new humanism, one in which man is defined first of all by his responsibility toward his brothers and toward history". (GS 55) The relationship between the new humanism and Christology is significant in the theology of new plenary humanism.

The theology that became dominant in the Council stresses that Christianity is primarily the humanization of man and his divinization in Christ.

---

[17] *Lumen Gentium* 1,9,48.

Within Christology we see the significance of the relationship of divine to human as these exist in the person of Christ. "The Word of God, through whom all things were made, became man and dwelt among men: a perfect man, he entered world history taking that history into himself and recapitulating it... and is now at work in the hearts of men through the energy of the Spirit". (GS 38)

Christianity regards the truth of human development as the eschatological transformation of man by God who surpasses even the greatest possibilities of man's self-realization within history. Everything human must somehow find its fulfilment in the humanity of Christ; for in assuming human nature Christ manifested the ultimate plan of God for all human development. Remaining human they are destined to transcend themselves through the action of God.

The answer to the problem of the meaning of human life is given in the revelation in Christ, the divine Word who became man. "Whoever follows Christ the perfect man becomes himself more a man". (GS 41) Fr Bernard Lonergan says: "(For) revelation is God's entry into man's making of man, and so theology not only has to reflect on revelation, but also it has somehow to mediate God's meaning into the whole of human affairs"[18].

Christ is presented as the true answer to the question of being human and therefore of true humanism. Christ as the true image of God transforms man once more into likeness to God. Human being is interpreted Christologically. "In reality it is only in the mystery of the Word made flesh that the mystery of man truly becomes clear... Christ the new Adam, in the very revelation of the mystery of the Father and of his love, fully reveals man to himself and brings to light his most high calling. It is no wonder then that all the truths mentioned so far should find in him their source and their most perfect embodiment. He who is the "image of the invisible God" (Cor. 1.15) is himself the perfect man who has restored in the children of Adam that likeness to God which had been disfigured ever since the first sin. Human nature by the very

---

[18] See his *Theology in its new context*, in L.K. SHOOK (ed.), *Renewal of Religious Thought*, Vol. 1, Herder and Herder, New York, 1968, p. 41.

fact that it was assumed, not absorbed, in him has been raised in us also to a dignity beyond compare. For by his incarnation he the Son of God has in a certain way united himself with each man. He worked with human hands, he thought with a human mind. He acted with a human will, and with a human heart he loved. (GS 22) All this holds true not only for Christians but for all men of good will in whose hearts grace works in an unseen way. (Ibid.) "For though the same God is creator and saviour, Lord of human history as well as of salvation history, in the divine arrangement itself the rightful autonomy of the creature, and particularly of man, is not withdrawn. Rather it is reestablished in its own dignity and strengthened in it". (GS 41) To christianize the human must mean, not to make it any less human but to help it become more completely itself. But the human is not absolute, independent of the divine. The role of grace would be to keep men open to God.

Christ is the Lord and centre of history (GS 10 and 45). Above all Christ is the revealer of the truth about man. Christ can show man the way and strengthen him through the Spirit in order to be worthy of his destiny. The key, the centre and the purpose of the whole of man's history is to be found in its Lord and Master. Beneath all that changes there is much that is unchanging, much that has its ultimate foundation in Christ. (GS 10) Constituted Lord by his resurrection and given full power in heaven and on earth, Christ is now at work in the hearts of men by the energy of his Spirit; not only does he arouse in them a desire for the age to come but he animates, purifies and strengthens the noble aspirations of mankind to make life more human and conquer the earth for this purpose. (GS 38)

In other words Christ is presented as the true answer to the question of being human, and therefore to the question of true humanism and of atheism. Christ is the true image of God which transforms man once more into likeness to God. Here the whole theology of man as the image of God and of Christ gives a profound meaning to the understanding of man.

Man as the image of God

"Man was created to the image of God, as able to know and love his Creator, and as set by him over all earthly creatures that he might rule them, and make use of him, while glorifying God... By his innermost nature man is a social being; and if he does not enter into relations with others he can neither live nor develop his gifts". (GS 12) There are three elements that define man as the image of God: his relation to God that makes him capable of knowing and loving him who is his creator and last end; his relation to the world which makes him lord of all creatures because as an incarnate spirit man expresses himself by means of science and techinique; his relation to other human beings, apart from whom he cannot live and act. In order to be an authentic image of God, man must cultivate right relations to God; right relations to the world; because man is the lord of creation; he is a creator of meanings; he is the master and not the slave of science and of tool; he must cultivate right relations to his fellow humans. We can say that man is an image of God, a reflection of God and a sacrament of God. God's sovereignty over the world is reflected in man in the sense that he is called to dominate creation, to submit it to himself, to be its king. Man is the sacrament of God in the sense that the theme of the image of God is set in relation to the spiritual interiority that reunites man to God.

Man as the image of Christ

The theme of creation is profoundly linked to Christology. In the image of man as he concretely exists there are also negative aspects: sin, human suffering and death. "He who is the image of the invisible God is himself the perfect man who has restored in the children of Adam that likeness to God which had been disfigured ever since the first sin. Human nature by the very fact that it was assumed, not absorbed, has been raised in us also to a dignity beyond compare. For by his incarnation, he, the Son of God, has in a certain way united himself with each man". (GS 22) Christ is seen as the antitype of the first Adam, the man from the earth; the risen

Christ is the man from heaven to whose image we must be conformed. (1 Cor. 15.47ff; Rom. 8.29) The formation of a new man, a man conformed to Christ is a process which will achieve its completion only at the second coming of the Lord. (Phil. 3.21) Christ gathers up in his own person that manifestation of the invisible God which was to be found both generally in the cosmos (Rom. 1.20) and more particularly in man. If man is in the image of God, then so is Christ *par excellence*. He is the perfect likeness of God. Jesus is the normative image for man who is called to become like it. Here the image is an eschatological one. It already exists within man in germs but it must attain to its full reality through progressive formation. Christ is presented as the eschatological Adam to whom the first Adam already pointed; as the true image of God which transforms man once more into likeness of God. The term 'similitude' is used for the restoration of the image of God in sinful man. Through sin man's similitude to God (grace) was lost and the image of God (nature) was wounded, thus making a distinction between similitude and image[19].

Jesus is not only the sacrament of God for man but also the sacrament of man for man. Jesus, being a sacrament, reveals man to himself. For in knowing Jesus we not only know his Father and his Spirit; the knowledge of Jesus also reveals man to himself, both in his present reality and under the aspect of his eschatological future. To know Jesus is to come to know the eschatological image of man. St Paul speaks of Christ as the first-born of all creation: i.e., the one who is supreme over all creation, since Christ's agency in creation is affirmed and Christ is the divine and pre-existent Wisdom. We can say that Christ is also the sacrament of man for God. As the first-born of creation Christ gives expression to man before God. As the perfect image of man, Jesus is the prototypical, supreme and perfect embodiment of man's response to God's invitation to every man to achieve his fulfilment as image of God. In God's eyes Jesus is the perfect expression and embodiment of humanity. In this sense we can say that Jesus is the sacrament of man for God.

---

[19] See H. VORGRIMLER (ed), *Commentary on the Documents of the Vatican II*, Herder and Herder, Vol. V, 1969, pp. 158-63.

Christian tradition points out three different directions with regard to man as the image of God. Clement, Origin, Gregory of Nyssa (the majority of Greek and Latin Fathers) consider the Logos as the model and the image is in the human soul. For Augustine the model is the Trinity which is reflected in the human soul as "mens-notitia-amor". Tertullian, Prudence and Ireneus propose the incarnate Logos as the perfect model and think that the image is in the body spiritually animated, in the "resurrected body". It appears that the third line of reflection is the most complete model in harmony with the whole tradition[20]. Resemblence to God becomes resemblence to Christ. It is Christ who is the true image of God. In the understanding of man the dynamic perspective of the history of salvation prevails. That is why through the Christological aspect of anthropology, it is also the escathological fullness of the former that is brought out. In other words, the order of "creation" is not considered absolutely in itself, separate from the order of redemption. The perspective is at once of creation and redemption.

Let us probe more deeply into the relation between creation and Christology.

In the Christological passages of the New Testament the relation of the person of Christ to the Old Testament doctrine of creation is very striking. Christ comes into the world as the completion and fulfilment of creation. Without Christ creation is a mystery without a solution.

> "He has let us know the mystery of his purpose, the hidden plan he so kindly made in Christ from the beginning to act upon when the times had run their course to the end: that he would bring everything together under Christ, as head, everything in the heavens and everything on earth. And it is in him that we were claimed as God's own, chosen from the beginning". (Eph. 1.9-11)

The whole of creation, having been cut off from the Creator by sin is decomposing, and its rebirth is effected by

---

[20] See CHARLES MOELLER, *Renewal of the Doctrine of Man*, in *Renewal of Religious Structures*, L.K. Shook (ed.), Vol. II, Herder and Herder, New York, 1968, pp. 460f.

Christ reuniting all its parts into an organism with himself as the head, so as to reattach it to God. The faith of the Old Testament rests not only on the fact that God is the Creator of all things but on the hope of a fulfilling Messiah. The coming of the messianic age affects the whole of creation, as the idea of "meassianic fertility" (Is. ch. 11; Hos. 2.23) implies. Christ himself is the Creator; "the image of God... by him were all things created" (Col. 1.15 and 16). He is the firstborn (Col. 1.16; Heb. 1.6; Ps 36.6); the firstborn not in time but he who takes precedence over all creation. His priority over all creatures provides a just lordship over all creation. He is Heir of all things by whom God made the worlds. (Heb. 1.2) Paul in the Colossians (1.15-20) indicates two ways in which Christ can claim to he the 'head' of everything that exists: he is the head of creation; he is the head of the new creation and of all that exists by being saved through his grace. it is as the incarnate God that Jesus is the image of God; i.e., his human nature was the visible manifestation of God who is invisible; and as such in this concrete human nature, and as part of creation, Jesus is called the firstborn of creation.

Christ is the wisdom of God by which he made all things (1 Cor. 1.24,30) and is the creative Word made flesh (Jn 1.14). Christ is the personal fulfilment of creative wisdom. Paul connects Christ as the wisdom of God with the power of God, the creative power which works through wisdom.

Christ's close connection with the whole of creation is an essential part of his fullness (pleroma). The pleroma of the Godhead (Col. 2.9) is the whole of the divine attributes formed into one. He came to pass on to us the pleroma. (Jn 1.16; Eph. 3.19 and 4.13) which finds a prominent place in the doctrine of the Church and the Eucharist[21].

Christ as a theandric unity stands from the very beginning at the centre of the universe. The Father created the world for love of Christ, and in order that Christ might come, he also to this extend permitted sin as a condition for

---

[21] See W.S. BOYCOTT, *Creation and Christology*, in *Theology*, LII (1949), Dec. pp. 443-448.

the realization of the concrete image of Christ the glorious redeemer[22].

Hence the redemptive incarnation is not only a perfecting episode or a rectification of a deviation of human history but is a structuring element without which the concrete humanity, conceived and willed as a participant in the paschal mystery, would be a defective element in the universe. The event of the death and resurrection of Christ reveals God as one who since the creation calls a being of the world to become man in his likeness, by the conquest of freedom in order to put on immortality in Christ. God creates the human being by yielding preference to him and letting him arrive at his freedom. It is shown at the same time that God from all eternity according to his trinitarian being is in a relation of love with the world, called to be recapitulated in the firstborn of creation. By this bond woven in history the world is established as a partner of our destiny, and man as responsible for the destiny of the world[23].

Conclusion

Certainly one of the results of the rediscovery of the unity of God and man in the whole of salvation economy is none other than the understanding of what St Paul called "The Mystery" (Eph. 3.3ff; Col. 1.26-27); namely, that the salvation and happiness of man (nor separated from the universe) is realized by communion with God in Christ. More explicitly, the rediscovery is that there is no "theology for man" without "an anthropology for God". The greatest misfortune perhaps that has affected modern Catholicism is to have been preoccupied with theory and catechesis about the *en-soi* of God and religion without paying attention to the significance it has for man. Contemporary atheism was born as a reaction against such a God without man or the world. The answer to this problem is that we must bring out the human impact of the things of God. This does not mean that

---

[22] For the Christocentric view of creation see FLICK-ALZEGHY, *Fondamenti di una antropologia teologica*, Firenze, 1970.
[23] See JACQUES MOINGT, *Création et Salut*, R.Sc.R. 84/4 (1996), pp. 559-595.

we must present a purely humanistic programme in substitution. This means that we speak of the mysteries of God in such a way as to unite a profound perception of what they are in themselves in relation to what they are for men: uniting anthropology for God to theology for man. This is the essence of revelation, which is economic, in a unique way by its crowing point in Jesus Christ; for in him, the wisdom of God was made man[24].

The Creator Word was always present in the world. The Word was present in the world before the incarnation (Ireneus). The Word is present in the world as light (Justin, Ireneus, Clement). Everything that is true and good in world religions and cultures comes from the illuminating presence of the Word. This enables us to understand the theological approach to the problem of the relation between the history of the world and the history of salvation, between the history of religions and the salvation history. The largest part of the universe which lies outside the visible sphere of the Church and its preaching, in the order of cultures and religions, is not outside the mysterious domain of the illuminating presence of the Creator Word. Here meet the order of universal salvation and other world religions.

---

[24] See YVES CONGAR, *Christ in the Economy of Salvation and in our Dogmatic Tracts, Concilium* Vol. 1, n. 2 (1966 January), pp. 4-15.

Annunzio e Progresso Umano

PIERO GHEDDO

«Annunzio e progresso umano» è un tema trascurato dagli studi e dalla pubblicistica cristiana. Nella bibliografia internazionale missionaria[1], ci sono decine di titoli sul debito estero dei paesi poveri, i rapporti commerciali fra paesi ricchi e poveri, i finanziamenti dei «piani di sviluppo», ma non se ne trova uno solo che spieghi, illustri, documenti, ad esempio, questa frase della «Redemptoris Missio» (n. 58): «La Chiesa non ha soluzioni tecniche da offrire al sottosviluppo in quanto tale, ma dà il primo contributo alla soluzione dell'urgente problema del sottosviluppo, quando proclama la verità su Cristo, su se stessa e sull'uomo»[2].

«LO SVILUPPO DELL'UOMO VIENE DA DIO»

Eppure, visitando le missioni, dove si realizza l'«annunzio di Cristo ai non cristiani», questo dato di fatto (il Vangelo sviluppa l'uomo e i popoli) è spesso presente nelle conversazioni dei missionari specialmente in Africa, perché corrisponde alla loro esperienza quotidiana. La cultura moderna lo ignora e il motivo è facile da capire. Negli ultimi 30-40 anni, il mondo occidentale ha spiegato i meccanismi che causano il «sottosviluppo» (o che portano allo «sviluppo») in termini materialisti, con letture di tendenza marxista-rivoluzionaria o liberal-capitalista: finanze, piani di sviluppo, commerci, prezzi delle materie prime, tecnologie, sistemi di produzione dei beni materiali, colonialismo, neo-colonialismo, ecc.

---

[1] Vedi il volume annuale di «Bibliografia missionaria» edito dalla Biblioteca della Pontificia Università Urbaniana, Roma.
[2] Vedi anche la «Sollicitudo rei socialis» (1987), n. 41; e i Documenti della Conferenza del Celam a Puebla (1979), n. 3760.

Il mondo ricco non sa ancora come aiutare i poveri a superare il sottosviluppo, perché non ha capito le radici dell'abisso fra Nord e Sud. Si sono date letture «materialiste», in parte giuste ma insufficienti a spiegare il fenomeno del «sottosviluppo» (ad esempio, è vero che il colonialismo ha commesso crimini e danni, ma non spiega la differenza), senza tener conto dell'anima dei popoli; si è guardato più al denaro, alla tecnica e alla politica, che non alle culture e alle religioni dei popoli.

Da questa «lettura materialista» anche il mondo cattolico (e missionario, ad esempio le riviste ed editrici missionarie, i movimenti di volontariato cattolico internazionale) è stato influenzato. Quando si parla di «sviluppo» (o di «sottosviluppo»), si tratta subito di finanze, scambi commerciali, tecnologie. Si ignorano (o si mettono tra parentesi come ininfluenti) i valori culturali e religiosi, l'educazione, le mentalità, i costumi, gli atteggiamenti di fronte alla natura e alla storia.

La gravità della spaccatura fra Nord e Sud sta nel fatto che non c'è solo un abisso economico e tecnologico fra ricchi e poveri: se fosse così, basterebbe trasferire in modo massiccio finanze e tecnologie (il che è stato fatto almeno in alcuni casi, e parlo soprattutto dell'Africa e dei «paesi del petrolio», con risultati deludenti); ma si tratta di un abisso culturale fra popoli che appartengono a mondi diversi, vivono in secoli diversi, sono separati da storia, cultura, religione, mentalità, lingua, costumi, strutture sociali (si pensi alla famiglia monogamica o poligamica!), visione dell'uomo (e della donna!), della storia, della natura.

Annunziare Gesù Cristo ai popoli è farli progredire umanamente per un motivo molto semplice: Cristo è venuto a rivelare quel Dio che tutti i popoli cercano ma non conoscono, un Dio che ama e perdona l'uomo, verità insospettabile se Dio stesso non l'avesse rivelata; ed a portare, attraverso la sua morte e risurrezione, il perdono di Dio, la pace, la fraternità e la giustizia, addirittura il modello molto concreto di un «uomo nuovo» descritto dal Vangelo. Il Papa scrive nella «Redemptoris Missio»: «Lo sviluppo dell'uomo viene da Dio, dal modello di Gesù uomo-Dio, e deve portare a Dio. Ecco perché tra annunzio evangelico e promozione dell'uomo c'è una stretta connessione» (n. 59).

Tutto questo noi lo crediamo per fede, ma la storia lo conferma. La storia cristiana dell'Occidente anzitutto. Perché il cosiddetto «progresso moderno» (ricerca scientifica, sviluppo tecnico ed economico, democrazia, giustizia sociale, diritti dell'uomo e della donna, strutture dello stato moderno, ecc.) è nato nell'Occidente cristiano e poi si è diffuso in tutto il mondo? Non perché in Europa ci fossero maggiori ricchezze naturali o perché i nostri antenati fossero più intelligenti di africani, indiani, cinesi, giapponesi, indios americani, ma perché l'uomo occidentale ha portato avanti nella sua storia una logica interna di sviluppo che ha radici lontane nella nostra cultura e nella nostra religione[3]. Tutto nel progresso di un popolo (come di un singolo uomo) è consequenziale, nulla viene per caso.

In questo mio contributo vorrei centrare l'attenzione sull'Africa e sui popoli africani, per i quali entrare nella dinamica del «progresso» e raggiungere il nostro livello di vita è un processo difficile, complesso: le loro culture, mentalità, strutture sociali, le stesse fedi religiose, sono impreparate, inadeguate al mondo moderno. Naturalmente, il progresso realizzato nei paesi occidentali non è tutto positivo, ma rappresenta comunque un passo in avanti dell'umanità: gli afri-

---

[3] Quello che conosciamo come «progresso moderno» (naturalmente non tutto positivo, ma questo è un altro discorso!), storicamente è nato nell'Occidente cristiano e poi è stato esportato ed ha attecchito in tutto il mondo. Pochi si chiedono perché. Oggi ci sono autori indiani e giapponesi che si pongono questo interrogativo e riconoscono che tutto quanto è «progresso moderno» è venuto dall'Occidente, ma spiegano il fatto in modo evasivo (il colonialismo, la maggior potenza militare dell'Occidente) o generico: l'Occidente è partito prima perché aveva stimoli al progresso che l'Oriente non aveva. Già, ma e perché? Ecco un tema da esplorare: la radice sta nella Bibbia. Questo non è per noi un vanto, ma una responsabiltà!
Il sociologo Franco De Marchi, in uno studio su questo tema (nel volume «Evangelizzazione e promozione umana», Pontificia Università Urbaniana, 1982) scrive che «la tendenza attuale del terzo mondo è di accogliere la tecnologia occidentale e le sue premesse scientifico-positive, ma resistere alla matrice filosofica dell'Occidente, specialmente a quei temi religiosi che la spiegano e la volgono a servizio dell'uomo... È molto difficile che un progresso così concepito possa dirsi vero sviluppo, perché finora non si sa davvero quali premesse valide alla motivazione psicologica del cambiamento drastico, alla socializzazione universale (ritornano i temi di persona, progresso, perdono, che sono propri della cultura occidentale a sfondo cristiano) si possano ricavare dalle tradizioni religiose orientali. Sembra evidente che quella stessa matrice dello sviluppo che, come abbiamo segnalato, è lo spirito cristiano, debba essere anche l'artefice del decollo delle altre culture e stimolo alla correzione di marcia della stessa imprenditorialità pragmatica occidentale».

cani lo imitano superficialmente, ma le sue motivazioni e radici profonde sfuggono a molti, per cui le basi del «progresso» in Africa sono precarie.

Come avviene il «primo annunzio» ai non cristiani?

Qual è il contributo che l'annunzio cristiano dà all'evoluzione di una tribù africana? Ecco l'esperienza della missione di Suzana tra i Felupe, in Guinea-Bissau, esemplare perché c'è stata continuità dal 1952 ad oggi: due soli missionari del P.I.M.E. (Pontificio istituto missioni estere), p. Spartaco Marmugi (1952-1973) e p. Giuseppe Fumagalli (1968-1998), per quasi mezzo secolo sono rimasti sul posto (Fumagalli è tuttora parroco), hanno fondato la missione e orientato l'annunzio: un caso raro (purtroppo i missionari, per mille motivi indipendenti dalla loro volontà, cambiano spesso di posto)!

Esemplare la missione di Suzana anche perché è in una etnia di religione tradizionale, in una regione isolata, non ancora influenzata dall'islam e dal «mondo moderno» (anche se oggi la situazione cambia rapidamente). La situazione che nel 1952 trovarono a Suzana padre Spartaco Marmugi e p. Luigi Andreoletti era «preistorica»: il «mondo moderno» tra i Felupe non era ancora arrivato. Ecco il racconto di padre Fumagalli su come avviene il primo annunzio ai non cristiani[4]:

> «Quando un nuovo villaggio viene a dirmi di voler 'conoscere Gesù', io chiedo perché fanno questa richiesta: voglio conoscere bene le loro aspirazioni e mi stupisce sentire che sono quasi sempre alte, nobili. Non vengono per avere aiuti materiali, ma perché hanno visto i cristiani, hanno sentito parlare della religione cristiana e vogliono saperne di più. Hanno fame e sete di conoscere Dio, 'il Dio dei cristiani'. Le motivazioni sono importanti, ma è importante anche il mio annunzio esplicito. A chi mi chiede perché sono venuto in Africa, io rispondo: 'Per amore di Gesù Cristo, per far conoscere e amare Gesù Cristo'.

---

[4] Giuseppe Fumagalli, «Il Vangelo felupe», «Mondo e Missione», ottobre 1988, pagg. 531-549. I brani citati alle pagg. 541-547.

Quando mi chiedono di conoscere il mio Dio, combiniamo un incontro con il villaggio. Io vado là e sono atteso. Ci sediamo per terra, sotto un albero, e incomincio col chiedere che mi parlino del loro Dio. Parlano volentieri e mi raccontano cosa pensano di Dio, come lo pregano, le loro tradizioni sul mondo misterioso della divinità. Poi chiedono a me cosa penso e io dico: 'Io ho il massimo rispetto delle credenze che vi hanno lasciato i vostri antenati; essi hanno cercato Dio nell'oscurità, come quando si cammina nella notte con la lanterna. Ma io vi porto una novità: Dio ha parlato, Dio si è fatto uomo in Gesù Cristo. Non c'è più bisogno della lanterna, perché è sorto il sole che ci illumina il cammino verso Dio'. Questo discorso li interessa profondamente. Ai non cristiani io parlo subito di Cristo, seguendo il Vangelo di Marco, che salta la nascita e l'infanzia e presenta fin dall'inizio Gesù sulla scena. Il Vangelo di Marco è tutto un rispondere alla domanda: chi è costui? E Cristo dice: 'Avete udito che vi fu detto dagli antichi, ma io vi dico...'. Gesù si presenta come colui che parla in nome di Dio e io racconto la storia di Gesù, figlio di Dio morto e risorto per liberarci dal peccato e dalla morte; e di come la Chiesa continua la testimonianza degli Apostoli su Cristo.
Questa è la mia catechesi di 'primo annunzio', tutta basata sulla parola di Dio e su Cristo. Ai non cristiani io non porto altro che la Bibbia e Gesù Cristo, parlando subito di fede e di conversione a Cristo».

Perché la missione è fattore di progresso umano

Il «primo annunzio» di Cristo ai Felupe ha un forte impatto sociale-culturale, come ho visto nelle due visite fatte a questa missione (1988 e 1997): quando i Felupe si convertono a Cristo e al suo Vangelo, acquistano una mentalità nuova che libera le loro potenzialità umane e li sviluppa socialmente, culturalmente, economicamente. Scrive p. Giuseppe Fumagalli[5]:

---

[5] Giuseppe Fumagalli, «Il Vangelo felupe», «Mondo e Missione», ottobre 1988, pagg. 531-549.

«Nella mia esperienza sono giunto a questa conclusione, che la causa radicale del sottosviluppo in Africa è la mentalità tradizionale e conservatrice, per la quale conta solo la tradizione che non deve cambiare in nulla. L'anziano della famiglia e il capo villaggio hanno essenzialmente questo compito: di consegnare ai figli il villaggio così come l'hanno ricevuto dai padri. Ora, la cultura e la tradizione sono elementi positivi se dinamici, ma negativi se statici. La cultura dei Felupe (e più in genere delle tribù africane) è statica per natura sua, perché, non conoscendo Dio che si è rivelato in Gesù Cristo, non ha sbocchi verso il futuro: è una cultura tradizionalista, conservatrice, non progressista. Manca il concetto stesso di 'progresso', cioè del cammino in avanti verso una vita migliore. Io tocco con mano che il 'primo annunzio del Vangelo', la conversione a Cristo e l'inserimento in una comunità cristiana sono fattori di progresso per tutti gli aspetti della vita africana.

Il Felupe ha una concezione della vita dell'uomo che è tutta in un recinto chiuso. Quando muori, pensano che rinasci in un'altra persona. Quando nasce un bambino che assomiglia al nonno, dicono: 'È il nonno che è tornato tra noi'. Il vivere quindi diventa senza scopo, senza meta. È un ripetere quello che è già stato, senza progredire, anzi senza cambiare nulla. Infatti quando tu rinasci devi ritrovare il tuo villaggio come l'hai lasciato, altrimenti non ti ritrovi più. Questa è la vita, non c'è nessuna possibilità di sfuggire al destino, non c'è nessun futuro se non quello di vivere giorno per giorno conservando la tradizione della tribù...

Cristo è venuto a spaccare questo recinto chiuso e a dare all'uomo, ad un popolo, uno scopo, una meta. Allora, il valore assoluto non è più la tradizione, ma il cammino verso il Padre, il progresso, la marcia in avanti, il messianismo dei 'cieli nuovi e terra nuova in cui avrà stabile dimora la giustizia' (2 Pt. 3, 13).

Può sembrare che tutto questo abbia scarso peso nella vita di una etnia africana. Invece no: l'uomo si muove in base alle idee che ha, in base all'educazione, alla mentalità, alla cultura, alla fede religiosa. Vivendo in Africa, in una tribù ancora non toccata dal mondo moderno, mi rendo conto delle diversità abissali che ci sono nella mentalità, nella cultura, nell'educazione fra Africa ed Europa. L'uomo africano ha tutte le qualità umane dell'europeo, tutte le possibilità di sviluppo, ma è bloccato in una cultura statica, volta al passato e non al futuro».

Gesù Cristo libera gli africani dalla paura

Chiedo a padre Fumagalli come e perché avvengono le conversioni a Cristo tra i non cristiani e cosa significa Gesù Cristo per quelli che si convertono[6].

«Il primo senso dell'annunzio cristiano è di liberare dalla paura. Tra i Felupe, la mentalità comune, in dipendenza dalla loro religione tradizionale, è questa: si vive bene quando tutte le forze della natura sono in equilibrio. Se succede qualcosa di spiacevole, ad esempio la malattia o la morte o una disgrazia, allora bisogna cercare il colpevole, cioè chi ha rotto l'equilibrio. Il pagano non concepisce la morte o la malattia come un fatto naturale, che prima o poi capita: tutto è dovuto agli spiriti cattivi, quindi bisogna cercare il responsabile che ha provocato negativamente questi spiriti. Si fanno cerimonie e sacrifici di animali, si «interroga il cadavere», e salta fuori il colpevole: allora seguono le punizioni e le vendette. Tutti accettano anche se nessuno ne è convinto. In privato dicono che sanno che non è vero, però in pubblico nessuno osa dire il contrario od opporsi alla punizione del colpevole. La ricerca pubblica di cause morali, di tabù, di peccati personali, diventa angosciosa per tutti.

– Tu pensi che questa è la prima spinta alla conversione?

– Tra i miei Felupe certamente sì. La vita di quelli che seguono la religione tradizionale è dominata dalla paura[7]. Cre-

---

[6] Intervistato a Suzana il 21 febbraio 1997.
[7] In Costa d'Avorio, un altro missionario del PIME, p. Giovanni De Franceschi, studioso della tribù e della lingua dei Baoulé tra i quali vive dal 1975, scrive (in «Cristo, la maschera, il tam-tam», «Mondo e Missione», dicembre 1985, pagg. 673-677): «Noi cristiani non ci rendiamo conto di come la vita del pagano è una

dono in Dio creatore, ma non lo conoscono e lo immaginano talmente lontano dall'uomo e inaccessibile, che la vita dell'uomo dipende dalle forze della natura e degli «spiriti» buoni o cattivi. Il cristianesimo libera dalla paura. Il cristiano sa che Dio è Padre che perdona e non si vendica, sa che Dio protegge l'uomo, gli vuole bene anche quando soffre e quando muore. La sofferenza, la malattia e la morte non sono «punizioni» di Dio, ma fatti naturali. Quando il cristiano entra in questa logica dell'amore, allora si rasserena, diventa gioioso anche nel dolore, accetta tutto dalle mani di Dio, ha sempre la forza di ricominciare da capo, non pensa a «difendersi» dagli spiriti e dal malocchio, ma ad amare il Padre buono che è nei cieli.

L'annunzio di Cristo e la conversione a Cristo sono i primi passi per lo sviluppo di una personalità equilibrata e serena, che affronta la vita con ottimismo e speranza nel futuro. Il paganesimo è senza speranza, è rivolto all'indietro verso i tempi mitici degli antenati, non verso la costruzione di un futuro migliore per tutti. Il concetto stesso di «progresso», di marcia in avanti verso la giustizia, la pace e i diritti umani, è sconosciuto alla cultura africana tradizionale.

- A volte in Italia qualcuno mi dice: «Perché voi missionari andate in Africa ad annunziare Cristo, quando gli africani hanno già una loro religione? Perché disturbarli?».

- Chi dice così non conosce i popoli africani che, ripeto, nella religione tradizionale sono dominati dalla paura. Credo-

---

continua paura che gli vien messa dentro fin dall'infanzia: temono di aver fatto torto al feticcio, che il feticcio si vendichi per motivi misteriosi. Ho sentito parecchie volte delle persone adulte, colte, psicologicamente mature, dire: «Mi arriverà una disgrazia perché ho trascurato il feticcio, ho offeso il feticcio». Hanno la ferma convinzione che la disgrazia gli capiti da un momento all'altro, ma non sanno cosa sarà: può essere un incidente d'auto, un avvelenamento, un cadere dalle scale. Vivono male, a volte impazziscono. Il terrore psicologico può distruggere una persona.

«Il dato di fondo è questo: il pagano non conosce Dio, il perdono di Dio, non sa che Dio è un Padre amorevole che ci vuole bene e ci perdona... Il primo passo per lo sviluppo è liberare l'uomo dal terrore del feticcio, rivelargli che l'amore di Dio lo rende libero e gioioso. Ecco perché sono convintissimo, per esperienza personale, che il più grande contributo che noi missionari portiamo allo sviluppo dell'Africa non sono gli aiuti economici, le scuole, gli ospedali (tutte cose indispensabili), ma la rivelazione dell'amore di Dio in Gesù Cristo».

no in Dio ma non lo conoscono. Noi missionari non veniamo a portare la fede in Dio perché ce l'hanno già, ma la rivelazione di Dio in Gesù Cristo, che umanizza la loro vita e le loro culture e li mette in un cammino di progresso non solo personale, ma anche come popolo. È un fatto che si vede in tutta l'Africa: le comunità cristiane, i villaggi cristiani progrediscono più in fretta di quelli non cristiani. Non perché ricevono più aiuti, perché noi aiutiamo tutti; ma perché cambiano mentalità, visione di vita: la loro cultura tradizionale, a contatto col Vangelo, evolve in senso positivo (pensa solo a come cambia radicalmente la situazione della donna!). Gesù Cristo è la vera rivoluzione umanizzante di cui i popoli africani hanno bisogno, perché rivela loro il vero volto di Dio che è amore, è libertà, è ottimismo, dà senso alla vita, dà un futuro».

«Chi va con i preti non fa più la guerra»

Oggi in Guinea-Bissau ci sono 1.000-1.200 Felupe battezzati, su un popolo che conta circa 12.000 individui (certamente di più, perché nel censimento parecchi bambini e anziani non vengono denunziati per via delle tasse!). Chiedo a padre Giuseppe Fumagalli quali frutti positivi il cristianesimo ha portato ai suoi Felupe. Mi risponde ricordando che in passato fra i villaggi di questa tribù c'era un perenne stato di inimicizia e di guerra. Si combattevano con archi, frecce e coltellacci, imboscate nelle campagne, si ammazzavano per nulla. I villaggi erano difesi, si viveva nel terrore di assalti notturni.

In un'inchiesta fatta tra i cristiani nel 1996 sul tema «Chiesa-famiglia», la gente ha discusso ed ha dato risposte. Tutti concordano nel dire che uno dei migliori risultati del cristianesimo è questo: ha fatto superare le antiche inimicizie che c'erano tra i villaggi e le famiglie. Una donna anziana dice che quando lei era bambina, la gente del suo villaggio e i suoi genitori non la portavano mai nel villaggio vicino pochi chilometri, perché era considerato nemico. «Oggi, dice, i bambini giocano assieme e questo è grazie a Gesù».

Un uomo ha testimoniato che nel 1979 e 1981 doveva esserci la guerra tra Edgin e Katòn per problemi di terre e proprietà di palmizi. In passato tra questi due grossi villaggi è corso molto sangue. I cristiani ed i catecumeni dei due villaggi nemici si sono intesi e hanno evitato la guerra. La gente lo sa e dice apertamente che sono stati i cristiani a fare la pace. La cappella di Kassolòl è stata costruita sul campo di battaglia tradizionale. Il terreno è stato concesso perché, hanno detto i capi (non cristiani), chi va con i preti non fa più la guerra, siamo tutti fratelli. Chiedo a padre Giuseppe se tutti sanno, tra i Felupe, che il cristianesimo porta la pace.

«Sì, lo sanno, lo dicono — mi risponde — e la storia lo conferma tante volte. Tra Edgin e Ehlalab in antico c'era un ponte. Poi l'hanno distrutto perché era sfavorevole a Ehlalab, in quanto si prestava ad imboscate da parte di quelli di Edgin. I nostri cristiani hanno proposto di ricostruirlo. Ci hanno pensato un po', ne hanno discusso, e poi hanno dato il permesso dicendo: «Tanto, ormai, voi cristiani non ci lasciate più fare la guerra, possiamo anche fare il ponte». L'abbiamo ricostruito in ferro e cemento, un'opera notevole da queste parti, che fa un grande servizio alla gente.

Il mio sforzo oggi — riprende Fumagalli — è di far capire alla gente che la cultura è una cosa viva, che cambia: per cui non bisogna ripetere ciecamente quello che facevano in passato, ma capire i valori da cui gli antenati partivano e incarnarli nella situazione attuale. Se in passato si lasciava morire il gemello più debole per salvare l'altro, oggi si possono salvare tutti e due. Se in passato i lebbrosi, i pazzi, gli incurabili venivano segregati in una capanna lontana dal villaggio e lasciati morire di fame, perché non si sapeva cosa fare per loro e per difendersi dal male, oggi si possono curare senza rischi per sè.

Io dico loro: bisogna capire il progetto primitivo di Dio nella vostra cultura. I vostri antenati hanno capito molto bene il progetto di Dio riguardo al matrimonio, che era monogamico. Tant'è vero che ancor oggi la prima moglie è quella che conta, anche se poi uno ha tante mogli. Questo vuol dire che i vostri padri avevano una concezione giusta del matrimonio, che poi nella storia è cambiata. Bisogna ricuperare i valori antichi e incarnarli nel mondo moderno. Nel matrimonio bisogna andare verso la monogamia. Su questa strada il Vangelo vi aiuta molto. Gesù Cristo non è venuto ad abolire la vostra cultura, ma a purificarla, a completarla, a renderla più umana e adatta al mondo moderno.

Ad esempio, l'iniziazione della tribù è riservata ai maschi, perché la femmina non conta. Ma questo è sbagliato, anzi chi trasmette la cultura è più la donna che l'uomo. Oggi la situazione è cambiata. A scuola bisogna mandarci non solo i maschietti ma anche le bambine: il Vangelo ci dice che l'uomo e la donna hanno la stessa dignità di creature di Dio e quindi bisogna dare le stesse possibilità al bambino come alla bambina».

Solo giustizia e carità contro la fame nel mondo?

Tra Vangelo e progresso umano c'è stretta connessione. La Chiesa l'ha sempre saputo, ma non l'ha richiamato con forza né approfondito quando dagli anni cinquanta in avanti è emerso il problema nuovo del «sottosviluppo» dei paesi poveri. Pio XII, Giovanni XXIII e lo stesso Concilio parlavano della fame e del sottosviluppo impostando il discorso sul binomio «giustizia e carità»: i popoli ricchi debbono comportarsi verso quelli poveri rispettando la giustizia internazionale e intervenendo con aiuti nei momenti di emergenza alimentare o dopo disastri naturali. L'annunzio di Cristo era fuori di questo quadro. Anche i documenti episcopali e sinodali sul tema del sottosviluppo ignorano il contributo dell'annunzio evangelico al progresso dei popoli[8].

Il p. Bartolomeo Sorge, nella «Presentazione» al secondo volume segnalato qui sopra (alla nota 8), sintetizza il contenuto di quei documenti ecclesiali affermando che «il contributo della Chiesa alla soluzione del grave problema della fame nel mondo» è triplice:

a) dare essa stessa «la testimonianza evangelica di una gioiosa austerità»;

b) «sensibilizzare ed educare le coscienze al grave problema della fame nel mondo»;

c) «l'impegno fattivo e concreto a cambiare le cose» nel senso della giustizia e di una politica coraggiosa e attenta ai più poveri...

---

[8] Si vedano: «Il problema della fame – Documenti pontifici» (a cura di Piero Gheddo), E.M.I., Milano 1965, pagg. 170; «La fame interpella l'uomo – Il contributo della Chiesa, Documenti di due decenni dello sviluppo» (a cura di Mani Tese), Ediz. La Civiltà Cattolica, Roma, senza data (edito nel 1981), pagg. 382.

Ma l'annunzio di Cristo non è il contributo più importante? Paolo VI nella «Populorum Progressio» (1967) parla della «visione cristiana dello sviluppo» (n. 14) e introduce il concetto di «sviluppo integrale» che «non si riduce alla semplice crescita economica», ma è «il passaggio da condizioni meno umane a condizioni più umane», fino alla fede in Dio alla carità di Cristo (n. 21). Secondo Paolo VI, per giungere al progresso dell'uomo, anche a quello sociale-economico, bisogna partire e mirare ai valori dello spirito, culturali e religiosi («Avere di più, per i popoli come per le persone, non è dunque lo scopo ultimo», n. 19): discorso che in quel tempo non venne recepito né approfondito.

Il 20 luglio 1991, «La Civiltà Cattolica» lamentava che «il numero dei documenti ecclesiali riguardo al problema del debito internazionale è tale da rendere impossibile una panoramica esauriente»: in pochi anni la macchina ecclesiastica aveva «prodotto più di 250 prese di posizione da parte di Conferenze episcopali, di singoli Vescovi, di gruppi ecclesiali locali». Ma non esiste nessun documento sul tema: «Vangelo e progresso dell'uomo»!

Del resto, il Documento «La fame nel mondo» di «Cor Unum» del 24 ottobre 1996 è un'ordinata e diligente elencazione delle «strutture di peccato» a livello internazionale già note (debito esterno, termini iniqui di scambio commerciale, ecc.). Manca del tutto il tema «Vangelo e sviluppo», fatto abbastanza «scandaloso»: un testo della Santa Sede che non spiega perché il Vangelo è il massimo contributo che noi cristiani diamo alla lotta contro la fame nei popoli poveri! Bisogna documentare la forza del Vangelo anche in campo economico-politico-sociale: altrimenti, a cosa servono l'annunzio e l'evangelizzazione? Ecco il tema che nei discorsi sulla fame nel mondo non compare mai.

CULTURA E RELIGIONE PER LO SVILUPPO DEI POPOLI

Giovanni Paolo II, nel discorso all'Unesco[9], pone con forza il tema della cultura al centro del dibattito sullo svilup-

---

[9] Parigi, 2 giugno 1980. «La Civiltà Cattolica» (5 luglio 1980, pag. 72) ha scritto che questo discorso è stato «fondatamente definito importante come una enciclica per la sua strutturazione e per la profondità del suo contenuto».

po dell'uomo e dei popoli. Il Papa parlava al termine dei due primi Decenni per lo Sviluppo, quando gli ambienti internazionali (Nazioni Unite, università, esperti, paesi ricchi), scoraggiati dalle esperienze precedenti, si chiedevano se e come il Nord poteva aiutare il Sud a liberarsi dalla miseria e dalla fame. Il Papa, dopo aver detto che «nessun uomo, nessun paese e nessun sistema del mondo possono rimanere indifferenti dinanzi alla 'geografia della fame'» e dopo aver invitato a cambiare «in modo essenziale e radicale..... tutto l'orientamento della politica economica e in particolare la gerarchia degli investimenti», aggiunge subito: «Per questo anche insisto, riferendomi alle origini della vostra Organizzazione, sulla necessità di mobilitare tutte le forze che orientano la dimensione spirituale dell'esistenza umana, che testimoniano il primato dello spirituale nell'uomo».

Il Papa parla della cultura: «L'uomo vive di una vita veramente umana grazie alla cultura»; poi accenna al «legame organico e costitutivo che esiste fra la religione in generale e il cristianesimo in particolare da una parte, e la cultura dall'altra», affermando il valore centrale dell'uomo («bisogna affermare l'uomo per se stesso e non per quasiasi altro motivo o ragione....amare l'uomo perché è uomo»); infine, per la soluzione del problema dello sviluppo, afferma che «il compito essenziale e primario della cultura è l'educazione, che consiste in sostanza nel fatto che l'uomo divenga sempre più umano, che possa 'essere di più' e non solamente 'avere di più'». In sostanza, il Papa riconosce l'importanza del problema economico nella lotta contro fame e sottosviluppo, ma pone a fondamento di tutta l'azione per lo sviluppo dell'uomo l'educazione dell'uomo, la cultura e il primato dei valori spirituali.

Con la «Redemptoris Missio» (1990) Giovanni Paolo II fa un passo avanti e proclama il valore del Vangelo per lo sviluppo. La missione della Chiesa non è di «operare direttamente sul piano economico o tecnico o politico o di dare un contributo materiale allo sviluppo, ma consiste essenzialmente nell'offrire ai popoli non un 'avere di più', ma un 'essere di più', risvegliando le coscienze col Vangelo» (R.M., n. 58).

Il contributo essenziale della Chiesa allo sviluppo dei popoli sta nell'annunzio del Vangelo, che è «una forza liberante e fautrice di sviluppo, proprio perché porta alla conversione del cuore e delle mentalità, fa riconoscere la dignità di ciascuna persona, dispone alla solidarietà, all'impegno, al servizio dei fratelli, inserisce l'uomo nel progetto di Dio, che è la costruzione del regno di pace e di giustizia già a partire da questa vita. È la prospettiva biblica dei 'cieli nuovi e terra nuova' (Is. 65, 17; 2 Pt. 3, 13; Ap. 21, 1), la quale ha inserito nella storia lo stimolo e la méta per l'avanzamento dell'umanità» (R.M., n. 58).

IL «TERZO MONDO» HA BISOGNO DI UNA «RIVOLUZIONE DELLE IDEE»

Le affermazioni del Papa possono sembrare teoriche, trionfalistiche: perché lo sviluppo anche socio-economico di un popolo è stimolato dall'annunzio evangelico? Normalmente, anche da parte di studiosi cristiani, le due cose sono separate (ecco la grave lacuna nella riflessione della Chiesa in questi anni!): da un lato c'è il «progresso», lo «sviluppo», la «liberazione dalla schiavitù e dal bisogno», quindi le finanze, la tecnica, la politica, i piani di sviluppo, la riforma agraria, gli aiuti economici, il commercio internazionale, la rivoluzione politico-sociale; dall'altro c'è il Vangelo, l'annunzio, la conversione a Cristo e l'opera «spirituale» della Chiesa. Siamo su due piani diversi.

La «Redemptoris Missio» congiunge strettamente le due cose ed afferma chiaramente che «il miglior servizio al fratello è l'evangelizzazione, che lo dispone a realizzarsi come figlio di Dio, lo libera dalle ingiustizie e lo promuove integralmente» (n. 58). L'enciclica afferma (n. 58) che «lo sviluppo di un popolo non deriva primariamente né dal denaro, né dagli aiuti materiali, né dalle strutture tecniche, bensì dalla formazione delle coscienze, dalla maturazione delle mentalità e dei costumi. È l'uomo il protagonista dello sviluppo, non il denaro o la tecnica».

Dopo aver detto che lo sviluppo viene dall'educazione dell'uomo, l'enciclica così continua (n. 58): «La Chiesa educa le coscienze rivelando ai popoli quel Dio che cercano e non conoscono, la grandezza dell'uomo creato ad immagine di Dio e da lui amato, l'eguaglianza di tutti gli uomini come figli di Dio, il dominio sulla natura creata e posta a servizio dell'uomo, il dovere di impegnarsi per lo sviluppo di tutto l'uomo e di tutti gli uomini».

Perché c'è stretta connessione tra Vangelo e sviluppo dei popoli? Perché sono le idee che muovono la storia (come ogni singolo uomo) e il «terzo mondo» ha bisogno soprattutto di una «rivoluzione delle idee». Il cammino storico dei popoli è condizionato dall'idea che ciascuno di essi si fa dell'uomo, del cosmo, del senso della vita umana, della divinità. Maritain afferma (in «Religion et Culture», Paris 1946): «Poiché lo sviluppo umano non è solo materiale ma anche e principalmente morale, è logico che l'elemento religioso giochi il ruolo principale». Gli storici delle civiltà (Toynbee, Weber, Dawson, Laloup-Nélis) parlano di «civiltà progressiste» (o dinamiche) e di «civiltà cicliche» (o statiche), le prime volte al futuro (messianiche), le seconde al passato che tendono a conservare ed a cui vogliono tornare. Dawson afferma che «la religione è la chiave della storia» e l'emergere e l'affermarsi della civiltà occidentale su tutte le altre non trova altra spiegazione che nella visione messianica e ottimista della storia che ha dato il cristianesimo, che ha liberato le forze dell'uomo per il «progresso»[10].

Il concetto di una storia orientata da Dio verso un fine positivo è uno dei contributi più grandi che la Bibbia porta ai popoli, al progresso dell'umanità[11]. Un mio confratello, p.

---

[10] DAWSON C., «Il cristianesimo e la formazione della civiltà occidentale», Rizzoli («I libri dello spirito cristiano»), 1997, pagg. 19 segg. Non mi fermo a precisare i concetti di «sviluppo» e di «progresso», che andrebbero ampiamente discussi, partendo dalla «Populorum Progressio» già citata. Qui vengono usati nel senso comune di «marcia in avanti» dell'umanità, pur con tutte le contraddizioni di ogni opera dell'uomo. Se invece si pensa che il «progresso moderno» è sostanzialmente una «marcia indietro» rispetto alle condizioni di vita, ad esempio, degli indios amazzonici o di quelle popolazioni africane e della Papua Nuova Guinea che ancora vivono nella preistoria, allora non si capisce perché mai noi dovremmo aiutare questi popoli ad evolversi. Meglio chiuderli in «riserve naturali» (specie di «zoo antropologici») come si è tentato di fare per gli indios d'Amazzonia e di certe regioni del Messico o per i Karimojon del nord Uganda!

[11] Si veda lo studio del biblista Sandro Sacchi, «La missione cristiana, contributo indispensabile allo sviluppo dei popoli», «Mondo e Missione», gennaio 1984, pagg. 56-61.

Silvano Zoccarato, che vive dal 1971 presso i Tupurì, tribù del nord Camerun, commentando una raccolta dei loro proverbi scrive: «Il tempo in cui si muove l'africano è più una ripetizione del passato che novità del presente. Il futuro è la fedeltà al suo passato... Egli non riesce a fare il passo dal tempo mitico al tempo storico, che comprende passato, presente e futuro»[12].

L'AFRICA NON PUÒ FARE A MENO DEL VANGELO

Un missionario gesuita in Madagascar (dal 1959 al 1962 e poi dal 1970 in avanti), p. Gino Manzone, afferma[13] che «secondo la mia esperienza, la povertà africana ha essenzialmente radici culturali... La visione del mondo, della natura, dell'uomo, della storia che viene dalla Bibbia è de-sacralizzante. Cioè il mondo e la natura non sono Dio, ma creati da Dio per servire all'uomo, a sua volta creato ad immagine di Dio. L'uomo è il signore dell'universo e deve lavorare per esplorare e sottomettere la natura, in modo da avere una vita più degna della sua dignità di figlio di Dio. Questa secondo me è una visione 'progressista' che supera tutte le visioni 'sacrali' della natura proprie del mondo africano, le quali ostacolano il progresso dell'uomo o almeno non ispirano, non giustificano il suo sforzo per migliorare e sottomettere la natura.

In Africa mancano gli stimoli interni allo sviluppo, manca una preparazione di idee progressiste, per cui l'accelerazione del progresso in tutte le sue espressioni non è possibile. Voler imporre questa accelerazione con metodi brutali, come fanno diversi governi africani, è una violenza fatta all'uomo africano che produce frutti negativi. Prima bisogna educare l'uomo, cambiare le mentalità. Ti porto un esempio: prendiamo la tecnica che noi portiamo in Africa, la meccanica e molte altre tecniche, compresi i nostri metodi di produzione agricola o industriale. L'africano impara facilmente, ha un'in-

---

[12] ZOCCARATO S., «Cosa per saggi, 100 proverbi dei Tupurì del Camerun», EMI 1988, pagg. 89; si veda anche la sua lunga testimonianza: «Nord Camerun: come nasce la Chiesa fra i Tupurì», in «Mondo e Missione, aprile 1977, pagg. 231-254.

[13] Si veda l'intervista che gli ho fatto: «Quale progresso per l'uomo africano?», in «Mondo e Missione», novembre 1983, pagg. 632-635.

telligenza viva e pronta, ma anche quando fa quello che vede fare dall'europeo, la sua mentalità profonda è diversa: questo vale per il contadino o il meccanico o per il lavoratore dell'industria, come pure per il voto politico secondo schemi democratici europei.

I risultati — afferma p. Manzone — sono necessariamente diversi: questo spiega perché certi progetti di sviluppo dopo un po' decadono, sono lasciati andare, le macchine si rompono e non si riparano[14]. Il Madagascar è grande due volte l'Italia ed ha enormi potenzialità agricole, per non parlare di altre ricchezze. Se fosse coltivato da contadini italiani o francesi, anche con mezzi rudimentali, potrebbe mantenere 100 milioni di abitanti. Invece non mantiene nemmeno nove milioni di malgasci, perché la produzione agricola è insufficiente. E questo non è certo colpa del colonialismo o delle multinazionali. Il progresso, in tutte le sue espressioni, è opera dell'uomo e quindi della cultura e della mentalità e credenze dell'uomo: non è solo una crescita materiale, economica, ma culturale, spirituale. Se non c'è adeguamento della mentalità, dell'educazione e dei valori, anche la crescita economica non viene, non può venire...

Il cammino dell'Africa verso il progresso sarà ancora lungo. Il vero problema è quello della cultura africana: l'Africa non deve perdere la sua identità, pur assumendo i valori universali dell'Occidente, che vengono dalla Bibbia e dal Vangelo. Non è semplice: da un lato deve rifiutare i

---

[14] C'è, nel terzo mondo, una frattura drammatica fra la vita dei popoli e il mondo internazionale degli «esperti». Questo spiega perché buona parte dei «grandi progetti», studiati in Occidente e finanziati con milioni e miliardi di dollari, quasi sempre non producono sviluppo né aumento di ricchezza (ecco l'origine del debito estero!). In Guinea-Bissau, a poca distanza dalla capitale Bissau, si possono ammirare le rovine di un grandioso e moderno mulino costruito all'inizio degli anni ottanta dall'Italia, capace di lavorare quotidianamente 300 tonnellate di riso e di arachidi. Ma non è mai entrato in funzione e gli impianti arrugginiscono al sole e all'acqua dei tropici, semplicemente perché il contadino africano non porta i suoi piccoli prodotti al mulino (quel lavoro lo fanno le donne, produce troppo poco perché valga la pena di fare il trasporto, mancano le strade, non c'è elettricità sufficiente, ecc.). I casi del genere sono molto comuni in Africa. Il prof. Ki-Zerbo, del Burkina Faso, docente universitario a Parigi, in conferenza nel Centro missionario del PIME a Milano diceva: «Voi europei venite in Africa, costruite una grande industria moderna e ci date le chiavi in mano. Ma le chiavi dovreste mettercele in testa!».

modelli di sviluppo capitalista o comunista che l'Occidente vuole imporle, per trovare un suo cammino di progresso, secondo la sua originalità; dall'altro, non è possibile per l'Africa fare a meno dei valori universali di cui l'Occidente è portatore, così come non può fare a meno degli aiuti allo sviluppo, se dati in spirito di fraternità e non per imporre qualsiasi soggezione.

Io sono convinto — conclude p. Manzone — che l'evangelizzazione è il massimo contributo che noi possiamo dare all'Africa. Gli africani accolgono il Vangelo non come un qualcosa di estraneo, ma come un completamento della cultura tradizionale, una luce nuova che illumina la loro storia, un criterio di giudizio che permette loro di capire quali sono i valori umanizzanti della tradizione africana da conservare e potenziare e quali quelli disumanizzanti da eliminare. Anche la cultura africana infatti ha bisogno di essere giudicata dal Vangelo, ha bisogno di purificazione e di conversione».

«I MISSIONARI RICONOSCIUTI PROMOTORI DI SVILUPPO»

Ecco la «rivoluzione delle idee» che l'annunzio di Cristo porta al «terzo mondo», non come un'imposizione, ma partendo dalla carità, dall'attenzione all'uomo, ai poveri, dallo sviluppo socio-economico alla crescita spirituale, fino all'inserimento in Cristo salvatore, «finalità suprema dello sviluppo personale», come dice Paolo VI nella «Populorum Progressio» (n. 16). Per questo nella «Redemptoris Missio» Giovanni Paolo II scrive (n. 58): «L'autentico sviluppo umano deve affondare le sue radici in un'evangelizzazione sempre più profonda».

Nella stessa enciclica (n. 58) il Papa scrive: «I missionari più che in passato sono oggi riconosciuti anche come promotori di sviluppo da governi ed esperti internazionali, i quali restano ammirati del fatto che si ottengano notevoli risultati con scarsi mezzi». È quello che si nota in tutta l'Africa. Ricordo un viaggio in Burkina Faso nel gennaio 1985, durante il tempo della grande siccità che devastava i paesi del Sahel. Nel nord del Burkina la gente scappava da città e campagne, invase dalla sabbia, emigrando verso il sud del paese e la Costa d'Avorio. Grandi progetti realizzati anche dal governo italiano, dighe, canali, pozzi, rimboschimento, stavano fallendo per mancanza di manutenzione e di unione nel lavoro da parte della gente del posto.

Invece, nelle regioni delle due «fattorie-scuola» agricole dei Fratelli della Sacra Famiglia italiani (di Chieri, Torino), Gundi e Nanorò, tutto era verde, c'erano coltivazioni, laghetti pieni d'acqua. Come mai? Perché i Fratelli da trenta e più anni avevano educato giovani e ragazze della regione a trattenere l'acqua piovana, a riparare le pompe dei pozzi, a scavare canali e laghetti di villaggio, ecc. Inoltre, li avevano uniti in cooperative per l'acquisto di sementi, di macchine, per lo smercio dei loro prodotti... Il Ministro dell'agricoltura del Burkina, che avevo intervistato a Ouagadougou, mi diceva: «Padre, se nel nord del nostro paese, invece di due «fattorie-scuola» ne avessimo avute cinquanta o cento, non ci sarebbe il flagello della siccità...».

Non da oggi la Chiesa è impegnata sulle frontiere della fame e del sottosviluppo. Da secoli ha stabilito con i suoi missionari rapporti di solidarietà con i popoli poveri, costruendo scuole, università, ospedali, lebbrosari, opere sociali, tipografie, fattorie-scuola, cooperative, studiando e alfabetizzando le lingue locali, salvando le memorie delle culture in via di estinzione (quanti «Musei missionari» in Africa e in Europa sulle culture africane, quante grammatiche e vocabolari di lingue indigene, quante «Raccolte di proverbi»...). Ma il contributo più importante non consiste tanto in queste ed altre iniziative educative, assistenziali, sociali, culturali, quanto nell'annuncio del Vangelo, che è «forza liberante e fautrice di sviluppo» («Redemptoris Missio», n. 58).

La Chiesa ed i missionari (con i volontari laici) non possono naturalmente risolvere il problema del sottosviluppo: non è il loro compito. Essi danno al Sud del mondo un modello di approccio e di azione, finalizzando la loro presenza soprattutto all'educazione: la chiave del «progresso» è l'educazione dell'uomo! Purtroppo bisogna dire che missionari e volontari sono ammirati, applauditi, ma non studiati, né imitati. Quale lo spirito e quali i metodi della loro azione? Il tema è molto vasto. In sintesi si possono indicare quattro piste di ricerca:

a) Motivazione religiosa nell'approccio ai popoli diversi e poveri. Non esistono popoli atei e i più poveri sono quelli più religiosi. Non c'è scambio educativo se non c'è sintonia profonda nella vita: per educare bisogna incontrarsi nella fede in Dio, nella preghiera, nella moralità naturale. Quante volte nel Sud del mondo (specie in Africa) ho sentito dire da missionari che sono sul posto da decenni: «Vengono qui tecnici e cooperanti laici dall'Europa per realizzare piani di sviluppo e si presentano come atei e uomini senza moralità. Non li vedi mai pregare, avendo molto denaro si comportano male con le donne, fanno una vita che la gente giudica scandalosa. Possono fare grandi opere materiali, ma non educano nessuno, perché la gente li disprezza, si crea fra loro e il popolo una barriera di incomprensione e di rifiuto». In Somalia, nel 1978, il Vescovo di Mogadiscio, il francescano mons. Salvatore Colombo, si lamentava di non pochi insegnanti e operatori culturali italiani venuti in aiuto al Governo locale per le scuole e l'Università: in mezzo a un popolo musulmano profondamente religioso, non pregavano mai e davano cattivo esempio sul piano morale. Gli studenti stessi lo riferivano al Vescovo, il quale mi diceva: «Come possono pretendere di educare?».

b) Condividere la vita (la legge dell'incarnazione). Il missionario si inserisce pazientemente e umilmente in un popolo, ne impara la lingua, la cultura, si adatta al cibo, ai costumi, è formato per saper ascoltare e imparare dall'altro, in spirito di fraternità: dona tutto se stesso e la propria vita all'incontro e all'amicizia con l'altro. Per educare bisogna condividere: ecco perché la vocazione missionaria è il modello profetico di come il Nord può gettare ponti di comprensione, di scambio e di aiuto autentico con il Sud.

La diminuzione delle vocazioni missionarie a vita (e anche dei volontari laici animati dallo stesso spirito) è un segno estremamente negativo per l'Italia. Quando un popolo come quello italiano, che ha preso coscienza dell'abisso esistente tra Nord e Sud del mondo e del dovere di impegnarsi a favore dei poveri, produce meno giovani che consacrano la vita alla missione o, come laici, alla cooperazione internazionale, questo significa che si parla molto di solidarietà, ma in sostanza si va nella direzione opposta, ci si disimpegna (come dimostra il disinteresse attuale per il «terzo mondo» e i suoi poveri, che «non fanno più notizia»).

Educare le coscienze con il Vangelo

c) Educare le coscienze col Vangelo e formare comunità solidali, impegnate, che sono il motore dello sviluppo e della lotta per la giustizia: lo scopo della missione è di rendere l'uomo più uomo annunziando e testimoniando Gesù Cristo e di far superare alle comunità la passività tradizionale e le divisioni che bloccano lo sviluppo. Sono numerosi gli esempi che si possono citare, di come le comunità cristiane sono state il motore dello sviluppo e della liberazione dall'oppressione. La fine della dittatura di Marcos nelle Filippine è frutto dell'azione delle comunità cristiane, che prima hanno coscientizzato per lunghi anni la gente (con centinaia di martiri fra i semplici cristiani), poi sono scese in piazza per protestare contro le elezioni truccate del febbraio 1986: è stata la «rivoluzione del rosario e dei fiori» che ha vinto sui carri armati schierati attorno al Palazzo presidenziale.

Anche in America Latina, i casi da citare sarebbero molti, nella lotta contro le dittature e per la democrazia, nell'impegno per la giustizia (si pensi a tutto il problema della terra in Amazzonia e nel nord-est brasiliano!), nella denunzia per la violazione dei diritti dell'uomo. Se non ci fosse un'educazione alla base, secondo i principi del Vangelo e delle Beatitudini, questo impegno non violento fino al martirio (quanti autentici martiri cristiani nelle giovani Chiese!) non sarebbe nemmeno pensabile. In Corea del sud, il passaggio dalla dittatura militare alla democrazia negli anni ottanta è da tutti attribuito all'opera della Chiesa cattolica e delle Chiese protestanti e delle loro comunità cristiane.

d) Aiuti allo sviluppo che partono dall'uomo, dal popolo: i piccoli progetti (micro-realizzazioni) che coinvolgono la gente e la uniscono per uno scopo comunitario, quindi creano sviluppo attraverso l'educazione. Gli aiuti non da stato a stato, ma da popolo a popolo, che creano solidarietà e scambio. In Africa, gli esempi di sviluppo creato a livello di villaggio o di regione, attraverso l'opera di missionari e volontari laici, sono quasi infiniti. Ne ricordo uno che ho visto da vicino nel 1994, esemplare per tanti altri[15]. Il missionario della Consolata padre Camillo Calliari, nei villaggi della missione di Kipengere sull'altopiano meridionale della Tanzania, ha realizzato un «polo di sviluppo» ammirato e proposto a modello dalle autorità e, quel che più importa, coinvolgendo la gente che lo segue con passione (lo chiamano con affetto «Baba – padre – Camillo»).

Le realizzazioni di Baba Camillo e del suo popolo, in vent'anni di lavoro, sono impressionanti solo a farne l'elenco: ospedale con 78 letti (400 parti l'anno); costruzione e riparazione di strade con mezzi propri, di seconda mano, quasi tutti venuti dall'Italia; acquedotto per portare acqua di fonte ai villaggi (serve 10.000 persone); opera di rimboschimento nella regione (ogni anno vengono piantati 70.000 pini, cipressi, eucaliptus, con l'aiuto dei ragazzi delle scuole); fattoria di 200 ettari coltivata con metodi moderni (per la prima volta si produce frumento a 2.000 metri); allevamento di vacche da latte (le vacche africane producono un litro di latte al giorno) e diffusione del latte nelle famiglie; caseificio-scuola, produzione di vino con uva locale; mulino che lavora a tempo pieno per la gente; scuola di falegnameria con 30 giovani residenti e molti altri esterni; officina-scuola meccanica per la riparazione di macchine d'ogni tipo; laghetto artificiale per la piscicoltura; vari tipi di scuole che dipendono dalla missione, per bambini e analfabeti adulti, per la promozione della donna; farmacie di villaggio e cooperative di vario genere, ecc.

Baba Camillo mi raccontava le difficoltà incontrate per convincere gli anziani e i capi della tribù dei «Wabena» (un tempo abili pastori e guerrieri, di grandi valori umani, ma ancora ai primi passi nell'agricoltura moderna), che proibivano ai giovani di cambiare i sistemi antichi di pesca e di agricoltura; poi, quando le cooperative hanno cominciato a produrre e si sono create piccole farmacie nei villaggi e altri servizi, c'era

---

[15] Il resoconto del viaggio in «Tanzania, Cammino in salita verso lo sviluppo», «Mondo e Missione», maggio 1995, pagg. 29-44. Si veda pure il libro di Giorgio Torelli, «Baba Camillo», De Agostini 1987, pagg. 176.

il problema che i capi e gli anziani volevano tutto gratis, rischiando di far fallire l'esperimento, ecc.

Il «Decennio mondiale per lo sviluppo culturale» (1988-1997)

Nell'Africa che soffre la fame, il contadino lavora ancora con la zappa, ignora l'irrigazione artificiale, i concimi anche naturali, la rotazione delle colture, la trazione animale e il carro agricolo (nei villaggi africani non si conosce la ruota, le donne portano tutto sulla testa), molte produzioni orto-frutticole (cipolle, carote, insalata, coste, cavolfiori, ecc... ma sono solo esempi!): com'è possibile che possa produrre a sufficienza per una popolazione in forte crescita? La radice della fame sta in questo: che molti popoli africani non sono stati educati ad un'agricoltura moderna, per cui, ad esempio, producono 5 quintali di riso per ettaro, mentre il contadino vercellese di quintali ne produce 70-80, nello stesso ettaro e in condizioni climatiche peggiori!

Nelle venti isole Bijagòs nell'Oceano Atlantico davanti alla Guinea-Bissau, con un mare pescosissimo, il popolo moriva di fame. Dal 1975 vive nelle Bijagòs il missionario del PIME p. Luigi Scantamburlo, che semplicemente ha insegnato a pescare e attrezzato i villaggi con barche da pesca a motore e strumenti adatti alla pesca; ha insegnato ai Bijagòs come costruire le barche, riparare i motori e le reti; poi ha fondato un'ottantina di piccole cooperative di villaggio per il possesso delle barche e la vendita del prodotto, ecc. Risultato: oggi l'evoluzione e il progresso dei Bijagòs è un esempio probante di cosa vuol dire l'educazione per lo sviluppo.

Ma per educare all'agricoltura e alla pesca moderne ci vuole istruzione ed è indispensabile l'evoluzione delle mentalità e delle culture tradizionali. L'esperienza dei missionari dimostra che lo sviluppo di un popolo è un'opera di lenta educazione, di formazione, di apertura a idee e metodi nuovi. Non si ottiene tutto questo con leggi o con rivolte e proteste, ma partendo dall'interno delle coscienze, delle famiglie e dei villaggi.

L'opera dei missionari è orientata a questa educazione di base, che parte dall'uomo e dalla sua cultura, religione, mentalità, per arrivare anche alla tecnica di coltivare una risaia e di pescare nell'Oceano Atlantico. I metodi di inserimento e di presenza educativa dei missionari dovrebbero essere oggetto di studio, di approfondimento, per servire di esempio a volontari e cooperanti inviati da governi e da associazioni non governative in Africa.

È da poco terminato il «Decennio mondiale per lo sviluppo culturale» (1988-1997), lanciato dall'UNESCO allo scopo di orientare studi e dibattiti alla scoperta «della dimensione culturale del progresso: è necessario trovare un legame tra la produzione e la creatività e capire che l'economia affonda le sue radici nella cultura»[16]. Ma l'iniziativa dell'Unesco ha avuto scarso seguito fra gli studiosi e nell'opinione pubblica: la cultura dominante non consente di andar fuori degli schemi consueti. Chi parla di «radici culturali e religiose del sottosviluppo» (com'è capitato al sottoscritto)[17], viene accusato di «spiritualismo» ininfluente nelle vicende storiche.

Mi auguro che questo quaderno di «Studia Missionalia» possa contribuire, almeno nel campo missionario e tra gli studiosi cristiani, a stimolare un settore di studi troppo trascurato: per far riflettere sul come aiutare i popoli poveri ad evolversi; ma anche per spiegare il significato della «missione alle genti» non solo in termini di salvezza extra terrena. Se le culture tradizionali africane (parliamo solo di quelle) non debbono essere giudicate e purificate dal Vangelo per il progresso dell'uomo africano; cioè se vanno già bene così come sono, vanno salvate così come sono (come dicono etnologi e antropologi): che senso ha l'evangelizzazione per il progresso dei popoli? Hanno ragione quelli che dicono (ed è una mentalità molto diffusa): i missionari non vadano a disturbare i popoli che hanno già culture e religioni, restino qui a chiedere più aiuti (economici) al governo ed a protestare per il «debito estero» e il «commercio ineguale»...

---

[16] «Il Corriere dell'Unesco», gennaio 1989, pagg. 4-6.
[17] Specialmente con questi volumi: «Terzo Mondo: perché povero?» (Emi 1972), «I popoli della fame» (Emi 1982) e «Nel nome del Padre: la conquista cristiana, sopruso o missione?» (Bompiani 1992).

Chiesa e Progresso Umano

Sergio Bernal

1. La complessità del concetto di progresso

Possiamo parlare oggi pacificamente di progresso, ma non è stato sempre così nell'ambito della Chiesa. Anzi, per secoli, essa ha manifestato una certa riluttanza ad accettare di stare al passo della storia. La nozione di progresso è infatti strettamente collegata con l'Illuminismo e con un periodo in cui nei movimenti storici serpeggiavano ideologie contrarie alla Chiesa. Il che, per motivi diversi, la portò ad assumere un atteggiamento di chiusura nei confronti di qualsiasi proposta proveniente da tali ambienti. Tuttavia, la riflessione più recente ha messo in evidenza come, di per sè, il termine stesso di *progresso* ha una connotazione positiva, «si può definire come l'idea che il corso delle cose, e in particolare della civiltà, ha avuto dall'inizio un graduale aumento di benessere o di felicità, un miglioramento del singolo e dell'umanità, un movimento verso un obiettivo desiderabile»[1].

Trattare il tema del progresso umano ci porta necessariamente a considerare l'altro, quello di sviluppo, per utilizzare la terminologia contemporanea, anzi parliamo di «sviluppo umano», nozione coniata di recente, alla quale si è arrivati dopo un lungo percorso. A questo riguardo vale la pena anzi rilevare l'interazione, anche se spesso non chiaramente percepita, fra Chiesa e ambienti secolari nei quali si è sviluppato questo concetto. La Chiesa e le altre istituzioni si sono reciprocamente avvantaggiate, per l'arricchimento del proprio pensiero e azione, con i frutti delle rispettive ricerche.

Intorno al concetto di sviluppo esiste comunque un ricco dibattito non privo di ideologia, per cui spesso viene ad

---

[1] Bobbio Norberto, *Dizionario di politica*, UTET, Torino, 1976, p. 794.

ingenerarsi confusione con altri concetti affini. Louis Baeck riassume in poche parole gli aspetti più salienti del complesso processo, descrivendolo come «rapida industrializzazione in campo economico, secolarizzazione delle ideologie e delle religioni, modernizzazione dei modelli comportamentali, urbanizzazione e adozione di comportamenti cosmopoliti (cioè occidentali) per facilitare la loro integrazione nella cultura mondiale»[2]. Appare così, per un verso, la complessità del fenomeno e, per un altro, il suo significato culturale ed etico, in quanto il processo incide sul sistema sociale e su quello culturale, modificandone i modelli di pensiero e di azione.

1.1. ALLA RICERCA DI UN MODELLO DI SVILUPPO

Nel delineare le strategie per il progresso, inteso come sviluppo, dei Paesi appena liberati dal colonialismo, si è passati da un progetto di ricostruzione, così come si era manifestato necessario dopo la seconda guerra mondiale per i Paesi europei, ad una nuova visione centrata su nuove proposte globali per i Paesi del Terzo Mondo. È da aggiungere che, nell'intero processo, gli Stati Uniti hanno avuto un protagonismo quasi egemonico, fatto questo che ha impresso un'impronta specifica alle varie proposte. Passati cinquant'anni caratterizzati dalla tensione Est-Ovest, durante i quali le due super potenze tentavano di imporre il proprio modello — capitalista o collettivista di pianificazione — ai Paesi che dipendevano politicamente ed economicamente da loro, oggi, la quasi assoluta egemonia degli Stati Uniti si accompagna alla proposta, sostenuta dai grandi Organismi Internazionali, di un modello unico che non consente alcuna libertà di scelta.

Si deve riconoscere, tuttavia, che le varie proposte e i diversi tentativi di portarle a termine negli ultimi 40 anni, sono state fallimentari, il che ha portato ad una revisione del concetto originario di sviluppo, tale da comprendere il riconoscimento della complessità dei processi di crescita e della di-

---

[2] BAECK LOUIS, «Cinquant'anni di cultura dello sviluppo: teorie e pratiche in questione» in *Abitare la società globale. Per una globalizzazione sostenibile*. A cura di Roberto Papini, Antonio Pavan, Stefano Zamagni. Napoli, Edizioni Scientifiche Italiane, 1997, 48.

versità delle situazioni che richiedono un adattamento dei modelli. Ma, soprattutto, si è palesata la necessità di pensare allo sviluppo come qualcosa a servizio dell'uomo, non come un processo finalizzato a se stesso, sotto un'ottica prettamente economica. Forse si potrebbe azzardare l'ipotesi che, pur senza un esplicito riconoscimento, in questo processo si scopre l'influsso della Chiesa che, con Paolo VI, lanciava la proposta di uno sviluppo integrale, vale a dire di tutto l'uomo e di tutti gli uomini. Il Programma delle Nazioni Unite per lo Sviluppo (PNUD), sin dal 1990, con il suo *Rapporto sullo sviluppo umano*, ha cercato di porre fine alla tendenza di misurare il progresso umano soltanto in termini di crescita economica, tanto che è ora in corso la elaborazione di un paradigma di sviluppo umano sostenibile. Anche gli esperti del PNUD sono arrivati alla conclusione che, affinché lo sviluppo possa essere valido e legittimo, deve essere centrato sulla persona umana, i suoi benefici devono essere distribuiti equamente e deve essere sostenibile dal punto di vista sociale ed ecologico. Ciò si è tradotto, nel *Rapporto 1996*, nell'accurata analisi del complesso rapporto fra crescita economica e sviluppo umano, secondo cui, malgrado una certa indipendenza dei singoli fattori a breve scadenza, a lungo termine si crea un reciproco influsso[3].

Non c'è dubbio che il progresso, sotto la categoria dello sviluppo, va visto in generale positivamente. Tuttavia, non possiamo ignorare alcuni aspetti negativi che si sono rilevati in questi ultimi decenni dedicati dalle Nazioni Unite allo sviluppo, come ad esempio le discriminazioni verso i Paesi sotto-sviluppati chiamati «tradizionali». Le loro culture, infatti, vengono viste, con una forte carica di etnocentrismo, come un vero ostacolo allo sviluppo che va superato. Una tale distorsione evidentemente non consente il necessario discernimento dei valori propri delle diverse culture e così ciò che viene a trovarsi in giuoco, nell'attuale processo di globalizzazione, è la stessa identità dei Paesi in via di sviluppo.

---

[3] Cf. *Informe sobre Desarrollo Humano 1996*, Publicado para el Programa de las Naciones Unidas para el Desarrollo (PNUD). Madrid, Ediciones Mundi-Prensa, 1996.

2. Rilevanza del tema nell'ambito pastorale

Or bene, il tema dello sviluppo non riguarda soltanto l'economia e la politica, come si è soliti pensare. Essendone stata superata la visione prettamente economica anche negli ambienti secolari, oggi si è arrivati ad una comprensione dell'importanza che esso ha per la pace nel mondo, strettamente vincolata ai rapporti fra le nazioni a diversi ritmi e livelli di crescita, come già rilevato da Paolo VI: «Ma deve essere ben chiaro ad ognuno che ciò che è in giuoco è la vita stessa dei popoli poveri, è la pace civile nei Paesi in via di sviluppo, ed è la pace del mondo»[4]. Ma, più che altro, oggi si sta arrivando a capire che vi è una dimensione umana all'interno di questa problematica, per cui lo sviluppo deve consentire a tutti, uomini e donne, di poter crescere secondo le proprie potenzialità per arrivare ad una piena umanizzazione. La preoccupazione recente degli Organismi internazionali per il grave problema della povertà, intesa come incapacità di accedere a quei beni ritenuti necessari per sopperire ai bisogni fondamentali, anzi come incapacità di trarre beneficio dal loro uso, è servita a far sì che la visione laica di sviluppo umano si avvicinasse di più a quella cattolica e viceversa.

Che la problematica del progresso non riguardi soltanto l'economia, appare assai evidente dal fatto che i rapporti interumani, come pure quelli fra Paesi ricchi e Paesi poveri, sono spesso segnati da una grande ingiustizia, specie per ciò che riguarda il mercato. Le condizioni che regolano le transazioni fra i potenti e i deboli, incidono sulla sorte delle persone, anzi, della intera società e, purtroppo, tali condizioni sono divenute troppo disuguali da paese a paese, motivo per il quale Paolo VI ha messo in causa il principio stesso del libero mercato, ritenuto dai capitalisti liberali in grado di garantire da solo la giustizia (cf. PP 58). Non si può continuare a pensare al progresso umano a livello soltanto della persona isolata e in se stessa considerata. Emerge con forza la profonda intuizione di Paolo VI quando pensava al necessario sviluppo di *tutti* gli uomini. La vita e il progresso di ogni persona risentono infatti fortemente delle condizioni dominanti i rapporti

---

[4] *Populorum progressio*, 55. Diventa chiara così l'espressione che appare nell'Enciclica, cioè lo sviluppo è il nuovo nome della pace.

internazionali. Appare così che, nell'ambito dello sviluppo, vi è una dimensione morale perchè è in giuoco la realizzazione o meno della vocazione umana e, di conseguenza, lo sviluppo della tecnica e della civiltà «esigono un proporzionale sviluppo della vita morale e dell'etica» (RH 15). La Chiesa, al centro della cui missione pone la cura dell'uomo nella sua integrità, non può perciò rimanere indifferente dinanzi alla complessa problematica della crescita economica, che costituisce una delle condizioni basilari per la crescita della persona. Anzi, essa «considera questa sollecitudine per l'uomo, per la sua umanità, per il futuro degli uomini sulla terra e, quindi, anche per l'orientamento di tutto lo sviluppo e del progresso, come un elemento essenziale della sua missione, indissolubilmente congiunto con essa» (Ib.). Più recentemente si sta facendo strada, in ambienti diversi, la preoccupazione per il bene comune, inteso come l'insieme delle circostanze favorevoli alla crescita dell'individuo e della società. In questa prospettiva, la ricerca di un minimo di benessere materiale e spirituale per tutti i membri della società, appare come l'obiettivo primario della crescita economica. Non a caso durante la Conferenza di Copenaghen, per evitare il predominio del fattore economico, è stato introdotto un concetto di «sviluppo sociale» che pone l'enfasi sulla persona considerata nei suoi rapporti sociali e, ancora di più, tiene conto delle società alle quali le persone appartengono.

Tuttavia, parallelamente al fatto positivo di una migliore comprensione del concetto di sviluppo, perdura la tentazione illuministica del sogno di un progresso illimitato, come risultato dello straordinario progresso della scienza e della tecnica, le quali in efetti trovano la soluzione ad antichi problemi considerati insolubili. Per questo motivo, Giovanni Paolo II ha preferito adoperare nel testo dell'Enciclica *Sollicitudo rei socialis* la parola «sviluppo» anziché quella di «progresso»[5].

Queste tracce d'Illuminismo costituiscono una tremenda sfida per l'evangelizzazione in quanto, dietro di esse, si nascondono tuttora le fallacie di un mondo senza Dio e di un «super uomo»: In questo modo si arriva a prescindere dal necessario riferimento ad una qualunque norma di moralità.

---

[5] Cf. la nota 50 dell'Enciclica.

D'altra parte, il processo di crescita, insieme al progresso tecnologico che l'umanità è riuscita a realizzare, mettono in crisi alcuni atteggiamenti della Chiesa che, per secoli, aveva guardato con diffidenza lo sviluppo della scienza e della tecnica, viste come una possibile minaccia alla fede dei cristiani. Ciò era dovuto, evidentemente, ad un concetto sbagliato della fede e della scienza. Così come la Chiesa trascinò per secoli il famoso conflitto fra scienza e fede, fu altrettanto difficile per essa accettare che la evangelizzazione avesse qualcosa a che fare con i problemi dello sviluppo, come uno degli elementi necessari per la sua completezza (cf. EN 31)[6].

3. L'EVOLUZIONE DEL CONCETTO DI PROGRESSO NELLA DOTTRINA SOCIALE DELLA CHIESA

3.1. *In principio creavit Deus caelum et terram (Gen 1,1)*

Questa semplice frase con cui si apre il messaggio della Rivelazione cristiana nasconde, sotto la sua apparente semplicità, tutta la complessità del rapporto fra uomini e donne e il loro mondo. Sembra che l'autore del libro sacro abbia capito benissimo che, al centro della esperienza umana, sta addirittura il problema della sopravvivenza che dipende da questo rapporto. Dal racconto biblico appare assai evidente che il meraviglioso e complesso mondo fisico è stato creato a servizio degli uomini, come loro «habitat». Si può parlare in questo modo, della «vocazione» del mondo fisico a servizio

---

[6] Vale la pena notare come già Pio XII anticipasse l'apertura di visione del Concilio in merito, quando, nel 1941, diceva, a proposito del progresso tecnico: «Noi non condanniamo ciò che è dono di Dio, il quale come ci fa sorgere il pane dalle zolle della terra, nelle viscere più profonde del suolo nei giorni della creazione del mondo nascose tesori di fuoco, di metalli, di pietre preziose da scavarsi dalla mano dell'uomo per i suoi bisogni, per le sue opere, per il suo progresso. La Chiesa, madre di tante Università d'Europa, che ancora esalta e aduna i più arditi maestri delle scienze, scrutatori della natura, non ignora però che di ogni bene e della stessa libertà del volere si può far uso degno di lode e di premio ovvero di biasimo e di condanna». *Radiomessaggio Natalizio sui presupposti per un nuovo ordine internazionale* (24-XII-1941) 8. Fra altri, spicca anche l'argomento di Giovanni XXIII nella *Mater et magistra»:* «Certo la Chiesa ha insegnato in ogni tempo e continua sempre ad insegnare che i progressi scientifico-tecnici e il conseguente benessere materiale sono beni reali; e quindi segnano un importante passo nell'incivilimento umano» (255).

dell'intera umanità. Dal racconto biblico scaturiscono tre verità che vanno al cuore della riflessione sullo sviluppo: la responsabilità, la gratuità e la comunità.

La vocazione del mondo a servizio dell'umanità trova la sua complementarietà nella vocazione che essa ha ricevuto di «dominare la terra», espressione che, purtroppo, per secoli è stata interpretata in senso completamente sbagliato, come se il dominio s'identificasse con un utilizzo egoista e irresponsabile. Il vero senso, invece, sta in un usufruire delle risorse che presuppone, da parte di chi domina, padronanza di sè e consapevolezza della sua responsabilità nei confronti degli altri. La volontà del Creatore, infatti, era *che l'uomo comunicasse con la natura come «padrone» e «custode» intelligente e nobile, e non come «sfruttatore» e «distruttore» senza alcun riguardo*[7].

Un secondo elemento che scaturisce dal racconto biblico è quello della «gratuità». Il Creatore, prima della creazione di coloro che avrebbero portato la Sua impronta, costruisce una stupenda dimora che sarà data loro in dono assolutamente gratuito, in modo tale che nessuno potrà legittimamente reclamare alcun diritto su di essa con esclusione degli altri.

La destinazione universale dei beni è un segno del destino comune dell'umanità che deve ricavare dalla terra quanto è necessario per la sopravvivenza. La retta comprensione di questa verità porterà alla conclusione della necessità di vivere in comunità. I misteri dell'Incarnazione e della Redenzione offrono il necessario complemento alla prima rivelazione della natura sociale (comunitaria) dell'uomo e della donna, creati e salvati in comunità (cf. GS, 32).

3.2. *La Missione della Chiesa e il progresso*

La Chiesa ha ricevuto la missione di evangelizzare (Mc 16,15), anzi, essa sta nel mondo per evangelizzare (cf. EN, 14). Ora, questa missione è stata intesa diversamente lungo i secoli di storia dell'evangelizzazione, durante i quali prevaleva piuttosto, una concezione della trasmissione del messaggio senza notevoli implicazioni per la vita quotidiana, soprattutto per ciò che riguarda gli aspetti materiali di essa. Le

---
[7] *Redemptor Hominis*, 15.

grandi trasformazioni sociali che hanno avuto luogo come risultato della rivoluzione industriale, portarono la Chiesa ad occuparsi, non senza grandi difficoltà, degli effetti che tali mutamenti avevano sulla vita della gente, mettendone a rischio la salvezza. Si trattava, all'inizio, soprattutto, di una preoccupazione morale e assai moralizzante, per i problemi che oggi chiamiamo dello sviluppo[8].

3.2.1. Il Magistero anteriore al Vaticano II

Pure senza un esplicito riferimento allo sviluppo, (impensabile d'altronde all'epoca), la prima Enciclica sociale, la *Rerum novarum* (1891), trattava già della problematica creata dalla crescita economica che, grazie all'innovazione tecnica, aveva assunto un ritmo tanto accelerato da superare la capacità di risolvere gli effetti negativi che essa stessa produceva sulla condizione dei lavoratori. Si può dire, tuttavia, che sin dagli inizi, i documenti sociali della Chiesa si sono occupati della problematica dello sviluppo. Già Leone XIII, sotto l'influsso di molti laici impegnati e di alcuni ecclesiastici, intuiva che la missione della Chiesa riguardava anche certi ambienti fino a quel momento visti come non confacenti con la missione di annunziare il Vangelo.

In questa maniera Leone XIII iniziava una autentica rivoluzione del pensiero e della prassi cristiana, pur cautamente, in un contesto in cui il mondo non cattolico appariva come nemico della Chiesa. La Chiesa provava una certa reticenza ad occuparsi di quegli aspetti della vita nella società che non apparissero direttamente collegati con la «vita spirituale» dei cristiani, sempre secondo una visione dicotomica della persona, che veniva esacerbata ancora di più dalla concezione liberale che propugnava la radicale separazione fra vita pratica e morale[9]. La Chiesa stessa non era arrivata anco-

---

[8] Pio XI, nella *Quadragesimo anno*, riteneva necessaria una «severa disciplina morale, rigidamente mantenuta dall'autorità statale» (QA 133).
[9] Nell'Enciclica sul comunismo, *Divini Redemptoris*, Pio XI descrive stupendamente tale atteggiamento: «taluni, mentre sono apparentemente fedeli all'adempimento dei loro doveri religiosi, nel campo poi del lavoro o dell'industria o della professione o nel commercio o nell'impiego, per un deplorevole sdoppiamento di coscienza, conducono una vita troppo difforme dalle norme così chiare della giu-

ra alla concezione integrale dell'anima e del corpo, della materia e dello spirito. Anche se, timidamente, la *Rerum novarum* apriva tuttavia una nuova via che troverà poi il suo sbocco nel Concilio Vaticano II.

Malgrado le grandi trasformazioni subite dalla società, la Chiesa manteneva una concezione di se stessa che rispondeva piuttosto ai primi tempi della cristianità. Infatti, sembra che lo stesso Leone XIII ritenesse ideale l'assetto dei tempi nei quali «la salutare influenza della Chiesa era, senza contrasto alcuno, penetrata in tutte le parti dello Stato»[10]. Anche se il contenuto di questi primi documenti era appropriato e oggi possiamo darne una retta interpretazione, tuttavia il linguaggio restava in certi passi assai ambiguo, lasciando spazio a d una lettura forse contraria al pensiero dei papi stessi. Così, per esempio, nella *Rerum novarum* si dice che l'unico rimedio ai mali sociali era «il ritorno alla vita e alle istituzioni cristiane» (RN 22). Quaranta anni più tardi, Pio XI ribadirà lo stesso principio (QA 128), anzi andrà oltre, sognando la restaurazione di un ordine sociale più vicino ai tempi medievali che non alle nuove strutture che la società del suo tempo andava assumendo[11]. L'unica via di soluzione consisteva, per Pio XI, nel «rinnovamento dello spirito cristiano» (Ib. 126), in una riforma cioè dei costumi.

Leone XIII riteneva che la soluzione ai mali creati dal progresso, nei diversi ambiti della vita nella società, poteva trovarsi soltanto all'interno della religione cristiana (RN 50). Ora, questo principio va interpretato rettamente, come giustamente fa Pio XI, quando dice, ben consapevole delle distorte letture, da parte di alcuni, del documento del suo predecessore, che vi sono alcuni cristiani che abusano della stessa religione «facendo del suo nome un paravento alle proprie ingiuste vessazioni per potersi sottrarre alle rivendicazioni pienamente giustificate degli operai» (QA 124).

---

stizia e della carità cristiana, procurando in tal modo grave scandalo ai deboli e offrendo ai cattivi facile pretesto di screditare la Chiesa stessa» (DR 55).

[10] 10. *Libertas* (20 giugno 1888) 23.

[11] Nella *Quadragesimo anno*, n.83 il Papa propone la creazione delle Corporazioni di mestiere come risposta alla lotta di classe propugnata dal socialismo. Si potrebbe discutere la possibilità di una tale riorganizzazione del lavoro. Sembra, tuttavia, dal contesto, che il Papa dimostrasse una certa difficoltà ad accettare l'evoluzione della società.

Nonostante questa visione, Pio XI entra nel merito dei problemi propri dello sviluppo quando parla dell'attività economica come espressione della volontà del Creatore «il quale ha posto l'uomo sulla terra perché la venga lavorando e facendola servire alle sue molteplici necessità» (Ib. 136). Contrariamente alle accuse mosse da alcuni contro la DSC, quasi che essa si opponesse alla creazione della ricchezza e insistesse soltanto sulla distribuzione, il Papa riconosce che la creazione della ricchezza è lecita, anche di quella personale, anzi, egli ritiene che, chi contribuisce con il suo sforzo al bene della comunità, può anche trarne qualche vantaggio personale, «purché tutto ciò si cerchi col debito ossequio alla legge di Dio e senza danno dei diritti altrui, e se ne faccia uso conforme all'ordine della fede e della retta ragione» (Ib). Pio XI apre il discorso sulla necessaria complementarietà fra carità e giustizia. Sempre con un chiaro riferimento alla vocazione del creato e degli uomini, il Papa riconosce che la sola giustizia potrebbe «togliere di mezzo le cause dei conflitti sociali, non già unire i cuori e stringere insieme le volontà (Ib. 137). Non basta dunque l'eliminazione dei conflitti. L'umanità deve progredire sempre di più verso l'ideale di un'autentica comunità[12]. È molto interessante notare che già la *Quadragesimo anno* introduce il discorso della solidarietà la quale trova il suo fondamento nel fatto che tutti, uomini e donne, apparteniamo ad una sola famiglia e siamo figli di uno stesso Padre celeste, anzi, «siamo tutti membri gli uni degli altri» (Ib. 138). Viene così giustificato l'mpegno della Chiesa in questo ambito, giacché un elemento basilare della sua missione è, propriamente, annunciare la vocazione comunitaria dell'umanità, il che presuppone modelli solidali di organizzazione economica.

---

[12] Nell'Enciclica *Divini Redemptoris*, sul comunismo, Pio XI dice che per salvare il mondo dalla rovina creata dal liberalismo, l'unico mezzo valido è «la penetrazione della giustizia sociale e del sentimento di amore cristiano nell'ordine economico e sociale» (32). Più avanti il Papa ribadisce ancora una volta questo principio: «una carità che privi l'operaio del salario a cui ha stretto diritto, non è carità. Né l'operaio ha bisogno di ricevere come elemosina ciò che a lui tocca per giustizia; né si può tentare di esimersi dai grandi doveri imposti dalla giustizia con piccoli doni di misericordia. Carità e giustizia impongono dei doveri, spesso circa la stessa cosa, ma sotto diverso aspetto; e gli operai, a questi doveri altrui che li riguardano, sono giustamente sensibili per ragione della loro stessa dignità» (49).

Data l'importanza dell'economia per la vita quotidiana delle persone, risulta assai evidente che le condizioni materiali costituiscono un aiuto, oppure un ostacolo, per la fedeltà alla propria vocazione. Pio XII giustifica la preoccupazione della Chiesa per la forma che assume la società, consona o meno con il disegno divino, quando dice che essa non potrebbe rimanere indifferente spettatrice dei pericoli che assediano i fedeli e tanto meno «tacere o fingere di non vedere e ponderare condizioni sociali che, volutamente o no, rendono ardua o praticamente impossibile una condotta di vita cristiana conformata ai precetti del Sommo Legislatore»[13]. Nel Messaggio di Natale del 1952, Pio XII avvertiva sui rischi della spersonalizzazione dell'uomo, come conseguenza di un modello di sviluppo economico basato esclusivamente sulla crescente produzione, che andrebbe ad incidere quasi meccanicamente, in modo positivo, soltanto sul tenore di vita. Questo messaggio è un buon esempio di evangelizzazione in un campo che sembrerebbe meramente tecnico. Il Papa fa leva sulla solidarietà, la cui mancanza sta alla base delle grandi ingiustizie economiche all'interno dei singoli Paesi e a livello internazionale. Viene così annunciata la verità sull'uomo, chiamato a vivere in solidarietà, per il fatto che tutti sono fratelli, figli dello stesso Padre e chiamati ad un destino comune.

Forse l'espressione più chiara del rapporto fra la missione della Chiesa e i complessi problemi sociali la troviamo nell'Enciclica *Mater et magistra* di Giovanni XXIII. Il Papa riconosce che «l'inserirsi della Chiesa in un popolo ha sempre riflessi positivi in campo economico-sociale, come dimostrano storia ed esperienza. La ragione è che gli esseri umani, diventando cristiani, non possono non sentirsi impegnati a migliorare istituzioni e ambienti dell'ordine temporale» (188). Non è semplice questione di precisione di linguaggio. In questo testo va sottolineata, innanzitutto, la comprensione della Chiesa come totalità dei battezzati, non più intendendo per Chiesa soltanto la gerarchia. Appare inoltre, nel testo, la concezione integrale della vocazione cristiana che non consente di trascurare gli aspetti pratici della convivenza. Di conseguenza il Papa ribadisce che «la dottrina sociale cristia-

---

[13] Radiomessaggio nel 50° della Rerum novarum (1-VI-1949) 5.

na è parte integrante della concezione cristiana della vita» (231). Tale dottrina scaturisce dai principi fondamentali contenuti nella Rivelazione.

La Chiesa ha il dovere di educare i suoi figli sui grandi principi del Vangelo. Il risultato di questa formazione sarà, fra l'altro, l'impegno con la storia. Infatti, «[q]uando si è 'luce del Signore' e quando si cammina come 'figli della luce' si colgono più sicuramente le esigenze fondamentali della giustizia (...) E quando si è animati dalla carità di Cristo ci si sente uniti agli altri e si sentono come propri i bisogni, le sofferenze, le gioie altrui» (267). Questa Enciclica che pone al suo centro i problemi dello sviluppo, è un richiamo all'impegno con i vari problemi concreti, che costituisce unaforma di cooperazione alla realizzazione del Regno di Cristo sulla terra (cf. Ib. 271).

3.2.2. L'apertura al dialogo con il mondo

Il Concilio Vaticano II che ha aperto in modo esplicito il dialogo della Chiesa con il mondo sui problemi concreti dell'uomo, in apertura della costituzione pastorale *Gaudium et spes* spiega in qual modo, mediante questo dialogo, la Chiesa renda un servizio in solidarietà all'intera umanità, essendo parte della sua missione proiettare su tali problemi la luce che viene dal Vangelo, «mettendo a disposizione degli uomini le energie di salvezza che la Chiesa, sotto la guida dello Spirito Santo, riceve dal suo Fondatore. Si tratta di salvare la persona umana, si tratta di edificare l'umana società» (2). La Chiesa attinge dalla Rivelazione i principi morali e religiosi per l'ordine sociale, politico ed economico e cerca di trovare, mediante il discernimento, di offrire agli uomini il necessario rapporto fra la Rivelazione ed il progresso della scienza e della tecnica (cf. 33). Questa verità sull'uomo e sul mondo costituisce «il fondamento del rapporto tra Chiesa e mondo, come pure la base del dialogo fra loro» (40).

Per ciò che riguarda il tema dello sviluppo, pur riprendendo quanto già affermato nei documenti sociali precedenti, il Concilio chiarisce tuttavia molte ambiguità del passato, superando dicotomie ormai inaccettabili: «l'attività umana individuale e collettiva, ossia quell'ingente sforzo col quale gli uomini nel corso dei secoli cercano di migliorare le proprie condizioni di vita, considerato in se stesso, corrisponde alle intenzioni di Dio» (Ib. 34). Il lavoro umano è il prolungamento dell'opera del Creatore.

A partire da questo momento la Chiesa assume come parte esplicita della sua missione quella di occuparsi direttamente dello sviluppo, offrendo su di esso una visione umanistica, riconoscendo in esso una scintilla della sapienza divina e ponendolo a servizio della persona integralmente intesa. Paolo VI con l'Enciclia *Populorum progressio* e Giovanni Paolo II con la *Sollicitudo rei socialis*, entrambi i documenti dedicati interamente allo sviluppo, offrono una visione che è riuscita ad entrare nella riflessione non ecclesiale, come dimostrato dal concetto di *sviluppo umano* introdotto dalle Nazioni Unite e dalla preoccupazione attuale della Banca Mondiale di indirizzare il progresso economico verso la lotta contro la povertà nel mondo. Nel documento più esplicito, riguardo alla missione della Chiesa, l'Esortazione apostolica *Evangelii nuntiandi*, documento conclusivo della III Assemblea Generale del Sinodo dei Vescovi, il Papa Paolo VI afferma che una Evangelizzazione che non tenga conto dello sviluppo, non può dirsi completa (29).

È la fede stessa che spinge la Chiesa ad occuparsi dello sviluppo, anzi a «considerarlo un *dovere del suo ministero pastorale*, a stimolare la riflessione di tutti circa la natura e le caratteristiche dell'autentico sviluppo umano» (SRS 31c). Ma il Papa va ben oltre. A suo avviso, quando la Chiesa si occupa della complessa problematica dello sviluppo, «adempie la missione di *evangelizzare*, poiché dà il suo *primo contributo* alla soluzione dell'urgente problema dello sviluppo quando proclama la verità su Cristo, su se stessa e sull'uomo, applicandola a una situazione concreta» (Ib. 41a).

4. IL CONTRIBUTO DEL PENSIERO DELLA CHIESA AD UNA NUOVA VISIONE DEL PROGRESSO

Come già accennato, sin dai primi documenti sociali, la Chiesa si è occupata della problematica creata dalla crescita dell'economia. Pur non trattando il tema dello sviluppo come tale, in quanto il concetto attuale è piuttosto recente, in questi documenti si offrono le fondamenta per ciò che costituisce l'insegnamento attuale in merito.

4.1. *La persona come centro e fine della vita in società*

Ispirandosi alla prima Rivelazione contenuta nel libro del Genesi, la Chiesa ha capito l'eccelsa dignità della persona creata ad immagine di Dio e destinata a rivelare in se stessa la Sua somiglianza. Appunto, perché l'uomo e la donna costituiscono il cardine di tutte le opere create da Dio, queste devono essere interamente a loro servizio affinché, servendosene, essi possano arrivare alla loro piena realizzazione secondo il disegno originale del Creatore.

Senza dubbio è dovuto a Pio XII il contributo maggiore alla riflessione sulla dignità della persona. Nella sua prima Enciclica che risulta programmatica di tutto il suo ricchissimo magistero, il Papa ci presenta il fondamento della concezione che la Chiesa ha dell'uomo e della donna: «Infatti, la prima pagina della Scrittura, con grandiosa semplicità ci narra come Dio, quale coronamento della sua opera creatrice, fece l'uomo a sua immagine e somiglianza; e la stessa Scrittura ci insegna che lo arricchì di doni e privilegi soprannaturali, destinandolo ad una eterna ed ineffabile felicità»[14].

Ed è appunto una tale altrettanto ineffabile dignità a costituire il fondamento dei diritti umani. Nel suo vastissimo magistero Pio XII mostra il legame insolubile esistente fra l'economia e la essenziale vocazione della persona. Commemorando il 50° della *Rerum novarum* il Papa ribadisce ancora una volta, la universale destinazione dei beni, presupposto dello stesso diritto di proprietà, il quale «assicurerà la dignità personale dell'uomo, e gli agevolerà l'attendere e il soddisfare in giusta libertà a quella somma di stabili obbligazioni e decisioni di cui è direttamente responsabile verso il Creatore»[15]. L'economia, di

---

[14] Lettera Enciclica *Summi pontificatus* (20-X-1939) 15. A questo riguardo è di particolare importanza il *Radiomessaggio di Natale* del 1942 sull'Ordine interno delle Nazioni. In esso il Papa ribadisce che «[o]rigine e scopo essenziale della vita sociale vuol essere la conservazione, lo sviluppo e il perfezionamento della persona umana» (7). L'ordine sociale poggia, addirittura, sulla dignità e sul rispetto dei diritti della persona umana.

[15] *La Solennità* (Radiomessaggio a Commemorazione del 50° della «Rerum novarum» 1-VI-41) 13.

conseguenza, «ad altro non mira che ad assicurare senza interrompimento le condizioni materiali, in cui possa svilupparsi pienamente la vita individuale dei cittadini» (Ib. 15). Perciò, tutto quanto riguarda l'economia, a cominciare dall'organizzazione del lavoro, nella quale prevale il diritto dei singoli all'iniziativa economica, deve tener conto del rispetto dei diritti fondamentali della persona la quale è misura, criterio di base, della giustizia di un determinato ordinamento.

La dottrina sociale della Chiesa può essere riassunta in poche parole, come impegno per la difesa della persona umana e della sua dignità che trova il suo fondamento nella sua natura intrinsecamente sociale e, soprattutto, nella sua elevazione all'ordine soprannaturale. Anzi, uomini e donne godono di una dignità che sta al di sopra di qualsiasi altra creatura, perché, redenti dal sangue di Cristo sono «divenuti figli e amici di Dio» (PT 3). La Chiesa, perciò, considera gli esseri umani come «il fondamento, il fine e i soggetti di tutte le istituzioni in cui si esprime e si attua la vita sociale» (MM 228). Paolo VI ritiene che ciò che la Chiesa ha da offrire all'umanità sia, addirittura, la sua visione dell'uomo (PP 13).

Sarà il Concilio Vaticano II, con la sua autorità, a dedicare un intero capitolo della Costituzione Pastorale *Gaudium et spes* alla fondazione della dignità della persona umana, a partire dalla riflessione sul mistero dell'uomo, offrendone così solidi fondamenti teologici. Infatti, solo nel mistero del Verbo incarnato si trova la comprensione totale della eccelsa dignità della persona umana: «Cristo, che è il nuovo Adamo, proprio rivelando il mistero del Padre e del Suo Amore svela anche pienamente l'uomo all'uomo e gli fa nota la sua altissima vocazione» (22).

Infine, Giovanni Paolo II costruisce l'intero suo magistero intorno a questo pensiero del Concilio. Non desta dunque alcuna meraviglia che la sua prima Enciclica sia dedicata al mistero della Redenzione con un chiaro taglio antropologico[16], e che colga, in tutta la sua profondità, il significato del-

---

[16] Nell'Enciclica *Dives in misericordia* il Papa ribadisce il senso pieno della sua prima Lettera: *Seguendo la dottrina del Concilio Vaticano II e aderendo alle particolari necessità dei tempi in cui viviamo, ho dedicato l'Enciclica «Redemptor Hominis» alla verità intorno all'uomo, che nella sua pienezza e profondità ci viene rivelata in Cristo* (DiM 1).

l'uomo redento da Cristo. «E perciò appunto Cristo Redentore — come è stato già detto — rivela pienamente l'uomo all'uomo stesso. Questa è — se così è lecito esprimersi — la dimensione umana del mistero della Redenzione. In questa dimensione l'uomo ritrova la grandezza, la dignità e il valore propri della sua umanità» (RH 10). Il cristianesimo è stupore riguardo al valore e alla dignità dell'uomo, «[q]uesto stupore giustifica la missione della Chiesa nel mondo» (Ib), che ha al suo centro, la preoccupazione per l'uomo storico, concreto, in tutte le sue dimensioni: «L'oggetto di questa premura è l'uomo nella sua unica e irrepetibile realtà umana, in cui permane intatta l'immagine e la somiglianza con Dio stesso» (Ib. 13). La Chiesa vuole che ogni uomo possa ritrovare Cristo per capire se stesso in profondità. Si capisce così la frase, tante volte ripetuta dal Papa, che l'uomo «è la prima fondamentale via della Chiesa» (Ib. 14)[17].

4.2. *Il nuovo concetto di sviluppo*

Contrariamente a quanto sperato, gli sforzi per promuovere i Paesi poveri ad un livello di sviluppo in grado di garantire alla maggioranza della popolazione un genere di vita degno, sono falliti. Questo fatto ha portato gli Organismi internazionali a ripensare il concetto stesso di sviluppo che supera la semplice categoria economica. Anche se in questi ambiti non viene riconosciuto alcun merito alla Chiesa, non c'è dubbio che essa ha contribuito ad una tale nuova concezione. Anzi, le grandi intuizioni dei documenti sociali si sono dimostrate giuste, malgrado le critiche rivolte alla DSC di ignoranza in materia economica ed altre simili, con le quali si voleva squalificare l'atteggiamento critico che la Chiesa ha sempre tenuto, appunto perché la sua preoccupazione è la persona, non in astratto, ma in quanto persona storica, quella di cui debbono occuparsi le istanze responsabili del benessere, localmente e a livello internazionale.

---

[17] Giovanni Paolo II conferma quanto detto, nella *Centesimus annus*, quando dice che la *Rerum novarum* fu una *difesa* dell'uomo, impegno al quale la Chiesa è rimasta fedele. Anzi, la Chiesa «ha posto la dignità della pesona al centro dei suoi messaggi sociali» (CA 61).

4.3. *Lo sviluppo integrale*

Il termine «sviluppo» appare per la prima volta così esplicitamente trattato, nella *Mater et magistra*. Tuttavia, nell'Enciclica si stabilisce una distinzione fra, da una parte, sviluppo economico, del quale si parla in riferimento al processo storico in cui si trovavano i Paesi in via di sviluppo, sotto la spinta degli Organismi internazionali che in quel momento accettavano la teoria dello sviluppo economico quasi come un processo meccanico che passava per stadi diversi[18] e, dall'altra, la visione che la Chiesa propone di sviluppo «economico e progresso sociale che rispettino e promuovano i veri valori umani, individuali e sociali; sviluppo economico e progresso sociale, cioè attuati nell'ambito morale, conformemente alla dignità dell'uomo e a quell'immenso valore che è la vita dei singoli esseri umani; e nella collaborazione su piano mondiale che permetta e favorisca un'ordinata e feconda circolazione di utili cognizioni, di capitali, di uomini» (MM 200). In queste espressioni si trovano già elementi che verranno sviluppati ulteriormente da Paolo VI e da Giovanni Paolo II magistralmente.

L'enciclica che Paolo VI ha dedicato interamente allo sviluppo, costituisce un tentativo di risposta al modello dominante di sviluppo meccanico, quasi fatalista, che doveva portare il benessere in pochi anni ai Paesi del Terzo Mondo, senza tener conto però nè delle implicazioni che tali processi avrebbero potuto avere sulle popolazioni stesse, nè, tanto meno, della giustizia dei rapporti internazionali di mercato. Tale Enciclica costituisce uno straordinario documento critico a queste proposte che, in modo profetico, venivano viste come fallimentari, ma soprattutto in se stessa costituisce la proposta, che troverà accoglienza solo molti anni dopo, di porre la persona umana al centro di questo necessario e inevitabile processo.

Secondo Paolo VI, vero sviluppo sarebbe «il passaggio, per ciascuno e per tutti, da condizioni meno umane a condizioni più umane» (PP 20), assumendo la persona nella sua to-

---

[18] Il periodo era dominato dalla teoria degli «stadi» dello sviluppo. Cf. W.W. ROSTOW, *The Stages of Economic Growth*, Cambridge, Cambridge University Press, 1960.

talità ed integrità e tenendo conto di tutti i suoi bisogni, da quelli più elementari per la sopravvivenza, a quelli più elevati ed esclusivi della persona umana, al cui culmine sta «la fede, dono di Dio accolto dalla buona volontà dell'uomo e l'unità nella carità del Cristo che ci chiama tutti a partecipare in qualità di figli alla vita del Dio vivente, Padre di tutti gli uomini» (Ib. 21)[19]. Non si arriverà dunque al vero sviluppo, finché ci saranno uomini e donne emarginati dal godimento dei beni della creazione, spirituali e materiali. Lo sviluppo, dunque, secondo Paolo VI deve essere integrale cioè, di tutta la persona. Il vero sviluppo non può trascurare alcun aspetto, in quanto la persona ha ricevuto la vocazione ad una crescita armonica in umanità. Con una lettura da un'altra prospettiva, Giovanni Paolo II conclude che pensare allo sviluppo significa anche pensare alla liberazione da tutte le servitù che inchiodano la persona e le impediscono di accogliere la salvezza, perché la missione della Chiesa riguarda la persona nella sua integrità: «La liberazione e la salvezza, portate dal Regno di Dio, raggiungono la persona umana nelle sue dimensioni sia fisiche che spirituali» (RM 14). In questo passo dell'Enciclica, il Papa dà un riconoscimento esplicito al contributo delle Chiese dell'America Latina al discorso sociale della Chiesa Universale riguardo alla promozione dello sviluppo come parte essenziale della sua missione: «il miglior servizio al fratello è l'evangelizzazione che lo dispone a realizzarsi come figlio di Dio, lo libera dalle ingiustizie e lo promuove integralmente»[20].

Essendo il Vangelo la via che conduce all'umanizzazione, progresso e sviluppo, visti alla luce dell'evangelizzazione, pongono ai cristiani molte domande, la prima delle quali è, se il progresso rende la vita umana «più umana», vale a dire, «se l'uomo, come uomo, nel contesto di questo progresso, diventi veramente migliore, cioè più maturo spiritualmente, più co-

---

[19] In modo simile si esprime Giovanni Paolo II in merito: «Non si tratta solo di elevare tutti i popoli al livello di cui godono oggi i Paesi più ricchi, ma di costruire nel lavoro solidale una vita più degna, di far crescere effettivamente la dignità e la creatività di ogni singola persona, la sua capacità di rispondere alla propria vocazione e, dunque, all'appello di Dio, in essa contenuto. Al culmine dello sviluppo sta l'esercizio del diritto-dovere di cercare Dio, di conoscerlo e di vivere secondo tale conoscenza» (CA 29).

[20] RM 57. Il riferimento è alla III Conferenza Generale dell'Episcopato Latino Americano a Puebla nel febbraio del 1979.

sciente della dignità della sua umanità, più responsabile, più aperto agli altri, in particolare verso i più bisognosi e più deboli, più disponible a dare a portare aiuto a tutti» (RH 15,c).

4.4. *Lo sviluppo solidale*

Sempre ispirandosi alla prima Rivelazione, la Chiesa propugna una crescita dei mezzi posti a disposizione dell'umanità, tali da consentire la realizzazione della vocazione della persona a vivere in comunità. Di più, come abbiamo visto, la solidarietà fa parte del disegno creatore di Dio che ha creato tutti uguali e li ha destinati alla filiazione senza alcuna distinzione. In comunità è stato creato l'uomo (uomo e donna) ed in comunità è stato redento dal Cristo. Sin dai primi documenti sociali, i Papi parlano della socialità della persona, ma dobbiamo riconoscere a Giovanni Paolo II il merito di aver approfondito questo concetto, pur certamente prendendo alcuni elementi dai predecessori e, soprattutto, dal Concilio,[21] ma rendendo l'idea con una chiarezza tale da non lasciare spazio ad ambiguità e, in modo particolare, assegnando al concetto il suo valore teologico fondante. Mentre nei documenti antecedenti al Concilio, la socialità appariva, piuttosto, con un taglio sociologico (l'uomo ha bisogno degli altri), Giovanni Paolo II, tornando al Vangelo, ribadisce la necessità del dono di sè per la piena realizzazione. Ecco il vero concetto della natura sociale dell'uomo in un linguaggio cristiano: non usiamo gli altri a proprio beneficio, ma, con la grazia di Dio, facciamo dono totale di noi stessi a beneficio dei fratelli e delle sorelle. In questo modo si chiude un cerchio meraviglioso di mutua complementarietà, perché chi si dà all'altro, riceve nell'atto stesso della sua donazione, il compimento della propria vocazione arriva cioè, alla piena realizzazione di sè come essere sociale.

Mediante il suo lavoro, la persona realizza se stessa, compie la sua missione di dominare la terra in modo di farla pro-

---

[21] Neppure il Concilio dà sufficiente chiarezza al concetto. Pur avendo offerto elementi in merito, tuttavia, in certi passi si lascia spazio a interpretazioni diverse, spesso troppo legate alla vecchia concezione che è piuttosto sociologica, come nel passo seguente: «L'uomo, infatti, per sua intima natura è un essere sociale e senza i rapporti con gli altri non può vivere né esplicare le sue doti» (GS 12d).

gredire secondo il disegno originale, collaborando così allo sviluppo. Orbene, il lavoro si realizza in comunione con gli altri uomini, in quanto che tutti lavorano su una materia che è dono di Dio, ma che contiene in sè il frutto del lavoro di tanti altri[22]. Pensare, dunque, allo sviluppo, presuppone pensare al lavoro umano, inteso come lavoro solidale. Di conseguenza, tutti gli sforzi per far progredire le risorse devono essere realizzati da tutti e a beneficio di tutti. Se così non fosse, lo sviluppo si farebbe «a spese degli altri; e là dove comincia, proprio perché gli altri sono ignorati, si ipertrofizza e si perverte» (SRS 32). E, purtroppo, questa è la realtà del mondo contemporaneo dove, per molti aspetti, alcuni Paesi hanno raggiunto un alto grado di sviluppo, in alcuni aspetti anche eccessivo, ma certamente non a beneficio di tanti altri. Anzi, forse a ragione, si pone la domanda se il livello raggiunto dai Paesi ricchi non presupponga addirittura il mantenimento dell'ordine ingiusto prevalente della distribuzione della ricchezza, dell'utilizzo dell'energia, della attuale divisione internazionale del lavoro e dell'esaurimento delle risorse.

5. Conclusione

Il problema dello sviluppo umano, dunque, riguarda la missione della Chiesa perché il Regno di Dio «mira a trasformare i rapporti tra gli uomini e si attua man mano che essi imparano ad amarsi, a perdonarsi, a servirsi a vicenda» (RM 15). Tali rapporti sono fortemente condizionati dalle strutture sociali, politiche ed economiche, vale a dire, dal grado di sviluppo raggiunto dalla propria società. Si tratta di un problema morale, un problema di giustizia nei rapporti interumani a tutti i livelli, aggravato ogni giorno dal formidabile processo di globalizzazione che, purtroppo, non ha come centro il bene della persona, ma il profitto senza riguardo per altre considerazioni. Il modello di sviluppo che domina l'economia e la politica mette a repentaglio la stessa umanità di tutti, uomini e donne, non solo di quelli che rappresentano la parte debole

---

[22] Giovanni Paolo II concepisce il mondo materiale come un grande banco di lavoro, creato da Dio, ma trasformato in tanti modi e perfezionato mediante il lavoro umano, sul quale tutti gli uomini lavorano. Si tratta di una visione cristiana sì, ma assai originale, che viene sviluppata in modo molto bello nella *Laborem exercens*.

dell'umanità. Mentre a questi viene negata la possibilità di crescere in umanità, coloro che pensano di avvantaggiarsi del modello apparentemente vincente, sono sottoposti ad un processo di crescente alienazione, di disumanizzazione.[23] Vi è, dunque, un intimo rapporto fra lo sviluppo umano e il Regno di Dio che «esige la promozione dei beni umani e dei valori che si possono ben dire "evangelici", perché sono intimamente legati alla "buona novella"» (Ib. 19).

La realtà contemporanea dunque, malgrado tanti aspetti positivi che potrebbero favorire lo sviluppo umano, costituisce per tutti i membri della Chiesa, ognuno secondo il proprio carisma, una sfida storica a pensare un modello di organizzazione della vita nella società che crei le condizioni atte alla crescita integrale e solidale di tutti, uomini e donne, del primo e del terzo mondo, un modello consono alla originaria vocazione del mondo e dell'umanità. La visione onesta e spregiudicata della situazione del mondo svela pienamente il senso profondo delle intuizioni di Paolo VI e di Giovanni Paolo II per i quali, sviluppo e solidarietà sono l'unica via per una pace vera e duratura.

Forse il modo migliore per concludere questa riflessione è ricordare le parole di Giovanni Paolo II che ha saputo presentare in modo magistrale l'impegno per lo sviluppo umano come parte essenziale dell'Evangelizzazione:

> «Col messaggio evangelico la Chiesa offre una forza liberante e fautrice di sviluppo proprio perché porta alla conversione del cuore e della mentalità, fa riconoscere la dignità di ciascuna persona, dispone alla solidarietà, all'impegno, al servizio dei fratelli, inserisce l'uomo nel progetto di Dio, che è la costruzione del Regno di pace, di giustizia a partire già da questa vita. È la prospettiva biblica dei "cieli nuovi e terra nuova" (cf. Is 65, 17; 2Pt 3, 13; Ap 21,1), la quale ha inserito nella storia lo stimolo e la mèta per l'avanzamento dell'umanità. Lo sviluppo dell'uomo viene da Dio, dal modello di Gesù uomo-Dio. Ecco perché tra annunzio evangelico e promozione dell'uomo c'è una stretta connessione» (RM 59).

---

[23] Cf. CA, 41.

Promotion Humaine dans Populorum Progressio

(*Populorum progressio*: la question sociale vue sous l'angle de la promotion humaine)

JOSEPH JOBLIN

Les encycliques sociales mettent en relief tel ou tel aspect de la question sociale qu'elles tiennent pour particulièrement actuel. Ainsi en fut-il, par exemple, dans *Mater et Magistra* qui souligna la gravité des déséquilibres à l'intérieur des nations et entre elles et conclut à l'urgence d'y remédier. D'autres marquèrent un moment dans l'histoire de la pensée sociale chrétienne en proposant une nouvelle approche des problèmes sociaux. Ainsi en fut-il avec *Rerum Novarum* qui, partant du principe que tout homme est appelé à une fin surnaturelle, en déduit les conditions d'un ordre social juste, légitimant ainsi, dans les conditions présentes, l'intervention de l'Etat en économie, la constitution d'organisations ouvrières et patronales indépendantes, la recherche d'un nouvel ordre social.

Populorum Progressio souligne l'urgence de mettre le développement au service de la promotion humaine[1]. Elle fait de cette dernière l'impératif moral à partir duquel doivent être pensées à l'heure présente les questions économiques, sociales, politiques ou culturelles. Elle appelle tous les hommes de bonne volonté à tenir compte de cette exigence dans les décisions qu'ils sont appelés à prendre au niveau qui est le leur.

---

[1] *Populorum Progressio* § 16: «la croissance humaine constitue comme un résumé de nos devoirs»; cf. Cardinal Paul POUPARD, *Le Père Lebret, le pape Paul VI et l'encyclique Populorum Progressio vingt ans après* in CENTRE LEBRET, *Lebret d'hier à aujourd'hui* Paris 1986 Colloque Lebret 1986; J. JOBLIN, *Pour un développement intégral* in *Revue international du Travail* (Genève) 1967/3 pp. 1-16.

Le fait qu'aucune autre encyclique ou document pontifical n'ait pris auparavant la promotion humaine comme point central de son enseignement s'explique aisément. Le discours social de l'Eglise porte sur les problèmes de société au moment où ils se présentent; l'originalité de *Populorum Progressio* ne vient pas de l'actualité du thème qu'elle aborde mais de l'approche qui est la sienne pour traiter de la promotion humaine. Les obstacles auxquels celle-ci se heurte dans la réalité deviennent pour elle un «fait d'ordre moral»[2] c'est à dire une donnée objective dont la conscience est appelée à tirer des conséquences pratiques. Tel est le point qui sera mis ici en évidence en étudiant la nouveauté de la méthode de *Populorum Progressio* et, en soulignant en conclusion, comment elle s'inscrit dans le mouvement de la réflexion des chrétiens sur la question sociale.

I. LA PROMOTION HUMAINE, POINT CENTRAL DE POPULORUM PROGRESSIO

L'encyclique *Populorum Progressio* contient tout un ensemble de textes dont les formules lapidaires constituent un véritable florilège de la promotion humaine; d'une très grande clarté et force d'expression, ils ne nécessitent, à première vue, aucune explication ou commentaire particulier. Qu'il suffise ici d'en citer quelques uns: «la croissance humaine constitue un résumé de nos devoirs» (16)[3] ou bien: «pour être authentique, le développement doit promouvoir tout homme et tout l'homme» (14) ou encore: «le développement exige des transformations audacieuses, profondément novatrices» (32).

Le vocabulaire de l'encyclique est certes nouveau puisque le pape y parle le langage de l'homme d'aujourd'hui; mais le contenu de son message n'est-il pas le même que dans les encycliques précédentes? Face à la «misère imméritée» des travailleurs[4], Léon XIII demandait des réformes sociales pour les tirer de cet état; devant le désordre de l'économie

---

[2] *Sollicitudo Rei socialis* § 9.
[3] Tout au long de cet article, les chiffres entre ( ) renvoient aux paragraphes de l'encyclique *Populorum Progressio* telle que publiée en 1967 par la typographie vaticane.
[4] *Rerum Novarum* § 2.

mondiale, Pie XI recommandait aux responsables de la vie politique et économique de s'inspirer du principe de justice sociale informé par la charité; les messages de guerre dans lesquels Pie XII déplorait les «ruines immenses»[5] provoquées par la poursuite des combats esquissaient les grandes lignes d'un ordre social qui apporterait la paix aux peuples; Jean XXIII voyait dans les déséquilibres entre régions une contrainte qui pesait sur le développement humain des peuples et demandait de les en libérer. Le message de *Populorum Progressio* s'inscrit donc dans un continuité; il reprend le thème que les papes ont mis en avant depuis un siècle, celui du poids que les structures économiques[6] et autres font peser sur certains peuples inhibant leur capacité d'«avoir plus pour être plus» (6). Les encycliques et messages précédant *Populorum Progressio* se préoccupaient bien de remédier aux inégalités et de libérer les potentialités des individus afin qu'ils puissent accomplir leur destinée; ainsi Léon XIII lorsqu'il affirma que nul n'avait le droit «d'entraver la marche de l'homme vers cette perfection qui correspond à la vie éternelle et céleste»[7]. L'originalité de *Populorum Progressio* vient moins de son contenu que de la méthode dont elle use pour traiter de la promotion humaine car, associant celle des individus à celle des peuples, elle renouvelle l'analyse sociale.

Les premiers chrétiens sociaux avaient eu recours à ce qu'on peut appeler une approche doctrinale des questions sociales[8]. Confrontés à la «misère imméritée» des travailleurs et aux tensions sociales qui en résultaient, ils opposaient à cette réalité l'image d'une société fondée sur les principes de la philosophie chrétienne. Leur argumentation reposait sur un double présupposé, celui de l'excellence de la doctrine chrétienne telle qu'elle était alors formulée et celui de fonder sur elle, *hic et nunc*, un nouvel ordre social; ils en concluaient

---

[5] PIE XII, *Message de Noël 1943*.

[6] Jean-Paul II dénoncera pour sa part les «structures de péché» qui oppriment les faibles, in *Sollicitudo Rei socialis* §§ 9, 36.

[7] *Rerum Novarum* § 32 sauf indications contraires, les encycliques sociales autres que *Populorum Progressio* sont citées d'après D. MAUGENEST (ed.), *Le discours social de l'Eglise. De Léon XIII à Jean-Paul II* Centurion Paris 1985 p. 744.

[8] J. JOBLIN, *Il movimento cattolico sociale e l'evoluzione del suo metodo d'azione* in *Civiltà Cattolica* 1983 III pp. 105-121.

que les Etats avaient avantage à donner à l'Eglise la plus ample liberté⁹.

La méthode de raisonnement qui vient d'être schématisée n'obtint que des résultats limités. Si elle eut l'avantage d'opposer aux philosophies du libéralisme et du socialisme une autre doctrine que la leur et de justifier de porter un autre jugement sur les réalités sociales, elle eut l'inconvénient d'introduire dans les sociétés une source supplémentaire de division: le lot de l'Occident n'a-t-il pas été, depuis deux siècles, d'opposer entre eux des partis ou des écoles de pensée et d'écarter de toute participation à la gestion de la chose publique ceux qui étaient minoritaires? Sans vouloir diminuer en rien la nécessité d'avoir des vues claires, fondées en doctrine, sur le devenir des sociétés, on peut penser qu'un défaut fondamental affecte cette approche des questions sociales; c'est à y remédier que contribua *Populorum Progressio*.

Lorsque le réformateur social part d'une «représentation internationale parfaite»¹⁰ afin d'établir quelle voie suivre pour y parvenir, son raisonnement est influencé par ses préjugés; il ne saisit pas ce qu'il y a d'humain et de juste dans les aspirations que peuvent avoir d'autres peuples ou couches sociales; il les tient même souvent pour irrationnelles et dangereuses; il ne peut alors que les combattre d'autant que la logique rigoureuse de son raisonnement confère à son jugement la force de l'évidence. Le traitement dont la question coloniale a été l'objet avant *Populorum Progressio* en fournit un exemple évident.

Les bases du droit de la colonisation ont été élaborées par Vitoria. Celui-ci a certes ouvert une nouvelle voie en parlant de l'unité du genre humain et de l'obligation des peuples de communiquer entre eux; mais se plaçant dans une optique purement européenne et confessionnelle, n'a-t-il pas sous-estimé les droits des peuples autochtones à sauvegarder leur

---

⁹ LEON XIII, Lettre *Etsi magno* (12 mai 1885) à l'empereur du Japon: «tous ceux qui font profession de christianisme... écouteront la voix de la religion enjoignant de révérer l'autorité royale, d'obéir aux lois et de ne rien vouloir d'autre, dans le domaine des affaires publiques, que ce qui s'accorde aux normes de la tranquillité et de l'honnêteté. Aussi demandons Nous avec ardeur que vous accordiez aux chrétiens la plus grande liberté possible...».

¹⁰ *Code de morale internationale* Union internationale d'études sociales (Union de Malines) Spes Paris 1938 pp. 207-212.

propre culture et civilisation? Malgré sa préoccupation de dégager les enseignements de l'Eglise sur la société de vues qui tenaient aux circonstances historiques du Moyen-Age, il a, en toute bonne foi, conservé ceux d'entre eux qui maintenaient la prééminence politique de l'Europe dans le monde.

L'enseignement des théologiens de la Renaissance sur les rapports politiques et économiques entre peuples inégaux a pénétré profondément les mentalités occidentales; il a été, depuis deux siècles, à la base de presque tous les exposés de la doctrine sociale de l'Eglise. Un résumé de celle-ci se trouve dans le *Code de morale internationale*[11] publié par l'Union de Malines à la veille du deuxième conflit mondial»; se demandant si les entreprises coloniales peuvent être justifiées, il répond par l'affirmative en mettant en avant divers titres dont le droit du premier occupant et la destination universelle des biens. Dans l'un et l'autre cas, les sociétés indigènes sont jugées du point de vue du colonisateur et non en fonction de ce qu'elles sont pour elles-mêmes.

Le premier argument, celui du premier occupant, part d'une évidence: celui qui occupe une terre inhabitée peut en prendre possession et la mettre en valeur; ce cas fut celui de diverses îles du Pacifique. Une difficulté se présente si quelques habitants y vivent selon leurs modes d'existence traditionnels; tel fut le cas de conscience qui se posa aux Européens, notamment en Amérique latine. Ils se demandèrent quelle attitude prendre vis à vis des «peuplades ou tribus qui vivent dans l'anarchie des rapports sociaux et créent de ce fait un obstacle insurmontable à la civilisation». Ce point de départ les conduisit à affirmer qu'«en l'absence de société organisée», la puissance colonisatrice a le «droit incontestable d'organiser le territoire qu'elle soumet à sa domination». La conclusion qui fut tirée du principe sur lequel elle s'appuya

---

[11] *Code de morale internationale* op. cit. pp. 85-98; l'on consultera également à ce sujet les leçons consacrées par les Semaines sociales de France à la question coloniale avant la deuxième guerre mondiale, spécialement en 1908, 1923, 1925, 1926, 1929; de plus la question des colonies fut le thème des sessions de 1930 (Marseille), 1936 (Versailles) et, au sortir du deuxième conflit mondial à Lyon en 1948; cf. de même N. Politis (internationaliste de renom et jugé ouvert) faisant de l'Afrique le déversoir du trop-plein de la population européenne in *La morale internationale* La Baconnière Neuchâtel (CH) 1943 pp. 147 et sq.

en découlait logiquement certes, mais la valeur des prémisses posées était sujette à caution puisqu'elles en venaient à refuser le caractère d'organisation sociale à toute forme de vie collective autre que celle pratiquée aujourd'hui en Occident. Or on aurait dû s'interroger sur les formes propres d'organisation sociale de ces peuples et sur la portée du droit qui est le leur de vivre comme ils l'entendent sur leur territoire.

Le recours à la méthode doctrinale pour la mise en oeuvre du principe de la destination universelle des biens permet également de constater la facilité avec laquelle l'énoncé de la morale sociale peut être influencé par les préjugés; ainsi en est-il dans la manière dont la question coloniale a été traitée dans le Code de Malines. De ce que les biens de ce monde ont été répartis entre les régions et les peuples pour qu'ils les mettent ensemble au service de l'humanité, peut-on conclure que «le plan divin est déformé et l'humanité frustrée de ce qui lui revient quand (...) les peuples arriérés s'abstiennent de mettre en valeur les réserves que recèle leur territoire»? Il ne suffit pas de les accuser d'«incapacité, incurie ou paresse» pour justifier le pays colonial «de mettre en valeur» les richesses de leur territoire». Les «peuples arriérés», pourraient aussi bien accuser ceux qui se disent développés ou civilisés d'«incapacité, incurie ou paresse» pour le pillage qu'ils font des richesses naturelles de la planète et la menace qu'ils font peser sur l'exploitation des richesses de la terre. Bien mieux, le raisonnement par lequel les peuples colonisateurs entendent justifier leur entreprise de domination pourrait se retourner contre eux puisque tout Etat qui se croirait plus avancé serait en titre d'intervenir dans les affaires intérieures des autres.

Les auteurs du Code de Malines ont opéré inconsciemment un choix parmi les principes impliqués dans la solution de la question coloniale. Une faille s'est d'ailleurs introduite dans leur raisonnement quand ils en sont venus à affirmer qu'«à défaut d'une autorité internationale apte à pourvoir» à l'exploitation de leur territoire au bénéfice de tous «la tutelle sur des peuples encore mineurs revient «par droit de légitime occupation au premier Etat qui peut et veut (l') exercer». Ils justifièrent ainsi la politique coloniale des Etats occidentaux au lieu de se mettre en peine d'une procédure objective et contradictoire pour juger des intérêts d'une population, des objectifs qui doivent être poursuivis lorsqu'un territoire est mis en valeur ou des garanties à donner pour que celle-ci s'effectue au bénéfice de tous.

L'argumentation traditionnelle ignore l'égalité et la solidarité qui doivent exister entre les peuples; l'autorité internationale devient ici l'instrument des États qui ont la force d'imposer leur suprématie. La promotion humaine est ici considérée comme résultant de l'intégration d'une civilisation dite inférieure dans une autre, celle qui la domine.

Toute autre est l'approche du problème du développement par *Populorum Progressio*. Les aspirations des peuples les plus pauvres sont ici le point de départ de la réflexion. L'encyclique reconnaît un «signe des temps»[12] dans le désir de ces populations d'«être plus»(15) et de bénéficier d'un développement «autonome et digne» (6) grâce à des mesures d'ordre économique, social, politique et culturel; d'autre part, constatant que les inégalités entre les peuples constituent un obstacle à la promotion humaine et qu'il y a en conséquence devoir d'y remédier, elle cherche la solution du problème ainsi posé dans une double direction, l'une doctrinale, l'autre pratique.

Populorum Progressio ne fait pas de la mise en valeur des ressources de la terre l'objectif du développement; elle donne la première place à la croissance humaine des populations comme des individus. L'encyclique souligne la voie à suivre par quiconque entend promouvoir, pour autant qu'il dépend de lui, le développement intégral de tout homme et de tout l'homme (14). L'anthropologie mise en oeuvre par Paul VI est à la fois historique et englobante[13]; historique puisqu'elle voit les individus et les collectivités assumant leur destin dans une histoire: «Comme les vagues à marée montante pénètrent chacune un peu plus avant sur la grève, ainsi l'humanité avance sur le chemin de l'histoire. Héritiers des générations passées et bénéficiaires du travail de nos contemporains, nous avons des obligations envers tous, et ne pouvons nous désintéresser de ceux qui viendront agrandir après nous le

---

[12] *Gaudium et Spes* § 4.
[13] J. JOBLIN, *Pour un développement intégral* op. cit. p. 11.

cercle de la famille humaine. La solidarité universelle qui est un fait, et un bénéfice pour nous, est aussi un devoir» (17). Mais l'anthropologie de l'encyclique est aussi englobante, en ce sens que la croissance ne peut s'opérer qu'à travers une action d'ensemble portant sur les aspects économiques, sociaux, politiques, culturels et spirituels du devenir humain. «Toute action sociale engage (en effet) une doctrine» (39) et suppose chez les responsables une «échelle de valeurs» (18) centrée sur la dignité morale des personnes humaines et leur solidarité effective: «l'homme doit rencontrer l'homme, les nations doivent se rencontrer comme des frères et des soeurs, comme les enfants de Dieu. Dans cette compréhension et cette amitié mutuelles, dans cette communion sacrée, nous devons également commencer à oeuvrer ensemble pour édifier l'avenir commun de l'humanité» (43)[14].

L'originalité foncière de *Populorum Progressio* ne vient pas de ce qu'elle est consacrée au devoir de se développer aussi bien pour les individus que pour les peuples: elle se trouve dans la manière dont l'encyclique envisage de répondre à cet objectif. Si Paul VI s'en était tenu à l'approche traditionnelle, il aurait sans doute longuement épilogué sur les droits des uns et des autres comme sur leur devoir de collaborer; mais une telle méthode conduit souvent à une impasse car les points de vue sont divers et l'on n'entrevoit aucun terrain d'entente quelles que soient les exhortations qui sont faites en ce sens. L'application de la doctrine de la destination universelle des biens à la situation coloniale montre bien qu'aucune solution satisfaisante ne pouvait être apportée à l'exigence d'un développement solidaire en partant seulement de ce principe puisque peuples colonisés et peuples colonisateurs ne parlaient pas le même langage.

Paul VI privilégie la recherche de solutions ponctuelles aux difficultés qui font obstacle à la croissance humaine des peuples: «le vrai développement, écrit-il, est le passage, pour chacun et pour tous, de conditions moins humaines à des conditions plus humaines» (20); ainsi ne propose-t-il pas aux hommes de réaliser un modèle de société idéale sur lequel ils

---

[14] L'encyclique reprend ici nombre de termes de l'allocution adressée par Paul VI aux représentants des religions non chrétiennes de l'Inde (Bombay, 3 décembre 1964).

se seraient entendus; il sait qu'un tel accord n'est pas possible et, en toute hypothèse, ne peut durer car les conditions politiques, économiques et autres des sociétés sont en perpétuel changement. Il propose aux partenaires du développement de s'accorder sur des mesures concrètes mais limitées et adaptées aux circonstances.

II. La poursuite de la croissance humaine dans *Populorum Progressio*

La promotion humaine ou, pour s'en tenir à l'expression de *Populorum Progressio*, la croissance humaine, est présentée à l'intérieur d'une vision chrétienne du devenir des sociétés qui s'appuie sur une certaine anthropologie. Celle-ci prend comme point de départ de sa réflexion la capacité de l'homme de poursuivre son «progrès matériel et développement spirituel»[15] comme sa volonté d'y parvenir dès qu'il en entrevoit la possibilité.

Alors que les institutions internationales et les sociétés civiles envisagent la promotion humaine indépendamment de toute référence explicite à la dimension religieuse de l'homme, *Populorum Progressio* la considère dans cette perspective. La volonté d'«avoir plus pour être plus» est la réponse libre de l'homme «au dessein de Dieu» sur lui (15), dessein qu'il peut lire dans «l'ensemble d'aptitudes et de qualités à faire fructifier» (15) dont il est dépositaire. «Leur épanouissement, fruit de l'éducation reçue et de l'effort personnel, permettra à chacun de s'orienter vers la destinée que lui propose son créateur» (15).

La croissance humaine repose pour Paul VI sur deux piliers: l'ordre providentiel et la liberté des individus face à l'invitation qui leur est faite de croître en humanité; aussi peut-il affirmer que, «chacun demeure l'artisan principal de sa réussite ou de son échec» et que «par le seul effort de son intelligence et de sa volonté, chaque homme peut grandir en humanité, valoir plus, être plus» (15), cela quelles que soient les difficultés rencontrées et les influences qui s'exercent sur lui.

---

[15] *Déclaration de Philadelphie* 1944.

La vision humaniste de la promotion humaine présentée dans *Populorum Progressio* a rencontré un large écho dans l'opinion publique; elle correspond à cette aspiration qui s'empare aujourd'hui des masses à bénéficier d'un «épanouissement» de leur vie humaine, et cela aussi bien dans les pays riches que dans ceux qui sont encore soumis à la pauvreté. Mais on peut se demander si beaucoup de lecteurs de l'encyclique qui se sont dits enthousiasmés par ses enseignements en ont bien saisi la portée et la nature véritable. Ils semblent bien n'en avoir retenu que les accents individualistes qui, pris isolément, risquent de tourner le dos à la vision de la promotion humaine qui est ici proposée.

L'interprétation individualiste de l'encyclique, extrêmement flatteuse à l'amour-propre humain, se fonde sur une équivoque. Sans doute y est-il affirmé que «l'homme n'est vraiment homme que dans la mesure où, maître de ses actions et juge de leur valeur, il est lui-même auteur de son progrès» (34), mais il est ajouté aussitôt «en conformité avec la nature que lui a donnée son Créateur et dont il assume librement les possibilités et les exigences». L'humanisme que présente l'encyclique est «ouvert sur l'Absolu» et, ajoute le Pape, «dans la reconnaissance d'une vocation, qui donne l'idée vraie de la vie humaine» (42). Que l'homme soit riche de dons qui lui permettent de se comporter d'une manière libre dans l'existence nul n'en doute, qu'il doive reconnaître dans ses aspirations et celles qui traversent l'humanité un «signe des temps»[16] rien de plus certain mais, pour Paul VI, l'usage qu'il doit faire de ses facultés pour devenir plus homme et rendre la société plus humaine n'est pas abandonné à son caprice. La parole «vocation» revient ici à plusieurs reprises ainsi que l'idée qu'elle représente[17]. Ce n'est pas parce qu'il y a aspiration au développement dans l'ordre naturel et que des idéologies proposent d'y répondre que l'homme peut s'en remettre à sa seule raison; il doit apprendre à «discerner»[18] en fonction du plan de Dieu sur le monde entre les diverses pos-

---

[16] *Gaudium et Spes* § 41.5.
[17] Ibid §§ 15, 42.
[18] *Octogesima Adveniens* §§ 3, 4, 36; sur les critères de discernement cf. G. FESSARD, *France Prends garde de Perdre la foi* Julliard Paris 1979 pp. 136-145.

sibilités qui se présentent à lui pour poursuivre la réalisation d'un ordre social plus humain au sens chrétien du terme. Il lui faut résister à la tentation de réaliser un ordre moins humain (21) et s'attacher à la poursuite d'un ordre plus humain; la voie en est tracée dans l'encyclique: elle passe par les divers paliers du bien commun, à savoir: la possession du nécessaire et la victoire sur les fléaux sociaux; la considération accrue de la dignité d'autrui; la reconnaissance des valeurs suprêmes et de Dieu qui en est la source et le terme. «Plus humaines enfin et surtout la foi, don de Dieu accueilli par la bonne volonté de l'homme, et l'unité dans la charité du Christ qui nous appelle, tous à participer en fils à la vie du Dieu vivant, Père de tous les hommes» (21).

Paul VI propose dans *Populorum Progressio* de parcourir les diverses étapes de la croissance humaine en s'en tenant à la méthode qu'il a préconisée durant tout son pontificat. Déjà dans son encyclique inaugural *Ecclesiam suam*, il avait donné une place essentielle au dialogue car seul il pouvait prendre la place de la confrontation. Le dialogue fut encore un point central de son allocution devant la Conférence internationale du Travail en 1969; lui seul, en effet permet de surmonter les tensions qui existent entre les partenaires sociaux leur faisant découvrir ce qu'il y a de commun dans leurs aspirations et les incitant à les transformer en règles de comportement qui s'inscrivent dans l'éthique de la société:

> «Plus qu'une conception économique, mieux qu'une conception politique, c'est une conception morale qui vous inspire: la justice sociale à instaurer jour après jour, librement et d'un commun accord... Vous en faites prendre peu à peu conscience et vous le proposez comme idéal. Bien plus vous le traduisez en de nouvelles règles de comportement social, qui s'imposent comme des normes de droit. Vous assurez ainsi le passage permanent de l'ordre idéal des principes à l'ordre juridique, c'est à dire au droit positif»[19].

---

[19] PAUL VI, *Allocution* à la Conférence internationale du Travail Genève 10 juin 1969.

Un lien existe pour Paul VI entre la promotion humaine et les institutions que se donne une société; celles-ci doivent être démocratiques; leur but est de faciliter la «participation organique»[20] des populations aux décisions afin de servir au développement de tous les hommes et de leurs communautés et non à en faire des «rouages»[21] des mécanismes économiques alors qu'elles devraient en être la fin.

Les encycliques sociales du passé ont toutes insisté sur l'importance d'institutions *ad hoc* pour améliorer la situation sociale; l'une de celles qui se rapproche peut-être le plus de *Populorum Progressio* est *Quadragesimo Anno* qui envisag la réalisation de la justice sociale internationale: «il convient aussi, écrit Pie XI, que les diverses nations, si étroitement solidaires et interdépendantes dans l'ordre économique, mettent en commun leurs réflexions et leurs efforts pour hâter, à la faveur d'engagements et d'institutions sagement conçus, l'avènement d'une bienfaisante et heureuse collaboration économique internationale»[22]. Mais Pie XI ne précisa pas quelles devaient être ces institutions, tandis que Paul VI donna des indications précises en ce domaine, montrant que la promotion humaine dépend de la collaboration de tous à la poursuite d'objectifs prioritaires qui avaient alors pour nom: l'amélioration de la situation des populations rurales, l'industrialisation, le développement du commerce international ainsi que des échanges commerciaux ou financiers.

La poursuite de ces trois objectifs était alors considérée comme une condition *sine qua non* de la promotion humaine et du développement des peuples. L'encyclique n'éprouve aucune peine à entrer dans cette vue; elle précise en outre quels sont les critères sur lesquels doit se guider un décideur pour que cette croissance humaine soit effectivement au bénéfice de tous et de chacun.

Les critères que recommande l'encyclique ne sont pas d'ordre économique mais moraux. Pour elle, les mesures qu'on se propose de prendre ne doivent pas être appréciées du seul point de vue de l'efficacité économique mais en fonc-

---

[20] Ibid.
[21] *Divini Redemptoris* § 10.
[22] *Quadragesimo Anno* § 96 cf. également § 118.

tion de leur aptitude à favoriser un développement solidaire de l'humanité, l'intégration organique des populations marginales dans le processus du développement et la paix entre les communautés.

Il y a ici un retour à une doctrine anthropologique pour guider l'action mais celle-ci remplit une fonction différente de celle qui était la sienne dans le premier catholicisme social. On ne déduit pas de principes philosophiques comment organiser la société mais constatant les tendances qui emportent celle-ci, on se demande comment les infléchir «de l'intérieur et de façon progressive»[23] vers plus de justice et de solidarité. La manière d'en appeler à une «justice supérieure»[24] pour arbitrer entre les diverses tendances qui s'affrontent dans la société a changé. Il ne s'agit plus pour les catholiques sociaux de reprocher à ceux qui ne partagent pas leur vision du monde «l'oubli des préceptes essentiels à l'ordre et à la paix»[25] comme si la mise en oeuvre de ces principes ne permettait qu'un seul type de société temporelle. L'on part ici de l'aspiration des hommes à être plus, à agir comme des êtres libres[26]; considérant cette attitude psychologique comme un «fait d'ordre moral»[27], on se demande quels obstacles sont à écarter pour permettre sa réalisation progressive.

La confrontation des points de vue et la tentative d'inscrire une doctrine dans la réalité caractérisaient l'ancienne approche des questions sociales, on cherche aujourd'hui à créer les conditions d'une recherche commune de qui est plus humain.

---

[23] *Pacem in terris* § 162.
[24] Chanoine CALIPPE, La tâche des catholiques français depuis l'encyclique *Rerum Novarum* in SEMAINE SOCIALE DE FRANCE XIème session Metz 1919 p. 37.
[25] Chanoine CALIPPE, *La tâche...* op. cit. p. 49.
[26] *Pacem in terris* § 34; *Dignitatis humanae* § 2; cf. Cardinal Pietro PAVAN. Il momento della «Pacem in terris»; sua incidenza negli Atti conciliari e nella vita della chiesa e sua influenza nella Società contemporanea in F. BIFFI (a cura di), *I diritti fondamnetali della persona umana e la libertà religiosa*. Atti del V colloquio giuridico. Libreria editrice Vaticana e libreria editrice Lateranense 1985 pp. 149-156.
[27] *Sollicitudo Rei socialis* § 9.

CONCLUSION

Le mouvement social chrétien s'était déjà préoccupé entre les deux guerres de mieux connaître les fondements de l'ordre social. Face aux totalitarismes, Pie XI avait affirmé que la personne humaine était l'une des «colonnes»[28] sur lesquelles reposait tout l'édifice social; lors d'un congrès tenu à La Haye en 1938, le professeur M. Byé concluait sa relation en demandant que «tous les hommes et tous les peuples» soient les bénéficiaires de la croissance économique grâce à la «promotion de la solidarité des nations sous toutes ses formes»[29]. Le même langage devait être employé par François Perroux en 1958 lorsqu'il affirmait que le développement devait être au bénéfice de «tous les hommes et de tout l'homme»[30]. Cette école de pensée pénétra les milieux d'Eglise grâce entre autres aux *Semaines sociales de France* ainsi qu'à l'action du Père Lebret et de son mouvement *«Economie et humanisme»*; l'autorité de ce dernier en matière de développement humain lui valut d'exposer le point de vue du Saint-Siège lors de deux conférences internationales tenues à Genève en 1962 (UNCSAT) et 1964 (CNUCED I). L'écho rencontré par ces interventions fut considérable et persuada Paul VI que le moment était venu d'exposer la pensée de l'Eglise sur cette question d'actualité qu'était le développement des peuples[31].

Le message de *Populorum Progressio* est imprégné d'optimisme. Il dit aux hommes que l'appel à être plus qu'ils ressentent en eux correspond à la réalité de leur nature et qu'aucune loi économique n'impose d'envisager le développement selon les principes du capitalisme libéral ou du socialisme marxiste.

Populorum Progressio s'inscrit donc dans un mouvement, celui par lequel l'Eglise répond aux problèmes de son

---

[28] *Mit brennender Sorge* § 37.

[29] M. BYE, Economic Causes of economic Disorder in CATHOLIC SOCIAL YEARBOOK, *The Foundation on international Order* Catholic social Guild Oxford 1938 p. 99.

[30] Cité par G. FESSARD, *Eglise de France prends garde de perdre la foi* Julliard Paris 1979 p. 107 note 67.

[31] E. SOTTAS, *Une politique de développement, vingt ans d'activité du Saint-Siège à la CNUCED* Centre d'information des OIC Genève pp. 8-12; Cardinal PAUL POUPARD. Cf. note 1.

temps par les encycliques sociales; elle ne cache pas l'ambivalence que peut avoir la promotion humaine dans laquelle les sociétés sont engagées et dont l'antidote se trouve dans un discernement fondé sur des critères religieux comme devait le souligner quelques années plus tard la Lettre de Paul VI au Cardinal Roy, *Octogesima Adveniens*.

Die Soziallehre der Kirche und der Fortschritt der Völker

JOHANNES SCHASCHING

Die Soziallehre der Kirche ist kein geschlossenes System, sondern eher ein offener Prozeß. Sie entstand in einer bestimmten gesellschaftlichen Situation, nämlich der «geradezu sklavenähnlichen Situation» des Proletariates (Rerum novarum, 1891). Als sich 40 Jahre später die Arbeiterfrage zur Klassengesellschaft entwickelte, versuchte die Soziallehre der Kirche eine neue Orientierung zu geben (Quadragesimo anno, 1931). Eines ist allerdings auffallend: Die ersten Sozialenzykliken befaßten sich fast ausschließlich mit den Problemen der westlichen Industrieländer.

Nach dem 2. Weltkrieg bekam die Soziallehre der Kirche eine neue Dimension. Die bisherigen Kolonialländer erhielten ihre politische Unabhängigkeit, gerieten aber gleichzeitig in schwere innere wirtschaftliche und politische Krisen. Auf der anderen Seite wurde die westliche Welt durch zwei große Blöcke getrennt: im Westen die demokratischen Systeme, im Osten die marxistischen Diktaturen. Damit wurde klar, daß die soziale Frage zunehmend einen globalen Charakter annahm, und daß sich die katholische Soziallehre dieser neuen Situation zu stellen hatte. Sie tat dies in drei Sozialenzykliken, die in je verschiedener Weise das gemeinsame Thema hatten: die neue wirtschaftliche, soziale und politische Situation und der Fortschritt der Völker.

I. DER FORTSCHRITT DER VÖLKER - DER EINZIGE WEG ZUM FRIEDEN POPULORUM PROGRESSIO, 1967

Das war die große Sorge Pauls VI. und seiner Enzyklika: Es war eindrucksvoll wie schnell sich die vom 2. Weltkrieg zerstörten Länder Europas wirtschaftlich erholten. Das geschah zu einem guten Teil durch eigene Initiativen, aber ebenso durch massive Hilfe von den Vereinigten Staaten. Paul VI. begrüßte diesen Fortschritt, war aber überzeugt, daß der Friede in der Welt nicht von Dauer sein kann, wenn die Entwicklungsländer, die den weitaus größten Teil der Menschheit umfaßten, von diesem Fortschritt ausgeschlossen blieben. Darum enthielt seine Enzyklika nicht nur einen dringenden moralischen Appell, sondern gleichzeitig auch die wesentlichen Elemente für den Fortschritt der Völker. Sie lassen sich so zusammenfassen:

Die Kontinuität der Kulturen

Eine erste Sorge in der Entwicklung und im Fortschritt der Völker bestand darin, daß die wirtschaftlich-technische Entwicklung die bisherigen Werte und Kulturen der Entwicklungsländer auflöste und an ihrer Stelle nichts Gleichwertiges stellte. Die Enzyklika formuliert das Dilemma so: «Entweder die Gebräuche und Überzeugungen der Völker bewahren und auf den Fortschritt verzichten, oder sich der von außen kommenden Technik und Zivilisation öffnen und die Traditionen mit ihrem ganzen menschlichen Reichtum hingeben. In der Tat: Der sittliche, geistige, religiöse Halt von früher löst sich nur allzuoft auf, ohne daß die Eingliederung in die neue Welt genügend gesichert ist» (10).

Die integrale Entwicklung

Darum insistiert Populorum progressio, daß der menschliche Fortschritt nicht einseitig wirtschaftlich und materiell gesehen werden darf. Die Entwicklung ist nicht einfach gleichbedeutend mit wirtschaftlichem Wachstum. Wahre Entwicklung muß umfassend sein, sie muß jeden Menschen und den ganzen Menschen im Auge haben. Umfassend im Sinn der Enzyklika ist eine Entwicklung, wenn sie neben der wirtschaftlichen gleichzeitig auch die soziale und kulturelle Entwicklung anstrebt. Gerade der soziale Fortschritt fällt aber oft hinter dem technisch-wirtschaftlichen weit zurück. Multinationale Unternehmen «erweisen sich in ihrer Heimat durch soziale Verantwortung aufgeschlossen. Warum betreiben sie dann aber in den Entwicklungsländern Geschäfte nach den unmenschlichen Grundsätzen eines krassen Eigennutzes»? (70).

Wege der Entwicklung und des Fortschrittes

Es wäre aber einseitig zu glauben, daß Populorum progressio mit dieser Betonung der integralen Entwicklung die wirtschaftlich-technische Entwicklung als nicht mitentscheidend ansehen würde. Ausdrücklich betont der Papst: Wachstum «ist unentbehrlich, damit der Mensch mehr Mensch werde» (19). Dieses Wachstum aber braucht von Seiten der Industrieländer eine Reihe von Vorleistungen. Es ist bedeutsam, daß Populorum progressio hier nicht sofort und ausschließlich mit finanziellen Hilfen der Industrieländer argumentiert. Weil er überzeugt ist, daß die Entwicklungsländer selber die erste Verantwortung für den Fortschritt tragen, betont er, daß ihnen zuerst Gerechtigkeit in den Handelsbeziehungen eingeräumt werden müsse. Oft aber ist es der Fall, daß die Industrieländer den Entwicklungsländern wirtschaftliche Bedingungen auferlegen, die schweres Unrecht darstellen und damit die Entwicklung verhindern oder zumindest verzögern.

Selbstverständlich braucht der Fortschritt der Entwicklungsländer auch finanzielle Hilfe. Paul VI. weist in diesem Zusammenhang auf ein Problem hin, das gerade zu seiner Zeit höchst aktuell war: die militärische Abrüstung. Darum sein Vorschlag:

Die reichen Länder «möchten einen Teil der Beträge, die sie für Rüstungszwecke ausgeben, zur Schaffung eines Weltfonds verwenden» (51).

Es ist ebenso klar, daß das große Werk der Entwicklung auf Weltebene nicht durch einzelne Initiativen und auch nicht durch das Bemühen eines einzelnen Staates gelingen kann, sondern, daß es dazu internationale Institutionen braucht (78).

Fortschritt und Bevölkerung

Populorum progressio ist die erste Sozialenzyklika, die im Zusammenhang mit der Entwicklung der Völker bewußt auf das Problem des Bevölkerungswachstums eingeht. Die Einwände gegen die Soziallehre der Kirche sind bekannt. Man sagt: Der Fortschritt der Entwicklungsländer hängt wesentlich vom Wachstum der Bevölkerung ab. Das gegenwärtige überstarke Wachstum der Bevölkerung verhindert eine echte Entwicklung. Die Kirche aber, so sagt man, ist grundsätzlich gegen jede Geburtenkontrolle. Im Gegenteil, sie verpflichtet sogar zum Kinderreichtum und sieht darin einen Auftrag des Schöpfers.

Die Position von Populorum progressio ist viel differenzierter. Die Enzyklika sagt ausdrücklich, «daß zu oft ein schnelles Anwachsen der Bevölkerung für das Entwicklungsproblem eine zusätzliche Schwierigkeit bedeutet» (37). Darum hat der Staat «innerhalb der Grenzen seiner Zuständigkeit das Recht, hier einzugreifen, eine zweckmäßige Aufklärung durchzuführen und geeignete Maßnahmen zu treffen, vorausgesetzt, daß diese in Übereinstimmung mit dem Sittengesetz sind und die berechtigte Freiheit der Eheleute nicht antasten» (37). Das heißt mit anderen Worten: Populorum progressio verteidigt keineswegs ein unbegrenztes Wachstum der Bevölkerung. Ein ethisch verantwortbares Wachstum hängt von zwei Voraussetzungen ab: vom Wissens- und Bildungsstand der Ehepaare, aber ebenso von ihrer wirtschaftlichen und sozialen Absicherung. Die Verwirklichung dieser beiden Voraussetzungen ist wesentlich wirksamer als staatliche Zwänge und Eingriffe in die Würde des Menschen.

Die Kraft der Solidarität

Populorum progressio gibt sich keiner Täuschung hin. Entwicklung und Fortschritt brauchen zweifellos wirtschaftliche, soziale und politische Maßnahmen. Diese brauchen durchaus nicht nur aus Selbstinteresse geleistet werden, sondern können bereits ein Stück echter Solidarität enthalten. Aber «die bisherigen Mittel sind unzureichend» (7). Ohne eine sehr bewußte Pflege der Solidarität können die Herausforderungen der Entwicklung nicht beantwortet werden. Hier wird Populorum progressio sehr konkret und geradezu leidenschaftlich: Ist gemand bereit «mehr Steuern zu zahlen, damit die öffentlichen Stellen ihre Entwicklungshilfe intensivieren können? Höhere Preise für Einfuhrgüter zu zahlen, damit die Erzeuger einen angemessenen Verdienst erhalten? Notfalls seine Heimat zu verlassen, wenn er jung ist um den zu höherer Zivilisation aufstrebenden Nationen zu helfen» (47).

Von einem ist Populorum progressio aber zutiefst überzeugt: Ein Aufschieben ist nicht mehr möglich. «Es eilt. Zu viele Menschen sind in Not und es wächst der Abstand, der den Fortschritt der einen von der Stagnation der anderen trennt»(29).

II. Der Fortschritt der Völker - im Randdruck der wirtschaftlichen und politischen Blöcke Sollicitudo rei socialis, 1987

Der Enzyklika Sollicitudo rei socialis Johannes Paul's II. liegt eine tiefe Besorgtheit zugrunde: 20 Jahre nach dem Rundschreiben Pauls VI. über die Entwicklung der Völker hat sich die Lage der Entwicklungsländer nicht gebessert. In einer Reihe von Ländern kam es zu einem Stillstand der Entwicklung, in nicht wenigen aber erfolgte ein massiver Rückschritt. «Man muß klar aussprechen, daß sich die Gesamtlage trotz der lobenswerten Anstrengungen ... erheblich verschlechtert hat» (16). Und das zu einer Zeit, in der auf der einen Seite die Überzeugung wächst, daß die Welt immer mehr eins wird und eins werden muß und auf der anderen Seite eine Menschheit, die über ein hochentwickeltes technisch-wirtschaftliches und politisch-soziales Instrumentar verfügt, um Probleme zu lösen, die früher unlösbar waren.

Natürlich weiß auch der Papst, daß die Entwicklung der Völker eine äußerst schwierige und komplexe Aufgabe darstellt. Darum geht es Johannes Paul II. nicht darum, konkrete Lösungen anzubieten. Dafür weiß er sich nicht zuständig. Aber er will die geistig-sittlichen Hintergründe aufzeigen, die das Werk der Entwicklung verzögern oder gar verhindern. Und er will ebenso die sittlichen Grundhaltungen darstellen, die für die Lösung des Dramas der Unterentwicklung notwendig sind. Davon ist Johannes Paul II. zuinnerst überzeugt, «daß die Fragen, vor denen wir stehen, vor allem moralischer Natur sind, und daß weder die Analyse des Entwicklungsproblems an sich noch die Mittel zur Überwindung der gegenwärtigen Schwierigkeiten von einer solchen wesentlichen Dimension absehen dürfen» (41).

Damit sind die zwei Dimensionen der Enzyklika bereits vorausgenommen: erstens die Analyse der Unterentwicklung, zweitens Wege zum Fortschritt der Völker.

Ursachen der Unterentwicklung: Strukturen der Sünde

Die Enzyklika Sollicitudo rei socialis kennt durchaus die unmittelbaren Ursachen der Unterentwicklung: die hohe Verschuldung, die Konflikte der beiden Blöcke Ost und West, die kostbare Ressourcen binden und die Versuche, die Entwicklungsländer in diese Konflikte mit einzubeziehen. Das verursacht ausgesprochene Formen des Neokolonialismus und Imperialismus, deren Hauptziel die Ausweitung der eigenen Vorherrschaft, nicht aber die Entwicklung der Völker ist. Die Entwicklungsländer werden «zu Rädern eines Mechanismus, zu Teilen einer gewaltigen Maschinerie» (22).

Hinter diesen vordergründigen Ursachen der Unterentwicklung gibt es aber tiefliegendere und grundsätzlichere. Sie sind nicht mit wirtschaftlichen oder politischen Kategorien zu messen. Sie entspringen sittlichen Fehlhaltungen und Verfehlungen. «Auf der einen Seite die ausschließliche Gier nach Profit und auf der anderen Seite das Verlangen nach Macht» (37). Diese sittlichen Fehlhaltungen erzeugen «Strukturen und Mechanismen ... die viel weiter reichen als die Taten selbst und die kurze Lebensphase des einzelnen Menschen» (36). Sie verfestigen sich zu wirtschaftlichen und politischen Machtsystemen. Das heißt konkret: auf der einen Seite der liberalistische Kapitalismus, auf der anderen Seite der totalitäre Marxismus. Im Westen besteht ein System, das sich historisch an den Prinzipien des liberalistischen Kapitalismus orientiert ... im Osten dagegen besteht ein System, das sich am marxistischen Kollektivismus orientiert. Die Enzyklika zögert nicht, sie als «Strukturen der Sünde» zu bezeichnen (36).

Beide Systeme bedingen nicht nur die wirtschaftlichen und politischen Strukturen der eigenen Länder, sondern haben ebenso einen direkten Einfluß auf die Entwicklungsländer, weil sie zwei Auffassungen von der Entwicklung der

Menschen und Völker darstellen, «die beide unvollkommen sind und als solche eine tiefgreifende Korrektur erfordern» (21). Damit stellt sich eine sehr grundsätzliche Frage: «Auf welche Weise oder in welchem Maß lassen diese beiden Systeme Veränderungen oder Anpassungen zu, so daß eine echte und umfassende Entwicklung des Menschen und der Völker in der heutigen Gesellschaft begünstigt oder gefördert würde? Solche Veränderungen und Anpassungen sind für die Sache einer gemeinsamen Entwicklung aller dringend und unerläßlich» (21).

Damit ist die zweite Frage in voller Deutlichkeit gestellt: Welche Wege gibt die Enzyklika an, um aus den «Strukturen der Sünde» zu einem echten Fortschritt der Völker zu gelangen?

Als Ausgangspunkt wiederholt die Enzyklika nochmals ihre feste Überzeugung: Wie wichtig auch die wirtschaftlichen und politischen Ursachen der Unterentwicklung sind, entscheidender aber ist es, «die wahre Natur des Bösen aufzuzeigen, mit der wir es bei der Frage der Entwicklung der Völker zu tun haben: Es handelt sich um ein moralisches Übel» (37).

Wenn dies feststeht, ist es klar, daß der erste und entscheidende Schritt ebenfalls moralischer Art sein muß. Das heißt mit anderen Worten: Es braucht eine moralische Umkehr und Bekehrung von der Gier nach Profit und Macht hin zu einer «völlig entgegengesetzten Haltung» (38): der Haltung der Solidarität. Sie ist nicht «ein Gefühl vagen Mitleids oder oberflächlicher Rührung wegen der Leiden so vieler Menschen nah und fern. Im Gegenteil, sie ist die feste und beständige Entschlossenheit, sich für das 'Gemeinwohl' einzusetzen, daß heißt, für das Wohl aller und eines jeden, weil wir für alle verantwortlich sind» (38).

Sollicitudo rei socialis gibt sich keiner Täuschung hin: Der Weg der Solidarität wird ein «langer und mühsamer Weg (sein), der zudem noch ständig bedroht wird, sei es durch die innere Gebrechlichkeit menschlicher Vorsätze und Taten, sei es durch die Wandelbarkeit der äußeren, oft nicht vorhersehbaren Umstände» (3 8).

Wird aber Solidarität grundsätzlich ernstgenommen, werden sich auch die konkreten Schritte der Verwirklichung finden lassen. Es ist nicht Aufgabe der katholischen Soziallehre, konkrete Lösungen vorzulegen. Sie kann aber durchaus Hinweise und Wegspuren solcher Lösungen angeben: z. B.: es braucht eine Reform des internationalen Handelssystems, das durch Protektionismus gekennzeichnet ist; es braucht eine Reform des Währungs- und Finanzsystems, das auf die besondere Situation der Entwicklungsländer eingeht; es braucht den Transfer von Technologien und ihrer möglichen Anwendung in den Entwicklungsländern, usw.

Sollicitudo rei socialis anerkennt durchaus, daß die Industrieländer und ihre Institutionen viel für die Entwicklung der Völker getan haben. Aber sie brauchen heute «angesichts einer neuen und schwierigen Phase ihrer echten Entwicklung ... einen höheren Grad internationaler Ordnung» (43).

Die Enzyklika versäumt nicht, immer wieder darauf hinzuweisen, daß die Entwicklungsländer selber einen entscheidenden Anteil an ihrem eigenen Fortschritt zu leisten haben. Das betrifft sowohl die wirtschaftlichen Grundlagen, die politische Ordnung und den Faktor der Bildung und Erziehung. Dazu kommt wesentlich, daß die Entwicklungsländer «neue regionale Organisationen aufbauen, die sich an den Kriterien von Gleichheit, Freiheit und Mitbeteiligung im Verbund der Nationen ausrichten» (45).

Eine Dimension der Enzyklika Sollicitudo rei socialis darf nicht übergangen werden. Der Papst ist davon überzeugt, daß sich die eingeforderte Solidarität zum Wohl der Entwicklungsländer nicht auf die wirtschaftlichen und politischen Autoritäten beschränken kann. Sie verlangt auch eine neue Solidarität innerhalb der moralischen und religiösen Kräfte. Darum richtet sich der Appell des Papstes nicht nur an die Katholiken und die anderen christlichen Gemeinschaften, sondern zum ersten Mal in dieser Deutlichkeit auch an die Juden, an die Muslims, an alle Anhänger der großen Weltreligionen und an alle Menschen guten Willens.

III. Der Fortschritt der Völker in einer globalisierten Welt Centesimus annus, 1991

Mit dem Zusammenbruch des Kommunismus ergab sich eine ganz neue Situation und Fragestellung für die Entwicklung der Völker. Sie mußte nicht mehr unter dem bisherigen Druck der beiden Blöcke gesehen werden, sondern in einer zunehmend globalisierten Welt. Genau das ist das Anliegen der Sozialenzyklika Centesimus annus.

Der Papst spricht zuerst von den drei Ursachen, die diese gewaltlose Revolution ausgelöst haben. Die erste war der Aufstand der Arbeiterschaft. Dieser Aufstand war deshalb für das System tödlich, weil es nach der kommunistischen Ideologie den «fortschrittlichen Teil» der Gesellschaft darstellte und daher der Träger der gesellschaftlichen Revolution sein sollte. Die zweite Ursache war der Zusammenbruch der Wirtschaft. Die marxistische Ideologie war überzeugt, daß im neuen System jeder nach seinem besten Können zum Gemeinwohl beitragen werde, für sich aber nur das nehme, was er braucht. Dies war eine wirtschaftliche Utopie und wurde durch die Privilegien der herrschenden Klasse widerlegt. Als dritte Ursache führte Centesimus annus den Verlust der Werte an: «Die wahre Ursache der jüngsten Ereignisse ist jedoch die vom Atheismus hervorgerufene geistige Leere» (24).

Auf Grund des Zusammenbruches des Kommunismus ergeben sich nicht nur für die Industrieländer, sondern in besonderer Weise auch für die Entwicklungsländer neue Herausforderungen und Aufgaben. Centesimus annus faßt sie so zusammen:

Die Gefahr des Neo-Kapitalismus

Johannes Paul II. stellt die Kernfrage so: «Kann man sagen, daß nach dem Scheitern des Kommunismus der Kapitalismus das siegreiche Gesellschaftssystem sei, und daß er das Ziel der Bemühungen jener Länder ist, die ihre Wirtschaft und Gesellschaft neu aufzubauen versuchen?» (42). Dann fügt er bewußt hinzu: «Ist vielleicht er das Modell, das den Ländern der dritten Welt, die nach einem Weg für den wirtschaftlichen und gesellschaftlichen Fortschritt suchen, vorgeschlagen werden soll?» (42).

Dann folgt die harte Kritik: Trotz gewisser Fortschritte herrschen gerade in den Entwicklungsländern «noch die Regeln des Kapitalismus der Gründerzeit mit einer Erbarmungslosigkeit, die jener der finsteren Jahre der ersten Industrialisierung in nichts nachsteht» (33). In dieser Situation der Ausbeutung «lebt leider noch immer die große Mehrheit der Bewohner der dritten Welt» (33).

Damit ergibt sich für Centesimus annus die entscheidende Frage, wie der Gefahr eines harten Neokapitalismus zu begegnen sei. Der Papst weiß sich nicht zuständig, ein alternatives Wirtschaftssystem zu erstellen. Aber er gibt eine Grundrichtung an: «Es geht um eine Gesellschaftsordnung der freien Arbeit, der Unternehmen und der Beteiligung. Sie stellt sich keineswegs gegen den Markt, sondern verlangt, daß er von den sozialen Kräften und vom Staat in angemessener Weise kontrolliert werde» (35).

Daß dies eine schwierige und langwierige Aufgabe darstellt, weiß auch der Papst. Aber er weiß ebenso, daß er mit dieser Aussage eine Grundsatzentscheidung getroffen hat.

Bausteine zur Entwicklung der Völker

Es wurde bereits gesagt: Johannes Paul II. weiß sich nicht kompetent, wirtschaftspolitische Details zur Entwicklung der Völker anzugeben. Aber er ist überzeugt, daß er aus dem Wissensgut der katholischen Soziallehre Bausteine dazu einbringen kann.

Ein erster Baustein ist die ethische Bejahung der Globalisierung. Nach dem Zusammenbruch des Marxismus «rückt die Wirklichkeit der gegenseitigen Abhängigkeit der Völker klarer ins Licht und ebenso die Tatsache, daß die menschliche Arbeit von Natur aus dazu bestimmt ist, die Völker zu verbinden, nicht aber sie zu spalten. Friede und Wohlfahrt sind Werte, die dem ganzen Menschengeschlecht gehören. Es ist nicht möglich, sie zu Recht und auf Dauer zu genießen, wenn sie zu Lasten anderer Völker und Nationen erworben und behalten werden, indem sie deren Rechte verletzen oder sie von den Quellen des Wohlstandes ausschließen» (27). Die letzte Begründung dafür aber heißt: «Gott hat die Erde dem ganzen Menschengeschlecht geschenkt... Hier liegt die Wurzel der universalen Bestimmung der Güter der Erde» (31).

Ein zweiter Baustein betrifft die Wirtschaft. Dieser Baustein ist deshalb so wichtig, weil er direkt einigen irrigen Auffassungen der Entwicklungsländer widerspricht. Noch vor wenigen Jahren wurde behauptet, die ärmsten Länder könnten sich nur dadurch entwickeln, daß sie sich vom Weltmarkt abkoppeln und den eigenen Kräften vertrauen. Die jüngste Erfahrung aber hat gezeigt, daß die Länder, die sich abgekoppelt haben, eine Stagnation und einen Rückgang erlitten haben. Eine Entwicklung hingegen haben jene Länder erfahren, denen es gelungen ist, in das allgemeine Gefüge der internationalen Wirtschaftsbeziehungen einzutreten.

«Heute stehen wir vor den Bestrebungen einer sogenannten 'Globalisierung der Wirtschaft', einem Phänomen, das sicher nicht zu verwerfen ist, enthält es doch außerordentliche Möglichkeiten zu einem größeren Wohlstand» (58).

Daraus folgt ein dritter Baustein. Es geht in der Frage der Entwicklung der Völker nicht zuerst um Almosen. Es geht darum, «ganzen Völkern den Zugang in den Kreis der wirtschaftlichen und menschlichen Entwicklung, von dem sie ausgeschlossen oder ausgegrenzt sind, zu eröffnen. Ein wesentliches Hindernis besteht in der Tatsache der gewaltigen Verschuldung der ärmsten Länder. Der Grundsatz, daß Schulden zurückgezahlt werden müssen, ist sicher richtig. Es ist jedoch nicht erlaubt, eine Rückzahlung zu erwarten oder einzufordern, die zu politischen Maßnahmen zwingt, die ganze Völker in den Hunger und in die Verzweiflung treiben würden... Darum braucht es Modalitäten, die mit dem Grundrecht der Völker auf Erhaltung und Fortschritt vereinbar sind» (35).

Dazu braucht es einen vierten Baustein: die internationale Solidarität und internationale Institutionen. Trotz aller Initiativen einzelner Länder und bilateraler Abkommen muß «das Übereinkommen zwischen den großen Ländern wachsen und in den internationalen Organen müssen die Interessen der großen Menschheitsfamilie gerecht vertreten werden» (58).

Einen letzten Baustein formuliert Centesimus annus sehr eindeutig: «Die Welt von heute ist sich immer mehr bewußt, daß die Lösung der ernsten nationalen und internationalen Probleme nicht nur eine Frage der Wirtschaft oder der Rechts- und Wirtschaftsordnung ist, sondern klare sittlich-religiöse Werte sowie die Änderung der Gesinnung, des Verhaltens und der Strukturen erfordert. Diesen Beitrag anzubieten, fühlt sich die Kirche in besonderer Weise verantwortlich» (60).

Aber dann folgt die entscheidende Ergänzung: Nicht nur die katholische Kirche hat dieses Angebot zu machen. Diesen Beitrag haben alle christlichen Kirchen anzubieten aber ebenso die großen Religionen der Welt: «Ich bin nämlich überzeugt, daß den Religionen heute und morgen eine herausragende Rolle für die Bewahrung des Friedens und für den Aufbau einer menschenwürdigen Gesellschaft zufallen wird» (60). Aber auch das genügt noch nicht. Es besteht die Hoffnung, aber auch die Notwendigkeit, «daß auch jene Großgruppe, die sich zu keiner Religion bekennt, beitragen kann, der sozialen Frage das notwendige Fundament zu geben «(60).

Wegspuren der katholischen Soziallehre

Sie wurden in Verbindung mit den drei erwähnten Sozialenzykliken zusammenfassend so formuliert: Populorum progressio — der einzige Weg zum Frieden; Sollicitudo rei socialis — der Fortschritt der Völker im Randdruck der wirtschaftlichen und politischen Blöcke; Centesimus annus - der Fortschritt der Völker in einer globalisierten Welt. In diesen drei Stichworten ist sowohl das Zeitbedingte als auch das Grundsätzliche der katholischen Soziallehre zum Fortschritt der Völker enthalten.

Das Zeitbedingte: Im ersten Rundschreiben ging es wesentlich darum, daß die wirtschaftliche Euphorie der Industrieländer im Wiederaufbau nach dem 2. Weltkrieg nicht den Fortschritt der Entwicklungsländer vergessen läßt und vor allem: daß der Auffassung widerstanden werden muß, daß das wirtschaftliche Wachstum das zentrale und einzige Problem im Fortschritt der Völker darstelle. Das zweite Rundschreiben war von der Sorge geprägt, daß sich die Konflikte der zwei Blöcke auf die Entwicklungsländer ausdehnen und sie zu einem bloßen Instrument im wirtschaftlichen und politischen Kampf der Großmächte degradieren würden. Das dritte Rundschreiben stand vor der völlig neuen Situation der Globalisierung und der offenen Gesellschaft. Werden die Entwicklungsländer schrittweise als gleichberechtigte Partner in die Weltwirtschaft eingebaut oder kommt es zu einer Zweiklassengesellschaft auf weltweiter Ebene?

Das Grundsätzliche: Hinter allen zeitbedingten Aussagen der drei Sozialenzykliken stehen grundsätzliche Inhalte, die zum Wesen der katholischen Soziallehre gehören. Der erste ist das Ernstnehmen der gemeinsamen Würde des Menschen. Wenn die Vereinten Nationen 1948 die Charta der Menschenrechte erlassen haben, dann muß das tiefgreifende Folgen haben. Für die katholische Soziallehre ist diese Menschenwürde nicht in einem bloßen Vertrag begründet, sondern im Schöpfungswillen Gottes. Sie stellt eine so schwerwiegende und vorrangige Wirklichkeit dar, daß sie zur Gesinnungsänderung und Strukturreform verpflichtet.

Der zweite Grundgehalt ist das Grundwissen über den Aufbau der Gesellschaft. Auch er hängt wesentlich mit der Würde des Menschen zusammen. Die soziale Dimension ist der menschlichen Person so wesentlich, daß er ohne sie oder gegen sie in seinem Menschsein verkümmern würde. Diese soziale Dimension hat zweifellos zwei Stufen und Grade der Intensität. In einer Zeit der Globalisierung aber verpflichtet sie zu neuen Dimensionen und zu neuen Solidaritäten, die ebenfalls einen tiefgreifenden Gesinnungswandel und eine Strukturreform bedingen.

Der dritte Grundgehalt betrifft die Überzeugung, daß menschliches Handeln nie aus bloß wirtschaftlichen oder gesellschaftlichen Interessen erfolgt, sondern daß sie auf Werten oder Unwerten aufruhen. Darum ist die Begegnung und Einübung der Werte eine entscheidende Voraussetzung dafür, daß der Fortschritt der Völker menschengerecht und demokratisch erfolgen kann.

LITERATUR

O.v. NELL-BREUNING, Texte zur katholischen Soziallehre, 8. Aufl., Kevelaer 1992, Butzon & Bercker.
O.v. NELL-BREUNING, Gerechtigkeit und Freiheit, Grundzüge katholischer Soziallehre, Wien 1980, Europaverlag.
PETER LANGHORST, Die Kirche und Entwicklungsproblematik. Paderborn 1996, Schöningh.
J. SCHASCHING, In Sorge um Entwicklung und Frieden, Wien 1988, Europaverlag.

Justice and Peace and the Integrity of Creation
(An African view on Evangelization and Human Progress)

Rt. Rev. Peter K. Sarpong

Preamble

If the words *"evangelization"* and *"progress"* are relevant to any continent, it is surely the continent of Africa. Many parts of Africa still need primary evangelization. Some parts of the same continent that have already received primary evangelization require to be regularly re-evangelised due to the influence of modernity that has gripped the whole world.

In the case of Africa, evangelisation implies the animation of the African with the Gospel imperative to make him realise that he has a dignity and that he is the beloved of the Lord. The existential reality of Africa is such that evangelisation and human progress must go together, as I think is the case everywhere in the world.

Human progress, or lack of it, takes different forms in Africa. That is why I have to choose one angle for discussion. To this effect, I have chosen *Justice and Peace and the Integrity of Creation*. I hope to link this up with evangelisation and human progress.

Personal

I am a simple priest from a rural area in Ghana. I was born in a village and brought up in what I now know to be very harsh conditions. My father and mother were subsistence farmers. My mother gave birth to eleven children, of whom six are alive, the four before me and the one immediately after me having died. Those who knew me as a child consider it a miracle that I am still living. I suffered from all kinds of illnesses, including hook worm, terrible ulcers of the body and, naturally, malaria. It was by pure chance that I went to school at the age of 10 and began to learn the alphabet.

Isaiah's Message

How I became a priest and later a bishop, only God can tell. As a priest, I have come to realise that the conditions in which my people live are not the conditions God intended for them. Holy Scripture is full of references to the plan of God for all of us to live in peace.

Talking of a shoot that springs from the stalk of Jesse on whom the spirit of Yahweh rests, a spirit of wisdom and insight, a spirit of counsel and power, a spirit of knowledge and of the fear of Yahweh, Isaiah is at pains to point out that this shoot does not judge by appearances. He gives no verdict on hearsay, but judges the wretched with integrity and with equity gives a verdict for the poor of the land. His word is a rod that strikes the ruthless, his sentences bring death to the wicked. He is incorruptible and faithful. In short, for Isaiah, the key virtue of the Messiah, the Saviour, is *JUSTICE*. Hence in his kingdom: Wolves and sheep live together in peace; leopards lie down with young goats. Calf and lion cubs will feed together, and little children take care of them. Cows and bears are friends, and their young lie down together. Lions eat straw like oxen. A baby is not harmed when it plays over a cobra's hole (cfr. Isaiah 11:1-9).

Elsewhere, the same Isaiah explains that in that kingdom:

No more will the sound of weeping be heard there, nor the sound of a shriek;
never again will there be an infant there who lives only a few days,
nor an old man who does not run his full course;
for the youngest will die at a hundred,
and at a hundred the sinner will be accursed.
They will build houses and live in them,
they will plant vineyards and eat their fruit.

They will not build for others to live in, or plant for others to eat;
for the days of my people will be like the days of a tree, and my chosen ones will themselves use what they have made.
They will not toil in vain, not bear children destined to disaster,
for they are the race of Yahweh's blessed ones and so are their offspring.
Thus, before they call I shall answer,
before they stop speaking I shall have heard. (Is. 65:19-24)

IMPORTANCE OF JUSTICE

All this shows that the justice of the Messiah causes the peace of his kingdom. How can a wolf live with a lamb? How can a cow make friends with the bear? How can an infant play over the cobra's hole and come to no harm? And how does a lion make straw its food, like an ox?

This will be possible only when the wolf forgets that it is a wolf, the lion empties itself of its "lion-ness" and the cobra does not insist that it is a cobra. In other words, the wolf must imagine that it is a lamb, the lion put itself in the place of a calf, and the bear consider how the cow must live in fear at the thought that it could become the bear's food. Humility, to forget who or what one is, is the key to justice.

There is no doubt that the injustices of this world stem from pride. Far too often we irrationally insist on what we are and only think about ourselves, without giving attention to what happens to other people. Rarely do we place ourselves in the position of the other person. In this way, we do injustice to the world itself, and erode its integrity.

PROBLEMS

The problems of injustice in the world, with special reference to Africa, are too well-known for there to be any need to recount them all again. In some countries, good food is thrown away or stored up or given to dogs; in others, millions of human beings starve to death. The majority of African nations lack the basic health requirements. According to the United Nations, 30% of Africa's children under the age of five go through a period of malnutrition, severe enough to cause permanent mental or physical damage. The infant mortality rate in Africa is around 130 per every 1,000 live births. Medicines that have been banned in advanced nations easily find their way into Africa. The illiteracy rate in Black Africa is very high.

The refugee situation of Africa is yet another instance of injustice to humanity. African refugees represent more than half of the world's homeless and they are larger in number than the combined population of ten smaller African nations.

There is injustice in the strings attached to loans and the high rates of interest and unrealistic debt repayment schedules that plunge African nations deeper into an economic quagmire and have created the debt crisis.

It was a travesty of justice that under the *apartheid* system, human beings should be classified as first class and third class and that 5 million whites should arrogate to themselves some 80% of the most arable land and reserve 20% to more than 28 million others. Thank God, *apartheid* is now a thing of the past, like the infamous slave trade that once reduced the humanity of the African to a mere commodity.

The economic system that makes Africans the producers of raw materials, the prices of which are determined by the rich nations, is unjust.

The same injustices against Africans continue under African leadership. The leadership of many African nations has turned out to be corrupt, inept, power-drunk, oppressive and discriminatory. The words "bribery and corruption", "nepotism", "intimidation" have become so common that they have lost their venom. In recent years, many African nations, notably Sierra Leone, Liberia, Congo, the Republic of Congo, Rwanda, Burundi, to name just these few, have witnessed the sadistic slaughtering of their own kith and kin. Fundamental human rights are flouted everywhere. Many leaders indulge in personality cult. Newspapers are censored or banned, unless they faithfully echo the government's propaganda. The combined daily circulation of papers on a continent of more than 500 million people is about that of the single London newspaper, *The Daily Mirror*.

The woman in Africa is physically and spiritually remarkable. Her comforts are few, her burdens many. She works hard and is responsible for 70% of the food grown on the continent. Yet African women generally are treated as second-class citizens. The illiteracy rate among women is double that of men.

The youth in Africa are fast losing their sense of identity and purpose. For fulfilment in life, many of them have recourse to drug-taking, alcohol and other forms of illusory satisfaction. Rural dwellers continue to be held in contempt, treated and looked down upon by urban dwellers, and so we could go on.

Faith

All this is a savage attack on the integrity of creation. Whether the account of creation in Genesis should be taken literally or not, the salient points are clear and these form the firm basis of our faith. It is fundamental to our faith that God created all human beings; and that he created all of us equal, in his own image and likeness. Everything that God created was good. He created the human person to rule the world, responsibly. His plan to entrust the mastery over other items of creation to the human person was clear (Gen. 1:28-3 1).

The integrity of this creation was savagely assaulted when Adam and Eve, our fore-fathers, succumbed to the temptation of the devil to try to be like gods, knowing good and evil (Gen. 3:5).

Pride

Do injustices not stem from the fact that we want to be more than what we are?

After Adam's disobedience came the episode of Cain who slew Abel for the simple reason that his sacrifice was not acceptable to God as that of Abel. Again, pride had the upperhand. As if this was not sufficient, human beings who spoke the same language with the same vocabulary, decided to build a tower with its top reaching heaven, in order to make a name for themselves. In answer to their pride, God confused them with different languages and scattered them. The integrity of creation had been dealt another fatal blow.

Role of spirit

This integrity, so badly shattered right from the beginning by man's pride, greed and selfishness, was to be restored on Pentecost day.

When the Spirit of love descended on the apostles, each one heard them in his or her own native language. The Acts of the Apostles is at pains to explain that they were from different parts of the world. Territorially, they were dispersed but in the Spirit of the Lord, they were united.

Equality

The point is that we are all human beings subject to the same laws of nature.

Africans are not inferior beings because they have melanin in their skin to protect them from the ravages of the sun. Africans can be as murderous as Germans and as merciful as Germans, as hypocritical and as rude as the British and as honest and polite as the British, as sinful and hypersensitive as the Irish and as saintly and tough as the Irish, as selfish as the Americans and as generous as the Americans. There is nothing to choose between them and any other species of *homo sapiens*. I have been to all six continents of the world and tasted life in many cities. If after my death, God were to send me back to the world and asked me to choose which race I wanted to belong to, I would plead with him to make me a black Ghanaian, Asante negro with kinky hair, thick lips and a flat nose.

Victim of injustice

From all angles the African is the victim of injustice which imposes on him a state of under-development. Surrounded by violence from stranger and brother alike, he is caught up in the vicious circle of poverty, disease, hunger and the resultant misery. His dignity as a human person is badly dented. Pope Paul VI exhorts the more fortunate to do something about this deplorable state of affairs by reminding us of the words of John: *"He who has the goods of this world and sees his brother in need and closes his heart to him, how does the love of God abide in him?"* (1 John 3:17). If few heed these words, it is, as Pope Paul VI explains, because: *"Human society is sorely ill. The cause is not so much the depletion of natural resources, nor their monopolistic control by a privileged few; it is the weakening of brotherly ties between individuals and nations"* (*Populorum Progressio* 66).

Civilization of Love

Love then is the key to the solution of the problem of injustice in Africa as elsewhere. Love is the weapon against which there can be no defences. Love does not divide. It unites.

In the interest of the integrity of creation, all of us together must respond to the divine call to be men and women for Africa, architects of a Civilization of Love for the victims of contempt.

The Civilization of Love produces the joy of living with others. In the Civilization of Love, justice is held to be a sacred right of all men and women; hence no one is disadvantaged in his economic, political, cultural and social relationships to others; there is no trade imbalance; and aid does not impose a cruel choice on recipients. In the Civilization of Love, there is no winner. For the Civilization thrives on truth and truth is not co-existent with victory.

As Rabbi Nahman of Bratzlav has observed: *"Victory cannot tolerate truth, and if that which is true is spread before your very eyes, you will reject it, because you are victor. Whoever would have truth itself, must drive hence the spirit of victory; only then may he prepare to behold the truth"*.

The Civilization of Love tolerates no lions, wolves, bears, or serpents. In the Civilization of Love what begins as a recognition of massive injustice in Africa must grow into a commitment to global love, provided that care is exercised lest in the process the new order take on the bitterness of the old. The Civilization of Love should remind us that love is synonymous with the power of Christ himself and unless we believe in love, we cannot call ourselves the disciples of the one who said: "*I give you a new commandment: that you love one another as I have loved you*" (John 13:34).

The Civilization of Love busies itself with building the kingdom of God, a society in which there is no discrimination based on sex or colour of the skin. In that society, the transformation of a person into a thing is avoided, and the refusal to respond to one afflicted is seen as denial of his humanity and turning him into a corpse.

Let us listen to a spokesman of God on this: "*Is not this the sort of fast that pleases me — it is the Lord Yahweh who speaks — to break unjust fetters and undo the thongs of the yoke, to let the oppressed go free, and break every yoke, to share your bread with the hungry, and shelter the homeless poor, to clothe the man you see to be naked and not turn from your own kin?*" (Isaiah 58:6-7).

It would be hard to find such a civilization anywhere on the map. However, this fact alone should be enough to show us the tragedy of a world so gripped by worldly values that there is little room left for the expression of man's humanity and dignity. The contradiction of our time is that some Christians should be part of the process.

Ernie Levy once asserted: "*The Christians say they love Christ, but I think they hate him without knowing it. So they take the cross by the other end and make a sword out of it and strike us with it*" (*The Last of the Just*). This is a terrible indictment which we must convincingly answer in anticipation of Christ's 2000th birthday.

Affection for Africa

Fortunately, Africa enjoys the affection of millions of non-Africans who, by resolutely championing its cause, have every right to refuse to plead guilty. These are men and women whose noble deeds for the oppressed and marginalised of Africa are recorded in the book of remembrance (Mal. 3:16). Without them, Africa would be in devastating despair. We appreciate their human and Christian commitment. They are willing and ever ready to listen to the voice of the African. In many instances, they respond to the call but their concern and solicitude alone is a source of consolation and hope. They constitute an inexhaustible source of strength and courage to Africans.

COMMON HUMANITY

The effort to bring about justice and peace in Africa concerns all of us because it is an imperative of our common humanity.

If at any given moment conditions are such that human beings do not reflect the image of God, then the Christian conscience should be pricked. Furthermore, our faith tells us that Jesus is the Saviour of all humankind. In him we are all one family; there is no Jew or Roman, slave or free man. He identified himself with the least of our brothers. *"For as long as you did it to the least of my brothers, you did it to me"* (Mt. 25:40).

JESUS' EXAMPLE

In the last analysis, it remains true that our insularity and refusal to see the other person's point of view are the main causes of injustices that breed violence. It was to counter-balance this that Christ became man, as our faith tells us. The example of Christ is amazing. Although he was God, he did not cling to his Godhead but emptied himself, as it were, forgetting that he was God, and took on the nature of human beings. For this reason, the writer of Hebrews tells us that he is a High Priest who knows our conditions and sympathises with us. *"Our High Priest is not one who cannot feel sympathy for our weaknesses. On the contrary, we have a High Priest who was tempted in every way that we are, but did not sin"* (Heb. 4:15).

This is where, I think, evangelization and human progress converge. Evangelization is the proclamation of the Good News of Jesus Christ. It is the acknowledgement and acceptance of the liberating mission of Christ which He has entrusted to the care of His Church. Christ liberates us from all shackles. He liberates us from the chains of sin and oppression. He it is who restores us to our former dignity. He sets us on the course of salvation. He makes us members of His Universal family, the Church, which is His Body. His Church is at the service of the Kingdom He came to establish. That Kingdom comes into being whenever human beings love one another and are sensitive to one another's plight. As a Good Shepherd, He protects us against the attacks of the ravenous wolf. He is the Unique Mediator between human beings and God, the point of encounter between us and His Father.

Evangelization, in the words of Mother Teresa, is *making this Christ present in our hearts so that we may make Him present in the hearts of others*. With Christ in our hearts, injustices stop; the seed of peace is sown and true human progress begins.

The atrocities that go on in Africa are directly contradictory to human progress. They degrade human dignity and there can be no progress where the dignity of the human person is not recognized. All human beings have a common Father and a common Saviour. Therefore, all human beings form one global community without boundries, after the fashion of the Most Blessed Trinity, the Source of true love, unity and peace.

All this is a further confirmation that indeed human promotion is a constitutive element of evangelization whose hallmark is solidarity and communion.

Environmental desecration

It is this kind of solidarity and sensitivity that the integrity of creation calls for. It also calls for our responsible use of our resources, especially the land. In the 1940s, I used to pass through thick forests to go to my father's cocoa farms. He had five. Today those equatorial forests are no more. In Kumasi, my former house is alongside the main ring road. Everyday I see dozens of truck-loads of big logs being transported to the coast for shipment abroad.

Countries like Germany that guard their millions of acres of reserved forests with religious jealousy have no compunction in depleting ours. The injustice is terrible.

Just as distressing each year, Africans are working less and less land as the desert advances as a plundering army taking as its booty the lean hopes of a helpless people and leaving in its wake barren wastelands. The Sahara alone is said to be growing at the rate of 250,000 acres a year and in the north of Africa, once the bread basket of the Roman Empire, desertification is a visible phenomenon. Yet a country like Ghana continues to cut its wood at an alarming rate for a quick short-term economic gain.

To make matters worse, some powerful nations have begun to dump toxic wastes on African soil. They do this sometimes with the connivance of some unscrupulous African leaders who want quick money for themselves. With the desecration of the environment created for us by God, the very essence of human existence is being ruthlessly threatened. We have to do something about this. We have to take the created world seriously as the place in and through which God touches us.

Reverence for Creation

We must treat all things reverently. To diminish or to destroy anything is to diminish or destroy ways of God's presence among us. We have to embrace the earth and not exploit it arrogantly. We have to embrace Jesus Christ, the God who has entered into solidarity with the human race so as to enter into solidarity with all creation. We have to work for peace and justice, beyond our social context into a global context. No nation should seek its own well-being at the expense of those very conditions upon which our global well-being depends. In our effort at restoring the integrity of creation, we must do our best to take human cultural values into serious account so as not to destroy the humanity of those we want to help.

Unfaithfulness

We are faced with the reign of injustice and the reign of violence. We are also faced with the disintegration of creation. These dimensions of our crisis are inter-connected. We need to open up a means of communication among us. To achieve this, we have to accept that the world belongs to God and that the earth is the beloved of God. God wants to enter into a covenant with us. We have always been unfaithful to that covenant; we have been disobedient to that covenant. But God's mercy never ceases. What we need now is to repent.

Change of heart

Repentance is a change of heart. The lions of Euro-America must stop devouring the lambs of Africa, and start eating straw like oxen. It is unjust for the serpent of powerful nations to continue to be biting the human child of Africa. Africa needs brothers and sisters who are sympathetic and feel with it. We need friends, not exploiters. We invite you to play with us as friends. This is the example that the Second Person of the Most Blessed Trinity gave us when *"The Word became flesh, and dwelt among us"* (John 1:14).

Promotion humaine et mission évangélisatrice
(Quelques principes doctrinaux)

LES CONFÉRENCES ÉPISCOPALES D'AFRIQUE
ET DE MADAGASCAR (CEAM)

MISSION DE L'EGLISE (N. 100)

Il nous a paru intéressant de proposer aux lecteurs un texte qui s'est forgé sur un continent où les questions de développement et de promotion humaine ont été liées depuis longtemps aux initiatives missionnaires. Un texte qui doit sa force au fait qu'il se nourrit d'une longue réflexion. Dès 1969, le Symposium des conférences épiscopales d'Afrique et de Madagascar (SCEAM), réuni à Kampala, avait lancé ce cri angoissé: «Le problème prioritaire des temps actuels est la lutte pour le développement des peuples et pour la paix. L'épiscopat d'Afrique et de Madagascar [...] ne saurait ignorer, sans manquer gravement à sa mission, la misère, la faim, la maladie, l'ignorance, les atteintes à la liberté, les conséquences tragiques de la discrimination raciale, les ravages de guerres ou d'oppressions qui accablent tant d'êtres humains du Tiers-Monde».

Sept déclarations sur le même ont précédé la publication du document auquel nous faisons référence, et qui a couronné la 7ème Assemblée plénière du SCEAM qui s'est déroulée a Kinshasa du 15 au 22 juillet 1984. (Document publié le 5 mai 1985 à Lomé, avec les signatures de Mgr Malula, Ganaka et Dosseh-Anyron, respectivement président, 1er et 2ème vice-présidents du SCEAM).

Sous le titre «L'Eglise et la promotion humaine en Afrique aujourd'hui», l'introduction donne le ton du document:

«Donner la vie aux hommes, et la donner surabondante, c'est la visée fondamentale que le Christ a donnée à sa mission dans le monde, mission confiée aujourd'hui à l'Eglise. Oui, fils et filles bien-aimés, le Christ que nous prêchons est venu pour que les hommes aient la vie, et qu'ils l'aient en abondance. L'homme a du prix aux yeux de Dieu: il l'a créé à son image, et l'a investi d'une dignité exceptionnelle, "le couronnant de gloire et de splendeur". La gloire de Dieu, c'est l'homme vivant. C'est ce que nous révèle l'histoire du salut.

[...] Nous voulons non seulement nous mettre au service de ceux et de celles qui, au nom de leur foi en Jésus-Christ, s'engagent dans les tâches de promotion humaine, mais nous voulons également coopérer avec tous les hommes de bonne volonté qui travaillent à l'avènement d'un monde plus humain pour tous. Notre profond souci pour l'avenir du christianisme en Afrique, notre foi dans le Seigneur de l'Histoire qui nous parle concrètement dans l'aujourd'hui de notre propre histoire, dans le partage de nos joies et de nos tristesses, nous font solidaires de nos peuples dans leur lutte pour une existence humaine en plénitude».

L'exhortation comprend trois parties. La première évoque brièvement les problèmes de promotion humaine tels qu'ils se posent en Afrique. La troisième partie propose quelques directives pastorales. La deuxième partie que nous citerons largement expose «les principes doctrinaux qui doivent éclairer l'action au service de l'homme africain».

Nous citons à présent des extraits de l'Exhortation pastorale, sans commentaires.

L'HOMME, SOUCI DE L'EGLISE

«Nous croyons que l'histoire que nous vivons avec notre peuple, avec ses contradictions de domination et de libération, de discrimination et de fraternité, de vie et de mort, trouve son sens dans l'espérance chrétienne. Nous voulons ici "donner raison de notre espérance".

Dans son Encyclique Redemptor Hominis, Jean-Paul II affirme avec insistance que l'homme est la première route que l'Eglise doit parcourir pour accomplir sa mission: il est "la première route et la route fondamentale de l'Eglise", route tracée par le Christ lui-même [...]

Il s'agit de l'homme concret, l'homme saisi selon toutes ses dimensions et toute sa vocation, l'homme dans la pleine vérité de son existence, de son être personnel et communautaire, "dans sa continuelle inclination au péché et en même temps dans sa continuelle aspiration à la vérité, au bien, au beau, à la justice, à l'amour".

[...] Jésus proclame la présence nouvelle du Royaume de Dieu. Le Royaume qu'il annonce et manifeste dans sa vie et sa pratique messianique n'est rien d'autre que la volonté efficace du Père qui désire que tous ses enfants vivent. Et pour que nous ayons la vie en abondance, Jésus se dessaisit de la sienne: c'est la volonté du Père. Il l'a réalisée en se solidarisant en particulier avec les pauvres, en se faisant pauvre, afin d'annoncer de l'intérieur de sa propre pauvreté le Royaume de la libération et de la vie.

Action en faveur des pauvres

Trois textes d'Isaïe annoncent admirablement le sens profond de l'activité messianique de Jésus:

"En ce jour-là, les sourds entendront la lecture du livre, et sortant de l'obscurité et des ténèbres, les yeux des aveugles verront. De plus en plus, les humbles se réjouiront dans le Seigneur. Et les pauvres exulteront à cause du saint d'Israël".

"Alors les yeux des aveugles verront et les oreilles des sourds s'ouvriront. Alors le boiteux bondira comme un cerf et la bouche du muet criera de joie".

"L'esprit du Seigneur est sur moi:
Le Seigneur en effet a fait de moi un messie.
Il m'a envoyé porter un joyeux message aux humiliés,
panser ceux qui ont le coeur brisé,
proclamer aux captifs l'évasion,
aux prisonniers l'éblouissement.
Proclamer l'année de la faveur du Seigneur".

Sourds, muets, aveugles, boiteux, pauvres, coeurs brisés, captifs, écrasés: autant de noms pour dire les pauvres et les opprimés. De même, guérir, redonner la vue et l'ouïe, susciter la joie, mettre en liberté, annoncer la délivrance, la grâce, la Bonne Nouvelle: autant de façons de travailler au salut total de l'homme.

L'annonce de la Bonne Nouvelle elle-même apparaît ainsi comme une libération.

[...] En portant l'Evangile ou la Bonne Nouvelle aux pauvres et aux opprimés, Jésus proclame la venue du Royaume de Dieu pour eux, en particulier pour ceux que nos sociétés ont marginalisés, ceux qui vivent dans un état permanent de détresse et de souffrance, ceux qu'on prive de leurs droits humains fondamentaux, les réfugiés, les handicapés, les victimes du sous-emploi, de l'exploitation, de la discrimination pour motifs de race, de langue, de religion, de sexe et d'opinion.

Le cri de Jésus pour les pauvres, nous l'entendons dans ce passage de l'Evangile que nous appelons les Béatitudes, la charte du Royaume:

> "Heureux, vous les pauvres: le Royaume de Dieu est à vous.
> Heureux, vous qui avez faim maintenant: vous serez rassasiés.
> Heureux, vous qui pleurez maintenant: vous rirez".

L'Evangile ou la Bonne Nouvelle du Royaume de Dieu est donc l'annonce par Jésus d'un nouvel état de choses sur la terre. Un nouvel ordre social où les pauvres ne seront plus pauvres, où les affamés seront rassasiés, et les opprimés libérés. Jésus est venu "pour que le règne de Dieu vienne", "pour que sa volonté soit faite" [...]

Mission de l'Eglise

Le Seigneur ressuscité est entré dans la gloire du Père. Mais il répand son Esprit sur son corps visible qu'est l'Eglise, pour que, par sa vie même, elle soit le sacrement, le signe qui révèle son action libératrice dans l'histoire des hommes.

Sacrement de Jésus-Christ, l'Eglise se consacre en toute situation à cette action libératrice de Jésus. Cela signifie que la mission évangélisatrice de l'Eglise inclut, nécessairement, comme partie intégrante, la solidarité avec les hommes et la participation à l'effort de ceux qui luttent pour atteindre à une libération plénière et au progrès en tout domaine: socio-économique, culturel et spirituel. Par mission, elle est la conscience des sociétés humaines pour condamner le mal, dénoncer les projets pervers et les structures injustes. Consciente de la valeur infinie de la personne humaine, l'Eglise doit concentrer son effort sur le changement des esprits et des coeurs ainsi que des conditions de vie. Elle doit s'efforcer d'humaniser les modes d'existence, de travail, de relation et les libérer des conséquences du péché que sont les structures injustes, les forces d'oppression, les aliénations de toute sorte.

En annonçant la rédemption de tous les aspects de l'existence humaine, l'Eglise contribue à l'édification et la restauration de la communauté humaine, telle que Dieu l'a voulue, pour que toute l'exigence de la dignité humaine et de la fraternité, de l'amour et de l'amitié, de la justice et de la paix, soit respectée et satisfaite.

Après le Concile Vatican II, le Synode des Evêques de 1971 sur la justice dans le monde, l'a pleinement reconnu:

> "L'action pour la justice et la participation à la transformation du monde apparaissent clairement comme un élément constitutif de la prédication de l'Evangile, en d'autres termes, comme l'exercice de la mission de l'Eglise pour la rédemption du genre humain et sa libération de toute oppression".

Telle est la mission de l'Eglise: comme le Christ et en Lui, elle doit s'unir à tous les hommes sur leur route terrestre et les servir pour leur plein accomplissement. Entendez le pape Jean-Paul II:

> "Si ce corps mystique du Christ est le peuple de Dieu — comme dira le Concile Vatican II en se fondant sur toute la tradition biblique et patristique —, cela signifie que tout homme est dans ce corps pénétré par le souffle de

vie qui vient du Christ. En ce sens également, se tourner vers l'homme, vers ses problèmes réels, vers ses espérances et ses souffrances, ses conquêtes et ses chutes, fait que l'Eglise elle-même comme corps, comme organisme, comme unité sociale, perçoit les impulsions divines, les lumières et les forces de l'Esprit Saint qui proviennent du Christ crucifié et ressuscité, et c'est là précisément la raison d'être de sa vie. L'Eglise n'a pas d'autre vie que celle que lui donne son Epoux et Seigneur. En effet, parce que le Christ s'est uni à elle dans son ministère de Rédemption, l'Eglise doit être fortement unie à chaque homme".

On le voit, la responsabilité de l'Eglise ne saurait se limiter à des dons pécuniers et à des prestations matérielles comme solutions aux problèmes posés par la pauvreté et l'injustice; il s'agit d'apporter une inspiration chrétienne à la totalité de l'oeuvre du progrès et de la libération.

Car la promotion au plan matériel et social ne sera pleinement humaine que si la dimension spirituelle de l'homme trouve en Jésus-Christ son accomplissement. Il faut donc que le chrétien saisisse les opportunités de manifester sa foi en Jésus-Christ, Promoteur et Rédempteur de l'homme, en travaillant pour que la vision chrétienne donne au développement son plein épanouissement.

La question n'est donc pas: ou évangéliser, ou travailler au progrès humain. Dans le passé, l'Eglise d'Afrique a souffert d'une tendance générale consistant à considérer l'évangélisation et la promotion humaine comme deux projets parallèles. Il existait pour ainsi dire une juxtaposition des deux secteurs. Mais depuis le Concile Vatican II, l'Eglise reconnaît que l'un et l'autre impératifs sont partie intégrante de sa mission; les deux s'appellent et se conditionnent dans une sorte de causalité intime et réciproque comme la parole et l'acte, le témoignage de la vie et son expression en discours.

Une conscience plus vive de la nouveauté de l'Evangile du salut

Le Nouveau Testament assigne à la mission une portée cosmique et eschatologique. Le Christ enseigne que la parousie est le terme de l'histoire humaine. L'attitude fondamentale du disciple doit être la vigilance. Mais cette visée eschatologique ne signifie pas désertion du monde. Le Christ proclame en effet que le but de la vie est l'action empreinte de charité.

L'amour du prochain est le signe de l'amour de Dieu. Le Christ demande à ses disciples de mettre leurs talents à profit. Voyant dans la mort et la résurrection du Christ le commencement de la nouvelle création annoncée par les prophètes, les premiers chrétiens ont compris qu'il ne s'agissait pas de déserter le monde, mais de poursuivre résolument le travail quotidien. Songeons à la réaction de Saint Paul contre les fidèles qui attendent dans l'oisiveté le retour du Christ glorifié: "Si quelqu'un ne veut pas travailler, qu'il ne mange pas non plus. Or nous entendons dire qu'il en est parmi vous qui vivent dans l'oisiveté, ne travaillant pas du tout mais se mêlant de tout, ceux-là nous les invitons et les engageons, dans le Seigneur Jésus-Christ, à travailler".

Comme le Christ, l'Eglise primitive demande que le travail soit animé par la charité. Saint Jacques écrit: "Si un frère ou une soeur sont nus, s'ils manquent de leur nourriture quotidienne, et que l'un d'entre vous leur dise: "allez en paix, chauffez-vous, rassasiez-vous", sans leur donner ce qui est nécessaire à leur corps, à quoi cela sert-il?"

La réalisation du Royaume comme projet ultime de Dieu pour sa création n'est qu'à son stade initial. *Le Royaume se réalise dans les processus historiques de libération humaine. Et les libérations historiques incarnent et rendent visible le Royaume dans la mesure où elles humanisent la vie et engendrent des relations sociales plus fraternelles et plus justes.*

Le Christ a cependant affirmé solennellement: "Mon Royaume n'est pas de ce monde"; ce qui met en lumière la distinction entre Royaume de Dieu et théocratie. Le Royaume transcende les libérations humaines. Le Royaume est grâce. Tous les hommes sont appelés à l'accueillir comme un don, en rejetant l'injustice et les idoles pour servir le Dieu Vivant et vrai.

Le Royaume est ainsi l'horizon et le sens de l'Eglise. Il est important de le rappeler dans le contexte africain. *L'Eglise n'existe pas pour elle même, mais pour servir les hommes en vue du Royaume de Dieu, pour leur révéler le dynamis-*

me profond qui traverse leur histoire, pour témoigner de la présence du Christ Sauveur et de son Esprit. Cet Esprit nous aide à comprendre que le Royaume est aussi exigence de vie nouvelle, d'engagement résolu dans la libération solidaire des hommes, dans la construction d'une société juste.

Ni réduction ni ambiguité

Ces considérations sont basées au vrai sur la conviction que l'Eglise ne s'identifie pas au Royaume. L'Eglise, en effet, ne monopolise pas Jésus-Christ ni son salut éternel. En son sens profond et véritable, le terme de salut renvoie au Royaume: il exprime la présence de Dieu Sauveur agissant par le Christ partout dans le cosmos et à tous les âges de l'Histoire et en particulier dans le secret de chaque homme qui s'ouvre à son amour. Car Dieu fait coopérer au salut de l'homme l'effort même que celui-ci met à sa réaliser. En ce sens le Royaume est coextensif au monde des hommes. Il en épouse le destin pour le mener à sa fin. L'action évangélisatrice adhère aux sinuosités de l'histoire, à ses soubresauts et à ses renouvellements. Sous ce rapport, *le Royaume n'est rien d'autre que le monde converti à l'Esprit du Christ.* Il est donc loin de s'opposer au monde, comme il est loin de se résorber en lui. Il n'est acculé ni à se retirer ni à s'établir fatalement dans une histoire parallèle.

La parole du Christ: "Mon Royaume n'est pas de ce monde" retentit ici comme un avertissement éternel. Cette parole signifie que Jésus et ses disciples sont dans ce monde sans être du monde, c'est-à-dire sans souscrire aux valeurs, aux critères du monde [...]

Ainsi compris, *le Royaume juge l'Eglise.* Il la provoque à la conversion du coeur, en dénonçant ses contradictions, son péché dans les personnes et les structures. Il l'amène à confesser ses erreurs historiques, ses compromissions, ses trahisons dans la tâche évangélisatrice. Et dans cette humble confession, elle rencontre la grâce de son Seigneur qui la purifie, la sanctifie et la soutient tout au long de son pèlerinage sur terre. Il faut le dire et le souligner: le chemin de l'Eglise sur terre est pascal, car l'Eglise doit vivre toute l'expérience du Ressuscité. Nous sommes convaincus qu'il nous faut passer par bien des tribulations pour entrer dans le Royaume de Dieu, tout comme le Christ a dû souffrir sa passion pour entrer dans sa gloire. A tous ceux qui travaillent généreusement au service de l'Evangile en Afrique et auxquels nous réexprimons nos vifs remerciements, nous voudrions rappeler la parole de Saint Paul aux Thessaloniciens: "Nous-mêmes sommes fiers de vous [...] de votre constance et votre foi dans toutes les persécutions et tribulations que vous supportez. Par là se manifeste le juste jugement de Dieu où vous serez trouvés dignes du Royaume de Dieu pour lequel vous souffrez aussi".

AU SERVICE DES HOMMES POUR LA TRANSFIGURATION DU MONDE

Nous rejoignons ici les grandes perspectives ouvertes par le Concile Vatican II. La Constitution pastorale Gaudium et Spes *situe l'Eglise au milieu du monde et non en face*. Les problèmes des hommes de notre temps sont ceux du chrétien et de l'Eglise. Sans nullement prétendre apporter avec la solennité d'un magistère admis par tous une solution toute faite, *l'Eglise cherche avec tous les hommes de bonne volonté*, (selon l'heureuse formule de Jean XXIII), apprenant des spécialistes les données techniques de ces problèmes, mais mettant au service de tous ceux qui réfléchissent sur notre temps l'éclairage donné par l'Evangile de Jésus-Christ. Servante des hommes parce que servante de l'Evangile, l'Eglise a son rôle à jouer dans la transfiguration du monde. Dieu nous appelle à édifier une société solidaire, où les structures sont faites pour permettre aux hommes de vivre en enfants de Dieu et cohéritiers du Christ; biens, service, sécurité, paix et joie.

Chers Fils et chères Filles,

Si nous croyons en Dieu, nous nous mettrons au travail pour créer un monde où tout homme puisse se réaliser à l'image de Dieu et à sa ressemblance.

Appelés à participer à la vie du Christ, Roi de l'univers, les hommes sont comme le Christ, maîtres de la création. Ils sont invités à rendre le monde habitable, l'associant à la gloire à laquelle ils sont appelés. Telle est la vocation de l'homme: "nous avons été créés en Jésus-Christ pour les oeuvres bonnes que Dieu a préparées d'avance, afin que nous nous y engagions".

Dieu est amour. Voilà pourquoi, pour qui croit en Dieu, vivre, c'est aimer comme Dieu aime. La fraternité entre les hommes est signe de la présence de Dieu, dont le Concile rappelle que le commandement nouveau de l'amour est "la loi fondamentale de la perfection humaine, et donc de la transformation du monde". Paul VI l'explicite avec force dans Populorum Progressio: "*L'homme doit rencontrer l'homme, les nations doivent se rencontrer comme des frères et soeurs, comme les enfants de Dieu. Dans cette compréhension et cette amitié mutuelles, dans cette communion sacrée, nous devons largement commencer à oeuvrer ensemble pour édifier l'avenir commun de l'humanité*".

Destination universelle des biens

Nous devons prendre davantage conscience de la destination universelle des biens de la création. On sait avec quelle fermeté le Concile Vatican II a rappelé cet enseignement. "Dieu a destiné la terre et tout ce qu'elle contient à l'usage de tous les hommes et de tous les peuples, en sorte que les biens de la création doivent équitablement affluer entre les mains de tous, selon la règle de la justice, inséparable de la charité". Le saint Concile affirme que le droit et le devoir qu'a tout homme d'user de ses biens pour son entretien et son développement est prioritaire.

Le rôle central de l'Eucharistie

L'homme cependant ne vit pas seulement de pain, mais de toute parole qui sort de la bouche de Dieu. L'Eucharistie, où le pain de l'homme devient Pain de vie éternelle, est la source où nous puisons la foi, l'espérance et la charité qui nous donnent la force de nous replonger chaque jour dans la détresse des hommes et d'affronter le désespoir des misérables. Elle est aussi le gage que la promotion humaine pour laquelle nous nous dépensons se réalisera pleinement le jour où "cet être corruptible aura revêtu l'incorruptibilité, et où cet être mortel aura revêtu l'immortalité".

L'Eucharistie est le Sacrement, le signe de la dignité humaine. Mémorial de la Passion et de la Mort du Christ, elle montre de quel prix nous avons été achetés, comme le rappelle avec vigueur le Saint Père Jean-Paul II:

> "En célébrant l'Eucharistie et en y participant, nous sommes unis au Christ terrestre et céleste qui intercède pour nous auprès du Père, mais nous ne sommes unis à Lui qu'à travers l'acte rédempteur de son sacrifice par lequel il nous a rachetés de manière telle que nous avons été achetés à grand prix. Le grand prix de notre Rédemption montre tout à la fois la valeur que Dieu lui-même attribue à l'homme et notre dignité dans le Christ".

Mystère de divinisation et de promotion de l'homme, l'Eucharistie est exigence de pauvreté. Pauvreté radicale, parce que amour sans mesure. En Jésus de Nazareth, Dieu s'est fait semblable à nous, en toutes choses hormis le péché. Il s'est proposé en modèle de don de soi total et gratuit, de partage sans retenue, de liberté intérieure, de disponibilité sans calcul, de générosité, d'accueil. Lui qui, "de condition divine n'a pas considéré comme une proie à saisir d'être l'égal de Dieu. Mais il s'est dépouillé, prenant la condition de serviteur, devenant semblable aux hommes, et reconnu à son aspect comme un homme, il s'est abaissé, devenant obéissant jusqu'à la mort, et à la mort sur une croix".

"De riche qu'il était, il s'est fait pauvre pour nous enrichir de sa pauvreté". Nous enrichir de sa pauvreté, qu'est-ce à dire, sinon nous apprendre le véritable amour:

> "Nul n'a d'autre amour plus grand que celui qui se dessaisit de sa vie pour ceux qu'il aime".

En participant à l'Eucharistie, les chrétiens, les chrétiens célèbrent l'amour du Ressuscité pour l'homme. Mais ils ne peuvent le faire avec vérité sans passer par l'amour de l'homme comme par une "route obligée", sans se sentir sacramentellement et historiquement solidaires des pauvres, des humbles, des marginaux, des damnés de ce monde. Participer réellement à l'Eucharistie, c'est donc refuser de voir dans la communauté humaine des frères et soeurs croupir dans la misère, souffrir de l'exploitation, de l'injustice, ou de l'ignorance.

L'action de Dieu ne supprime par l'initiative et la responsabilité historique de l'homme dans l'édification de la cité terrestre. L'homme reste libre, capable de participer à la nature divine, comme de revêtir le masque horrible de la Bête de l'Apocalypse. Or, participer à l'Eucharistie, c'est mourir avec le Christ au péché individuel et collectif du monde et vivre avec lui pour Dieu et pour les hommes. "Si nous sommes morts avec le Christ, nous croyons que nous vivons avec lui [...] sa mort fut une mort au péché, une fois pour toutes; mais sa vie est une vie à Dieu. Et vous, de même, considérez que vous êtes morts au péché et vivants en Dieu dans le Christ Jésus". Ceci donne à l'oeuvre du Christ divinisateur une dimension de libération. Il est mort pour nous les hommes et pour notre salut.

Libération individuelle et aussi libération communautaire, celle des péchés collectifs inscrits dans les institutions et les structures injustes de la société. *L'action du Christ libère dans le chrétien le dynamisme nécessaire à la transfiguration du monde.* Participer à l'Eucharistie, c'est donc s'engager historiquement dans le combat pour l'avènement d'un monde plus juste et plus équitable pour tous.

La foi n'est pas démobilisatrice. Avec le dynamisme de l'espérance et la créativité de la charité, elle rassemble toutes les énergies des disciples au service de Dieu et des hommes. Le chemin qui conduit à cette divinisation est long sans doute, la conversion intérieure progressive, mais l'Eucharistie est déjà la présence et la garantie de la plénitude de vie, de la communion parfaite entre Dieu et l'homme racheté par le Christ et sanctifié par l'Esprit. Participer à l'Eucharistie, en effet, c'est vivre la réalité de la parole, du pain et du vin, comme lieu de la rencontre entre Dieu et l'homme, et des hommes entre eux.

Crédibilité de l'Église et chances pour l'évangélisation

[...] La crédibilité de l'Eglise et les chances de l'évangélisation seront à la mesure de sa solidarité avec l'aspiration légitime des Africains à prendre désormais en main leur propre destinée, à la mesure de sa disponibilité dans la recherche des solutions aux problèmes et la construction de ce continent.

Concrètement la crédibilité de l'Eglise et l'accueil réservé à son Message dépendent des réponses qu'elle donne à des questions comme celles-ci: quel rôle joue l'Eglise dans cette situation? Comment se situe la pensée chrétienne face à l'exploitation de l'homme qui continue aujourd'hui en Afrique? Quelle est la contribution de l'Eglise à la promotion des peuples opprimés depuis longtemps par la domination du sexe, de la race ou de la classe? Quelle action mener contre la corruption multiforme qui se développe dans nos pays?

Ces questions ne requièrent-elles pas une re-conversion, une réorientation de toute la pastorale pour qu'à travers la vie, les activités et les engagements de tous ses membres, l'Eglise apparaisse vraiment comme sacrement de salut pour les Africains, comme signe manifestant et actualisant tout à la fois l'amour de Dieu pour l'homme?

ÉVANGÉLISATION ET PROMOTION HUMAINE

Nous sommes convaincus que l'Eglise du Christ en Afrique doit faire prendre conscience à ses fils et à ses filles du rôle qu'ils ont à jouer dans la promotion humaine et l'éducation du peuple au développement et à l'auto-promotion.

Une conception dualiste de la mission, nous l'avons souligné plus haut, a longtemps marqué notre évangélisation. Il manquait une vision théologique unifiant ces deux aspects de la mission. *Ce qui n'a pas favorisé une évangélisation en profondeur* et une authentique promotion humaine. La foi chrétienne, telle qu'elle a été proposée et vécue, ne semble pas avoir influencé suffisamment les comportements et restait étrangère aux projets de sociétés qui s'élaborent et s'imposent.

Depuis le Concile Vatican II, nous l'avons également noté, toute la pastorale est marquée par une volonté de plus en plus affirmée de se mettre davantage au service du monde et de contribuer efficacement à l'édification de structures sociales plus humaines, plus justes, plus fraternelles. Ce faisant, *l'Eglise a la ferme conviction que son engagement au service de l'homme relève de sa mission qui est d'annoncer la Bonne Nouvelle aux pauvres.*

Approfondissant l'enseignement conciliaire, dans son Exhortation Apostolique Evangelii Nuntiandi, Paul VI montre que l'Eglise existe pour évangéliser et que rien ne peut la détourner de cette mission qui est sa mission propre. La tâche de promotion humaine n'est rien d'autre qu'une dimension intégrante, une exigence interne de l'évangélisation.

Il ne s'agit donc pas pour nous d'abandonner l'évangélisation pour la promotion humaine. Il s'agit tout simplement d'évangéliser autrement, d'une manière plus complète et plus crédible pour les hommes et les femmes de ce continent.

L'action évangélisatrice s'oriente non plus vers un individu isolé et comme extrait de son milieu mais plutôt vers l'homme, membre d'une communauté et sujet de culture. C'est ce qu'enseigne Paul VI, quand il dit qu'il s'agit désormais d'évangéliser non pas de façon décorative, comme par un vernis superficiel, mais de façon vitale, en profondeur et jusque dans les racines, la culture et les cultures africaines.

En effet, le but de l'évangélisation est de convertir la conscience personnelle et collective des hommes et de transformer en même temps l'activité dans laquelle ils s'engagent, la vie et l'environnement socio-politique et économique qui sont les leurs. *Une évangélisation authentique s'exprime nécessairement dans une action de promotion humaine.*

L'Eglise en Afrique est convaincue de l'urgence et de la nécessité de bâtir des structures sociales plus humaines, plus justes, plus respectueuses de la dignité et des droits de la personne humaine. Mais elle est aussi consciente que les structures les mieux conçues deviennent vite inhumaines, s'il n'y a pas une conversion du coeur de ceux et celles qui vivent dans ces structures ou les commandent.

Notre devoir de pasteurs, à cette heure de l'histoire africaine, est de nous poser la question suivante: *comment évangéliser, comment proclamer la Bonne Nouvelle, comment en témoigner par notre vie et nos engagements pour que l'Eglise soit aujourd'hui perçue comme Sacrement de Salut pour les hommes de ce continent?* La tâche de promotion humaine apparaît ainsi comme une dimension intégrale, de transformation profonde des personnes et de leur environnement. En cela, nous rejoignons Paul VI qui a thématisé le lien entre évangélisation et promotion humaine comme étant d'ordre anthropologique, théologique et de charité.

D'ordre anthropologique d'abord, "parce que l'homme à évangéliser n'est pas un être abstrait, mais sujet des questions sociales et économiques".

D'ordre théologique ensuite, "puisqu'on ne peut pas dissocier le plan de la création du plan de la Rédemption qui, lui, atteint les situations très concrètes de l'injustice à combattre et de la justice à restaurer".

Lien de charité enfin, car on ne peut proclamer le commandement nouveau sans promouvoir dans la justice et la paix, la véritable et authentique croissance de l'homme».

Fin de citation

La documentation Catholique a publié les résolutions et recommandations pastorales de cette VIIe Assemblée du SCEAM. Cf D.C. du 4 novembre 1984, n. 1883, pp. 1041 à 1043.

Religious Humanism Among the Yoruba of Nigeria

Muhib O. Opeloye

The Yoruba race is the only major Nigerian race that has experienced a high degree of heterogeneity of religious humanism. This is due to the wide acceptance of Islam and Christianity by the people who were hitherto practitioners of Indigenous Religion. In Yorubaland today, unlike the other major sections of the country, Islam and Christianity are widely practised side by side with the Indigenous Religion. The chronology of the three religions is epitomised in the Yoruba adage: *Aye la ba fa, aye la ba Imale, Osan gangan ni gbagbo wole de* (meaning, we met *Ifa** in the world, it was followed by Islam while Christianity gained entry late in the day).

There is no gainsaying the fact that the arrival of the acclaimed world religions, namely Islam and Christianity, have dealt a great blow to the growth of Indigenous Religion in view of the loss of most of its adherents to the new faiths. This is why the present day Nigerian governments are doing everything possible to revitalize the indigenous culture. It is pertinent to say that even though the Yoruba are today mostly Muslims and Christians, they still practise their religions within the context of their indigenous cultural background. The diversity in religious beliefs of the Yoruba shows that the people have wider religious experience. This article is therefore concerned with the religious aspect of the Yoruba culture. We shall examine the basic beliefs and practices of the three main religions practised in Yorubaland with a view to high-lighting their impact on their life.

The Yoruba Indigenous Religous Humanism

In this part of the world, extensive work has been done on this subject by eminent scholars such as Idowu, Awolalu and Dopamu, to mention a few. They have been able to correct certain misconceptions of the non-African writers about the subject.

The Yoruba Indigenous Religion is structured on the following beliefs: belief in the Supreme Deity; belief in divinities; belief in ancestral spirits, belief in moral order, and belief in the hereafter.

Many Western Writers have written to deny that Africans believe in the existence of a Supreme God. Some are of the view that God to the Africans is a *deus incertus* and *deus remotus*[1]. This view does not represent the view of the Africans about their religion. It has been argued that the strongest proof of their belief in God's existence is the fact that every ethnic group has names for the Supreme Deity in contradistinction to the divinities. In Yorubaland, the name for the Supreme Deity is Olodumare or Olorun[2]. What this implies is that God to the Yoruba is not merely an abstract concept, a vague entity, but a veritable reality. The name depicts their understanding of God. Apart from the names, the Supreme Deity possesses attributes ascribing traits, properties, qualities or characteristics to Him[3]. These demonstrate how the Yoruba perceive God and how He relates to creatures. It is to this Supreme Deity that the Yoruba direct their worship and supplications through the lesser gods.

The divinities known among the Yoruba as *Orisa* are phenomenological spiritual beings who serve the will of

---

[1] IDOWU, E.B., *Olodumare, God in Yoruba Belief*, (Longmans, London, 1962), p. 140.

[2] The word *Olodumare* which has three components is translated to mean "The unique King who holds the sceptre, wields authority and has the quality which is superlative in worth, and he is at the same time permanent, unchanging, and reliable". The world *Olorun*, on the other hand, has two components and it is simply translated "the Owner of heaven" or "the Lord of heaven". See J. OMOSADE AWOLALU and P. ADE DOPAMU, *West African Traditional Religion*, (Onibonje, Ibadan, 1979) pp. 37-39.

[3] Among the attributes of God as given by Idowu are Eleda (the creator); *Oyigiyigi Oba aiku* (The Immortal rock that never dies). *Adakadejo* (he who executes judgement in silence) etc.

Olodumare in the creation and the theocratic government of the world[4]. According to Yoruba theology, the divinities are not created, rather they have emanated from the Supreme Deity[5]. Consequently they are regarded as His offspring taking part in the running of the theocratic government of the world. The divinities serve as intermediaries between God and man. Prayers and sacrifices are offered to God through them. Prominent among the Yoruba divinities are *Obatala or Orisa nla* (the earth divinity), Orunmila (the Oracle divinity), Esu (divinity of Mischief), Ogun (god of Iron) and Oya (goddess of river), to mention a few.

The divinities form the Yoruba pantheon. Idowu[6] has argued that their preponderance does not suggest polytheism. To him the Indigenous Religion is monotheistic and more specifically diffused monotheism. This view is not plausible considering the fact that the divinities feature prominently in the Indigenous Religion, each of them having its temples, shrines, and priests. Sometimes because of adoration of the divinity, the worship tends to be an end in itself. It may not be appropriate to describe the Yoruba religion as monotheistic since it is believed that the divinities partake of the attributes of the Supreme Deity. One problem with the Yoruba divinities is the fact that some of them are used by the wicked men to inflict sickness, death and other misfortunes on the innocent[7]. Since they can be used for evil purposes, it means they sanction evil-doing. Esu, Sanpanna, Sango and Ifa are examples of Yoruba divinities usually employed for evil ends.

In Yoruba theology, distinction is made between ancestral spirits and divinities. While divinities are not related to the world, the ancestors are related to the living community as members of the earthly families to which they belonged before their death[8]. Death in the understanding of the Yoru-

---

[4] IDOWU, E.B., *op. cit.*, p. 57.
[5] AWOLALU, O., and DOPAMU, P.A. *op. cit.*, 132.
[6] IDOWU, E.B., *op.cit.*, p. 168.
[7] DOPAMU ADE, "The Weakness of the Yoruba Divinities", in Sam Babs Mala and Z.Z. Oseni (eds.) NASR Conference papers (NASR, No. 2 September, 1980) p. 10.
[8] EARDES, J.S., *The Yoruba Today* (Cambridge University Press, Cambridge, London) p. 123.

ba involves transformation of the personality of the dead into an ancestral spirit. It is believed that the ancestors take active interest in members of their earthly families, hence they give them advice through dreams and trances. Prayers and offerings are made to a dead parent for protection. The Yoruba take care not to offend the ancestors who they believe can cause disaster if offended. The ancestors are regarded as intermediaries between man and God or divinities. The significance of *egungun* cult lies in its commemmoration of individual ancestors.

The Indigenous Religion lays premium on the moral order of the society. The activities of man are not left unregulated. In Yoruba theology certain norms and codes of conduct are entrenched which facilitate orderly maintenance of the society. These form the moral values. Every man is endowed with the sense of right and wrong, he knows what is morally right and what is morally wrong. Those things which are morally disapproved by the society are known as *eewo* (taboos), the prohibited action. These are not contained in any revealed law, rather they are preserved in the tradition. To break a taboo or act contrary to the will of the Deity amounts to sinning against Him. The sinner can be punished or forgiven if the performs the necessary rites of atonement[9].

The Yoruba's belief in the hereafter has to be explained in the light of their understanding of death. Death in their belief marks the transition to the afterlife. It is a means of passing from the earthly world to the world of the spirits where the soul of the deceased continues to exist. Hence, much of the symbolism of Yoruba burial rituals is that of a journey. The eschatology consists of three phases: Separation of the deceased, transformation of the soul and incorporation of it into the spirit world[10]. The dead go either to 'good heaven' (*Orun rere*) or bad heaven (*Orun apadi*) depending on how they are judged by the Supreme Deity. This is to say that the Yoruba believe in man's accountability for his earth-

---

[9] AWOLALU, J.O., *Yoruba Beliefs and Sacrificial Rites* (Longman, Essex, 1981) p. 152.

[10] DOPAMU, P.A., "Towards Understanding African Traditional Religion", in Balogun, I.A.B. (eds.) *Religious Understanding and Cooperation in Nigeria* (Department of Religions, University of Ilorin, 1978) p. 143.

ly deeds in the hereafter, thus resting his salvation on his righteous acts. It is believed that there who go to good heaven would experience no sorrow and can choose to reincarnate while those who go to bad heaven would experience torments and they can never be reborn[11].

The Yoruba Indigenous Religion is not just a religion, it is also a culture. Consequently, apart from its sets of beliefs it has its cultural dimension which cuts across the different facets of Yoruba life. We would draw illustration from the major events of man's life circle, viz.birth, marriage and death, each of which has its traditional rites and ceremonies to be performed.

The birth of a child in the family is a thing of joy and it is regarded as one of the greatest blessings. Hence the event is greeted with joy and happiness. Once pregnancy is noticed in a woman there are traditional methods of ensuring protection of the pregnancy and also of the child after birth. Traditional medicine-men and diviners are usually consulted for this. Protection is sought for the baby against evil forces. Since the birth of a new baby is a thing of joy, feasting, eating, rejoicing and dancing are associated with it. A name is given to the new-born on the seventh day if it is a female and on the ninth day if it is a male. Many factors determine the type of name give: the circumstances of birth; events previaling at the time; family divinity; occupation or even the mood of the parents. This goes to show that names in Yoruba tradition are pregnant with meaning. On the naming day the child's hair is shaved (if it has not been shaved before) while prayer and sacrifice are made to appease God and thank him for his blessing. To make prayers efficacious some items used for offerings and sacrifices such as Kola nut, bitter kola, oil, salt, honey, money etc. are used. In some families the mother of a new baby is forbidden to eat certain foods thought to be harmful to her health. The rites of birth are not complete without circumcision of a baby boy or clitoridectomy of a baby girl. This is usually done at a very early age especially before the baby starts to crawl.

---

[11] IDOWU, E.B., *op. cit.*, p. 197f.

Marriage according to Yoruba tradition is a sacred duty which every normal person must perform because it is seen as a means of perpetuating the society. The 'Institution of marriage is the meeting point of the three layers of human life according to the general African Religion. These are the departed, the living and those to be born. The departed are the roots on whom the living stand, the living are the link between death and life, those to be born are the buds in the loins of the living and marriage makes them to germinate and sprout'[12]. Among the Yoruba serious importance is attached to marriage (and childbearing) because they are regarded as medicines against death. He who dies and leaves offspring still lives.

An important aspect of the Yoruba marriage custom is the choice of the life partner. This is done either by the parents or the children themselves. Even when the choice is made, the parents of the partners are brought into the knowledge because of their wider experience. The parents would sanction a marriage when they know it would be a source of happiness for the partners and the members of the extended families. People who are related by blood or by marriage are prevented from marrying one another.

Marriage gifts are important aspects of the tradition. They serve as symbols of the marriage bond. They are legal instruments which authorize the husband and wife to live together. The gifts often consist of yam, money, goat, cloths, ornament etc. They are given during engagement. It is not regarded as payment for the wife because the amount given is usually not exorbitant.

After fulfilling all the necessary requirements, the partners are joined on the agreed date. Prayers are offered by members of the two families for the welfare of the new couple. They are also given instructions on how to live successful material life. Marriage ceremonies are usually accompanied with feasting, feeding, rejoicing and dancing. Virginity of the bride is highly valued among the Yoruba. Women who until their marriage retain their virginity are usually highly respected. Multiple marriages (polygamy) is an essential fea-

---

[12] MBITI, J.S., Introduction to African Religion, (Heinemann, London 1981) p. 98.

ture of the Yoruba marriage custom. A man can marry several wives depending on his financial strength.

Death as earlier noted is not regarded as the end of a man's existence according to Yoruba belief. Here lies the significance of some of the rituals performed for the deceased before burial.

The rituals concerning the preparation of the corpse for burial consist of washing of the body, shaving of the hair, cutting of the nails and oiling of the bodily openings. Time is not wasted at all before burial takes place. It is customary for the deceased to be buried with his belongings in the belief that he will continue to use them in the next world. The rites performed at burial are intended to send off the departed peacefully. Wailing, weeping and lamenting accompany the burial while the funeral rites are followed by feasting if the deceased attained old age before he died. Feasting can be extensive and take several days. The Yoruba believe in resurrection of the dead during which they would stand before God to account for all their earthly deeds before receiving judgement. Hence, their belief in the good and bad heaven where the righteous and the unrighteous abide. According to Mbiti, this belief is not commonly held among many African Societies. It is therefore peculiar to the Yoruba-speaking people[13].

THE PENETRATION OF ISLAM AND CHRISTIANITY INTO YORUBALAND

As noted earlier Islam arrived in Yorubaland before Christianity. According to Fafunwa the former predated the latter by three hundred years[14]. With the arrival of Islam, there came to an end the era of Indigenous Religion which held unchallenged sway till about the middle of the 17th century. With the emergence of Islam, the gradual decline of the Indigenous Religion set in.

It is not easy to say with precision the date Islam penetrated into Yorubaland as this is still a subject of controversy

---

[13] *Ibid.* p. 117.
[14] FAFUNWA, BABS. A., *History of Education in Nigeria*, (George Allen and Unwin, London 1974), p. 70.

among scholars. Adam Abdullah has suggested that Islam was first known in Yorubaland during the reign of Mansa Musa of Mali (d. 1337). He argued that the Yoruba came to understand the practice of Islam at the hands of Mali traders and from some Mallian Ambassadors who used to visit the Old Oyo during the reign of this great Mallian King; hence the religion is known as Imale[15]. Ahmad Baba of Timbuktu (d. 1610) is reported to have mentioned the presence of Islam in Yorubaland in his work[16]. Gbadamosi[17] reported the incident of one Baba Kewu, a Muslim Mallam from Nupeland who challenged the action of Alafin Ajiboyede (1562-1570) for killing some people on account of this son's death. It is reported he later showed remorse and tendered apology in public. The presence of Baba Kewu in Oyo during the reign of that king indicates the presence of Islam in the town at the time. However, by the 18th century Islam had become widely accepted in Yorubaland considering the fact that by that time mosques had sprung up in the different parts of Yoruba country. Oyo Ile Mosque is dated 1550 A.D. Ketu Mosque 1760; Iseyin Mosque 1770, Lagos Mosque 1775 together with Idumagbo and Okunu Mosque in 1776 (all during the reign of Oba Adele I) and Oyo town had its recognised mosque in 1775 during the reign of Alafin Ayinde. After the Jihad of Uthman dan Fodio in 1809 and the Islamisation of Ilorin, Yorubaland experienced more influx of the Muslims from the Islamised areas.

Islam was introduced to Yorubaland through peaceful means by traders and scholars from the North. The traders settled in the urban centres to trade, in the process of which their hosts were fascinated by their practice of Islam. The itinerant scholars on the other hand spread Islam through preaching and education. They taught people how to read and write. Many factors contributed to the rapid spread of Islam among the Yoruba, including: conversion of family units rather than individuals, support of many tradition

---

[15] ADAM ABDULLAH EL-ILORIN, *Mujiz Tarikh Nigeria* (Beirut 1965) p. 147.
[16] The work is entitled *Al-Kashf al-Bayān li asnaf majlub al-Sudan*.
[17] GBADAMOSI, G.T.O., *The Growth of Islam among the Yoruba 1841-1908*, (Longmans, London, 1978) p. 6.

rulers and chiefs; the multi-functional roles of the scholar as man of God, preacher, trader, adviser and medicine man as well as introduction of literacy and civilisation[18]. The Islamic Institution of poligamy, the impressive Islamic festivals; the Mallams' use of talisman, charm and divination to offer protection were also admired by the people because they met their social and spiritual needs. The growth of Islam among the Yoruba was tremendous. The religion became the way of life of its adherents within a short time of its acceptance. Even when Christianity came early in the 19th century it did not retard the progress of the religion, rather it motivated its adherents to make Islam compatible with Western Civilisation. This was the concern of Muslim organisations like Ansar-ud-Deen, established early in this century.

As for the penetration of Christianity, three events of major historical significance occurred in Europe which paved the way for its introduction in West Africa and eventually in Yorubaland in the second half of the 19th century. These are the evangelical revival of the late eighteenth century, the formation of Christian Missionary societies and the abolition of the slave trade[19]. After the abolition of the slave trade in Britain in 1807 the British government founded the colony of Sierra Leone in order to resettle the freed slaves three. The colony was soon transformed into a Christian population through the Missionary activities of the Church Missionary Society (CMS) which first established their mission work among the liberated slaves.

It is a well-known fact that the first real missionary work in Nigeria began with the 1841 Expedition sent to the areas of modern Nigeria by the British government acting upon Sir Thomas Fowell Buxton's proposal. The close cooperation which existed between the missionaries and those interested in trade resulted from the dual aim of the missions, namely to encourage 'legitimate' trade between the Europeans and Africans as a substitute for the slave trade and to

---

[18] GBADAMOSI, G.T.O., "Islam and Christianity in Nigeria" in Obaro Ikime (ed.) *Groundwork of Nigerian History* (Heinemann Educational Books Ltd, Ibadan, 1984) p. 349.

[19] OLADOJA J.O., "African Response to Christianity: The Yoruba Episode", in Sam Babs Mala and Z. Oseni *op. cit.*, p. 80.

convert Africans to Christianity. If the Expedition failed to achieve most of its primary objectives, it at least succeeded in bringing missionaries into the country, and Yorubaland had her fair share.

The first Missionaries (the Methodist Mission) arrived in Badagry in 1842. They tried to make the town their base but found it unsatisfactory because the missionaries recieved little cooperation from the indigenous people. The missionaries nevertheless succeeded in establishing the first mission in the town, thus making it the cradle of Christianity in Nigeria. The Missionaries turned their attention to Abeokuta where they were accommodated after a protracted negotiation in 1846[20]. The Church Missionary Society (CMS) under the leadership of Townsend, Crowther and Gollmar embarked upon pioneering missionary activities in Abeokuta. They built schools and churches. The Methodists were equally actively involved in the pioneering missionary activities in the town. From Abeokuta Christianity spread to other Yoruba towns, thus making it the gateway of the missionaries into Yorubaland. The Baptist mission pioneered missionary activities in Oyo and Ogbomoso areas. African Independent Churches (Aladura Church) emerged much later, with the aim of relating the indigenous experience to Christianity.

THE BASIC TENETS OF ISLAM AND CHRISTIANITY

Islam is universally acknowledged to be a religion as well as a way of life. As such it lays down detailed regulations to guide man in all his earthly endeavours both spiritual and material. The superstructure consequently rests on faith, ritual observances and transactions. In a short chapter like this it is not possible to treat these subjects in detail.

The articles of faith in Islam are five, viz.belief in the existence and oneness of God, belief in the angels, the prophets, the revealed books, and the hereafter. Islam requires belief in God in recognition of His Being as the source of creation. Disbelief in God or to associate a partner with Him is a

---

[20] GBADAMOSI G.T.O., "Islam and Christianity ..." in Obaro Ikime *op. cit.*, p. 349.

heinous sin which is not forgiven[21]. Islam teaches that angels, unlike the devil, are agents of good inclination and good thoughts. They are sent on special errands by God. Belief in them is required in order to emulate their good qualities. Belief in the prophets and the revealed books is required in consequence of man's need for divine guidance to live a righteous life. Belief in the hereafter enables man to realise that he is to account for his earthly deeds in the hereafter.

The Islamic ritual observances (worship system) consist of *Salāh* (canonical prayer) *Zakāh* (alms giving) *Sawm* (fasting) and *hajj* (pilgrimage). These together with the belief system form the five pillars of Islam. Apart from the fact that all the rituals are instituted to promote equality and unity of the Muslims, each of them has other roles to play in the spiritual development of the individual Muslim. *Sallah* keeps man in constant remembrance of his Creator and it affords him the opportunity of being in communion with Him from time to time. *Zakāh* enables have-nots to share from the wealth of those who have, to alleviate their suffering. *Sawn* strengthens the will-power of a Muslim as he makes efforts to resist all temptations even when he is not seen by others. Lastly, *Hajj* inculcates in the pilgrim the lesson of detachment from the carnal-self and materialism[22].

The Islamic belief and worship system discussed above has to do with man's relationship with God. The aspect relating to man's relationship with man covers different facets of human endeavour: social, political, economic, moral, legal etc. The religion, being a way of life, has its tradition for the conduct of the life-circle ceremonies discussed under the Indigenous Religion.

Christianity, on the other hand, is based on faith and works. Unconditional faith in the redemptive role of Jesus Christ is required of a true Christian for salvation. This is emphasised in the Pauline epistles[23]. It is not just faith in the person of Jesus Christ which is required, it is faith in his crucifixion and resurrection as a result of which the Christian

---

[21] *Surah* 4 : 48.
[22] NOIBI D.O.S., Islamic Perspectives: A comprehensive Message (Shebiotimo Publications, 1988) p. 23f.
[23] ROMANS 2 : 21 - 3 : 10.

becomes justified, regenerated, adopted and sanctified[24]. It is the only condition for the atonement of his sins. The necessity for works as an additional condition for salvation is recognised by James in his epistle[25]. Thus in Christianity as in Islam a combination of faith and works is a necessary condition for salvation.

Interactions in Religious Beliefs and Practices

Each of the three religions discussed above has its tradition and culture within the context of which its adherent operates in his dealings and actions. However, interaction in diverse religious traditions are permissible where the teaching of one does not conflict with the other. This is why it is possible for a Muslim or a Christian to live according to the tradition of his religion and still retain elements of his indigenous tradition without commiting syncreticism. Syncreticism sets in where an attempt is made to live in two religious traditions. Let us illustrate with a few examples.

As already noted, belief in God is paramount in the belief system of the three religions. However, in spite of this common belief the conception of God greatly differs. In the Indigenous Religion the Supreme Deity is approached through intermediary divinities who are believed to be co-sharers of divine attributes which make the belief system polytheistic. In Christianity Unity of God is understood in trinity of the Godhead, Jesus Christ and the Holy Ghost being manifestations of divine presence. Islam, on the other hand, teaches absolute monotheism. Thus religion for the Yoruba Muslim and Christian has evolved from polytheistic tradition into monotheistic tradition of two different concepts. It has been plausibly argued that the understanding of God is reflected in man's theological reasoning which portrays the development the mind of man has undergone at different points in time[26]. Hence at the earliest stage God is per-

---

[24] WILEY, H.O. and CULBERTSON, P.T., *Introduction to Christian Theology* (Beacon Hill Press, Kansas, 1946) p. 275.
[25] JAMES 2 : 14 - 3 : 12.
[26] BALOGUN, I.A.B., "Religious Tolerance as a Pre-requisite for peace, Progress and Unity in Nigeria" in Balogun, I.A.B. *op. cit.*, p. 58.

ceived through several inanimate objects; at another stage through the Ark of the Covenant; at yet another stage, through Jesus Christ, and lastly religion reached a stage where no representation is sought for God. This is indeed an evolutionary process.

Since the belief system of the Indigenous Religion is generally incompatible with those of Islam and Christianity, they are not expected to be combined, otherwise that would mean syncreticism. Syncreticism means the practice of owning loyalty to and practising more than one religion at the same time[27]. Every religion frowns at it, particularly Islam and Christianity[28]. There is the tendency among the Yoruba Muslims to practise syncreticism, hence the adage: *Igbagbo* (or Imale as the case may be) *Ko ni ki a ma soro, a o soro ile wa*. Meaning, "Christianity could not prevent us from celebrating our indigenous rites, we shall celebrate it".

Hence it is not uncommon to find Muslims and Christians participating actively in Indigenous Religious rites. A research I recently conducted in Ile-Ife and Ila-Orangun, two ancient Yoruba towns, reveals that more than 40% of the egungun (Masquerade) cult members in the two towns are mosque and church goers; about 50% of those who put on *egungun* masks bear either Muslim or Christian names while an overwhelming majority of those entertained by the Masqueraders are Muslims and Christians.

Participation in the traditional religious rites and festivals always involves undergoing intensive rituals which are often not compatible with the tenets of the revealed religions. Those who are mostly involved in this are the traditional rulers and chiefs. Most of the *Obas* in Yorubaland as well as their Chiefs are either Muslims or Christians, yet they are active practioners of Indigenous Religion. This they usually want to justify by their claim to be father of all and custodians of indigenous tradition. It is equally found among the Yoruba instances when traditional taboos (eewo) are given reverence even when they contradict Islamic or Christian

---

[27] WILLIAM MORRIS (ed.), *American Heritage Dictionary of English Language* (Houghton Mifflin, Atlanta) p. 1304.
[28] See REVELATION 2 : 14 and Surah 2. : 208.

tenets. Syncreticism is usually the problem of someone who lives in a tradition that is not indigenous to him.

This is however not to say that every aspect of the Indigenous tradition is to be cast away in favour of Islamic or Christian tradition. Islam like Christianity absorbs elements of the indigenous culture and tradition that are amenable to it, it rejects some aspects while other aspects are modified. It would be appropriate to illustrate with the rites and ceremonies connected with life-circle events — discussed in the first section.

The distinctive characteristic feature of Islamic and Christian naming is the service associated with them with the prescribed recitations from their scriptures. In both cases, the naming ceremony takes place on the eighth day as against the traditional naming which takes place on the seventh day if the baby is a female or ninth day if it is a male. Babues born into islam are given Islamic names while those born into Christianity are given baptismal names. In addition to these, indigenous names including names determined by circumstances of birth are given, but not in the sense of idolatry. All the feasting, eating, dancing, rejoicing which accompany the child's birth and naming are permitted. The shaving of the baby's head, circumcision, clitoridectomy, burying of the placenta, are practices common to the adherents of the three religions. The indigenous tradition which forbids a woman who has just delivered a baby to eat certain foods in the belief that they are harmful to her health is observed in many Muslim and Christian homes believing that they do not conflict with scriptural teaching[29]. The use of food items such as alligator pepper, salt, bitter kola, kolanut, honey etc. to invoke God in prayer for the baby is not tolerated in Islamic naming and it is also frowned at by some denomina-

---

[29] Qur'an is explict on the kinds of foods that should not be eaten as evident in *Surah* 2. : 172-173 and 5 : 3. Qur'an also warns against making unlawful what God makes lawful as evident in *Surah* 2. : 168 and 5 : 87-88. It would seem this latter verse contradicts the view expressed in the chapter but to my mind it is not necessarily a contradiction. In *Surah* 2 : 168 and 5 : 87-88 what God desires for man is ease and comfort and if man decides to disregard such an injunction for whatever may be his reason it is left to him. The wrath of God is not to be aroused for that. It would be a different matter if the tradition referred to above makes lawful what is forbidden. That would be a serious sin.

tions of Christianity including the Christ Apostolic Church. Using them in prayers is like praying through intermidiary gods, more so because the objects are materials offered as offerings to the idols.

With regard to marriage tradition, the same philosophy underlines marriage contract. The three religions see marriage as an institution legalising intercourse and procreation of children. Indigenous Religion and Islam attach serious importance to marriage. For them it is a sacred duty enjoined on their adherents. Christianity on the other hand permits celibacy for any one who chooses not to marry.

With regard to the number of wives a man is allowed to marry, again, Indigenous Religion and Islam have closer affinity, as the two allow polygamy while Christianity teaches monogamy. However, while the Indigenous Religion permits unlimited polygamy, Islam limits the number of wives to four. This is why one cannot but disagree with Adelowo when he opines, quoting Trimingham, 'that Islam allows unlimited polygamy but regulates it by introducing two categories of wives, usually called legal wives and concubines'. This view to say the least is misleading. The Qur'an in *Sūrah* 4 : 3 and 4 : 129 makes it explicit that a man cannot exceed the limit of four wives if he decides to be polygamous. It is also clear in the passages that monogamy is the rule while polygamy is only an exception to the rule[30].

The teachings of the two religions had effect on the attitude of the Yoruba when they were first introduced to them. Islamic polygamy, in spite of the limitation imposed, was more appealing to the Yoruba than the Christian monogamy. It is however important to note that polygamy is becoming increasingly popular among some Indigenous African Churches using the examples of some Biblical figures as justification.

The requirements to be fulfilled for the validity of marriage are essentially the same for the three religions. These are mutual consent of the partners, the sanction of the par-

---

[30] ADELOWO, E.O., "Islam and Yoruba in Religious contact: An Episode of Acculturation" in Sam Babs Mala and Z. Oseni (eds.) *op. cit.*, p. 70.

ents or guardians, payment of the dowry, and the presence of witnesses.

Belief in the hereafter during which man is expected to account for his earthly deeds is entrenched in the theology of the three religions. The traditional Yoruba belief in it, as noted, is not common among many African societies. However funeral rites and ceremonies are performed strictly according to Islamic and Christian traditions. The major Islamic rites performed are the ritual bath and the ritual prayer after which burial takes place. Similarly Christian rites involve washing of the corpse and conduct of the Christian service. All the wailing, weeping and lamentation are discouraged. The funeral tradition appears to be an example of the aspect of Yoruba culture that has been supplanted by the traditions of Islam and Christianity.

The focus of this chapter as we have seen so far has been the changing religious experience of the Yoruba and the effect religion has had on their life. When we speak of the Yoruba today we are speaking of the Yoruba living within three different religious traditions, the traditionists, the Yoruba Muslims and the Yoruba Christians. It can be said that this is divisive, as indeed it is. This is because there is the tendency these days among the Yoruba to think first in terms of their religious affliation or brotherhood before thinking of Yoruba as a racial entity. This is the magnitude of the influence which religion can have on the life of man. Be that as it may, religions should not be devisive in view of their common philosophical base. This is the aspect of religious culture which needs to be emphasised in the overall interest of the Yoruba as a race.

Christian-Muslim Collaboration in Human Development

PAUL JACKSON

The topic of "Christian-Muslim Collaboration in Human Development" can be seen from a number of different perspectives. One is that of blindly painting a rosy picture more appropriate to Alice in Wonderland than to the real world that we live in. Another extreme is that of the arch pessimist who sees no such collaboration anywhere and, moreover, insists that none is possible. Both of these extremes have to be rejected.

Well, what is the real situation, and what are the factors involved which will enable us to understand it as well as indicate practical considerations to ensure its further realization? We have to turn to history to gain the necessary perspective.

HISTORICAL PERSPECTIVE

The Life of Muhammad[1] is the oldest and most authoritative Muslim biography of the Prophet of Islam. It records the earliest known instances of collaboration between Christians and Muslims. Faced with persecution in Mecca, Muhammad advised some of his followers to go to Abyssinia, a Christian country, "for the king (Negus) will not tolerate injustice and it is a friendly country"[2]. Some eighty-three men migrated there, in groups, and some of them had their families with them. "They were safely ensconced there and were grateful for the protection of the Ne-

---

[1] A. GUILLAUME, *The Life of Muhammad*, Oxford University Press, Karachi, 1970. A translation of Ishaq's *Sirat Rasul Allah*.
[2] *Life*, p. 146.

gus; could serve God without fear; and the Negus had shown them every hospitality"³. The Quraysh sent two emissaries from Mecca laden with presents in an effort to bring them back. They presented their case but the Negus allowed the emigrants to defend themselves. He was impressed with what they said and permitted them to remain. "We lived in happiest conditions until we came to the apostle of God in Mecca"⁴, was how they summed up their experience. This episode has left an indelibly favourable imprint on the Muslim consciousness. Was it, however, a conscious form of collaboration for human development?

Before attempting to answer this question it is necessary to reflect on the term, "human development". What are some of the presuppositions of the term as used in the title of this article? Surely the very first is that the background envisaged in the title is that of a secular society? And is it not further true that this is a comparatively recent phenomenon dating back to the clarion call to "liberty, equality and fraternity" which resounded during the French Revolution at the end of the eighteenth century? This call was focussed on human beings. With its rationalist philosophical underpinning it clearly espoused a form of humanism which was untrammelled by religious affiliations. Unfettered human reason could work out what was best for human beings. This, in a nutshell, expresses the humanistic creed. It naturally envisages what is termed a secular society, meaning a society concerned with the affairs of this world, not of some nebulous world after death. Religion, at best, is relegated to the private concern of the individual. The decision to follow a particular religion could be compared to that of electing to smoke a particular brand of cigarette — with not dissimilar consequences.

This is the setting of the term, "human development". At best, it prescinds from religion. At worst, it considers it "the opium of the people". It envisages an uninterrupted stream of human advancement bereft of any transcendental dimension. It is concerned with feeding, clothing, housing and educating people, as well as providing them with health

---

³ *Life*, p. 148. "Negus" was the title of the Christian king.
⁴ *Life*, p. 153.

care and employment, while also diligently safeguarding their human rights. Much hope is put in scientific advancement as the tool par excellence for achieving this goal.

This is definitely not the setting in which Muhammad sent some of his followers to Abyssinia for their safety. Nor did it constitute the milieu of the ebb and flow of Christian-Muslim relations in the ensuing centuries. It was under the second caliph, Umar (634-44), that Jerusalem was captured. In 1084 a Turkoman chief, Urtok, began to rule in Jerusalem and the Christians suffered[5]. The call went out to liberate Jerusalem and the Crusaders began to gather for this enterprise. Ironically by the time they arrived the city had been captured once again by the Fatimid caliph of Egypt in August, 1098. Reports speak of some 10,000 Muslims slain when the Crusaders captured Jerusalem in 1099[6]. Another author writes: "All Muslims, men, women and children, as well as Jews, perished in the general slaughter that followed"[7]. This event sent shock waves among the Muslims on account of the barbaric nature of the killing, and Christians living as minorities in Muslim countries experienced hardships which previously had been unknown to them. The ensuing centuries of conflict associated with the Crusades did nothing to ameliorate the engendered mutual hostility. In 1453 Constantinople was captured by the Ottoman Turks. They made it their capital and the push into Eastern Europe gathered momentum. Their armies eventually reached the very walls of Vienna in 1529 and again in 1683. For a long time Europe lived under threat from the Ottoman Turks. Obviously the Christian naval victory at Lepanto in 1571 had not ended this threat. The next thrust was that of so-called Christian countries in Europe who proceeded to lord it over Muslims during the colonial period. In view of such a turbulent history, involving so much Christian-Muslim hostility, what possible scope exists for talking about "Christian-Muslim Collaboration in Human Development"? Even

---

[5] THOMAS PATRICK HUGHES, *Dictionary of Islam*, Oriental Reprint, New Delhi, 1976, p. 229.
[6] *Dictionary of Islam*, p. 229.
[7] *Encyclopaedia Britannica*, Macropaedia vol. 5, 1980, p. 300.

Vatican II openly acknowledged in 1965 that "over the centuries many quarrels and dissensions have arisen between Christians and Muslims"[8].

As already explained, specific collaboration for human development should not be looked for before the nineteenth century which saw the birth of secularism. Prior to this Europe had its political divisions but it also had its own form of unity which could be summed up in one word — Christendom. It was Christendom which launched the Crusades.

For a long time this even had a political expression in the form of the Holy Roman Empire. When Charlemagne was crowned Holy Roman Emperor on Christmas Day, in the year 800, in what is now the town of Aachen in Germany, a political reality was born which culminated in the sixteenth-century struggle between the Emperor Charles V and King Francis 1 of France. This heralded the emergence of the nation-state in Europe. The so-called Reformation of the sixteenth century led to the religious division of Europe and the political supremacy of the nation-state. Christendom was no longer a reality. Nation-states like England and Spain, frequently at war with each other, developed into colonial powers. For example, people speak and write about British rule in India, not Christian rule.

This situation was mirrored within the Muslim community also. Although the Caliphate perdured until around 1258 it had ceased to be a political unity by the end of the tenth century. Political power had passed into the hands of the rulers of various kingdoms usually called sultanates. The Caliph was merely a figurehead. It is true that the Ottoman rulers were not slow to appropriate the title of Caliph for themselves, but this was more of a political ploy than an expression of a religious reality. Although the term "colonial power" is not usually used to describe the Ottoman Empire, the fact remains that the subjugation of other countries, Christian as well as Muslim, was exactly the sort of thing done by, for example, England, and it was this that resulted in the creation of the British Empire. Although religious in-

---

[8] *Nostra Aetate*, no. 3.

terests may have been proposed as the motivating factor of the Ottoman expansion, hard facts, like the alliance between Francis 1 of France and Suleiman the Magnificent, which permitted the Turkish fleet to winter in French ports, for example, serves to underline the fact that the ultimate deciding factor was political in nature, not religious. Both the European colonial powers and the Ottoman Empire gained vast material riches as a result of their colonizing propensities. The only factor behind the Franco-Ottoman pact was mutual self-interest. There is nothing reprehensible about this. After all, this is the basis for all treaties. Each party strives for the best deal it can manage in the given circumstances. Nevertheless it scarcely allows us to label it as an example of Christian-Muslim collaboration for human development, for this implies a transcendence of narrow self-interest.

Present Situation

The present situation is quite new. The ebb of the colonial tide has witnessed the emergence of over fifty Muslim countries. The very latest additions to this expanding group of countries occurred as a direct result of the break up of the Soviet Union. Five countries with an overwhelming Muslim majority, and one with a 42% Muslim population, came into existence. All these countries strive for as much unity as possible. The political forum for the implementation of this desire is the Organization of Islamic Conference (OIC). Its most recent meeting was in Teheran in December, 1997. The very fact that the meeting was held in this venue, granted the tensions between Iran and Iraq, as well as Iran and Saudi Arabia, for example, is a triumph of the Islamic quest for unity. By implication it recognizes that differences of political and sectarian outlooks, although quite real, should not be allowed to stand in the way of an ever-increasing sense of unity among the global Muslim community. Although they may quarrel among themselves they would like to speak with one voice to the world community.

If one turns towards Christians one sees a disjunction. At the religious level the World Council of Churches and the Vatican strive for mutual understanding and unity. At the political level, however, there is no sign of nation-states seeking unity on the basis of Christianity. The powerful thrust towards a united Europe is ultimately based on financial considerations, not religious. Cultural factors, including religious aspects, are also operative and are freely acknowledged, but they do not provide the overriding impetus.

Thus our world of today highlights a clear-cut difference in perspective between Muslims and Christians. Both groups have a deep-seated preoccupation with religious unity even though regional and sectarian sentiments remain quite strong. Indeed these not infrequently erupt in violence. Moreover, this same violence not only tears the fabric of the particular religion involved but also sends shock waves among adherents of the other religion. One thinks of the massacres in Algeria, for example, even though it is difficult to establish who the perpetrators really are. If an issue is grave enough Muslim countries are ready to break ranks and align themselves to the perceived wronged party, as happened during the Gulf War. If there is no clear-cut issue involved, however, Muslims tend to support fellow-Muslims.

European countries tend to make decisions which are largely influenced by enlightened self-interest. They are normally secular in nature. In other words, religion is not the determining factor. People want to put the wars of religion behind them. They form an undeniably painful aspect of sixteenth and seventeenth century European history. No one wants a repetition of that horror! The Constitution of the United States is specifically intended to obviate such disruption of civil society. People are free to practise their religion and others have a similar right, but they cannot impose their views or practices on others.

Before examining what can be done in the present situation it will be instructive to examine an instance of collaboration from Medieval Spain. Tariq ibn-Zayd landed in Spain in 711 and defeated the Visigoth army under King Roderick. The Moors — as the Muslims were called — quickly overran the Iberian Peninsula. Only a small pocket of resistance remained in the North-West. Over the long centuries that followed the Christians inched their way South and, in 1492, Granada, the last Moorish kingdom, fell. Those centuries were certainly filled with many "quarrels and dissensions", but also with collaboration of various kinds. For example, when El Cid, the most famous Christian warrior of all these centuries, known as *Campeador*, the Winner of Battles, was unjustly exiled by King Alfonso VI of Castile, he offered his services to Counts Ramon II and Berenguer II of Barcelona. "His offer was scornfully rejected; and since it seemed that there was no Christian prince who valued his abilities, he addressed himself to al-Muqtadir, the Moorish king of Saragosa"[9]. Apart from Seville, Saragosa was the most brilliant court of eleventh-century Spain. Al-Muqtadir was a philosopher, mathematician and astronomer who had surrounded himself with Muslim and Jewish scholars. El Cid served his son, al-Mu'tamin, faithfully, but on the express condition that he would never do anything prejudicial to the interests of Castile, for he considered Alfonso to be his liege lord throughout his entire life, no matter how unjustly he treated him.

Towards Collaboration

The first thing to remember as we move towards collaboration is the *newness* of our present situation. Not only do we have more than fifty Muslim countries. We also have significant Muslim minorities in countries where few were previously to be found. This applies to many European countries, the United States and countries like Australia. On the reverse side you have, in the United Arab Emirates, for example, large numbers of Christians now rubbing shoulders with local Muslims who had, until a few decades ago, never seen a Christian. Even strictly sequestered Muslim girls at the Emirate university in Al-Ain have had male Christian mathematics teachers. For the first time ever large numbers of people are in a position to make judgements about Muslims or Christians which are based on their own experience, not on hearsay. Those who work together learn about each other. Never before in history have so many Christians and

---

[9] JAN READ, *The Moors in Spain and Portugal*, Faber and Faber, London, 1974, p. 132.

Muslims been interacting together. This leads to precious personal experience, which is usually overwhelmingly positive. This is the conclusion reached after personally interviewing about a thousand young Christian men and women from all parts of India over a period of fifteen years. The last statistical count revealed that 88% of their personal experience with Muslims was positive in nature. Moreover, the balance they exhibited in the opinions they expressed during discussions was usually in stark contrast to what was said by those who had never had any personal experience.

Some people may object that what applies to India need not necessarily be applicable in other countries. This is true, but only those with personal experience will be in a position to prove or disprove the wider applicability of these statistics. On the other hand, the very fact that they come from people living in many different parts of India already gives them a wider scope than would apply to more narrow, homogeneous situations.

It is impossible to exaggerate the importance of this current phenomenon. It is clearly important for people in authority to encourage and foster personal interaction on the part of Christians and Muslims. This has been done by the Catholic Church in the first aspect of the oft-repeated *fourfold dialogue*: "The *dialogue of life*, where people strive to live in an open and neighbourly spirit, sharing their joys and sorrows, their human problems and preoccupations"[10].

It is really very simple to meet and interact with others, once you start doing so. There can, however, often be massive yet unseen barriers preventing this simple exchange from taking place. For example the novitiate of a congregation of religious sisters in Calcutta is situated right next to a mosque. There is only a dividing wall separating them. Nevertheless it was only a couple of weeks ago, in mid December, 1997, that the first interaction took place. A sister with much experience in meeting Muslims was invited to give twenty-two novices an introduction to Islam. It was she who

---

[10] *Dialogue and Proclamation: Reflections and orientations on Interreligious Dialogue and the Proclamation of the Gospel of Jesus Christ* (Pontifical Council for Interreligious Dialogue and Congregation for the Evangelization of Peoples, 1991), n. 42.

took the novices to the mosque. The Imam gave them a warm welcome and showed them all around. It was all so easy, and such a pleasant experience. It was possible simply because no hidden barrier existed for the sister who was herself quite used to meeting Muslims.

Another example is that of a priest who spent more than twenty years as the parish priest in a town which contained the tomb of a very eminent Sufi. Not once did he visit the tomb. Even more, it can be doubted that the thought of doing so ever crossed his mind. This is not meant as a criticism. It serves to illustrate the strength of the invisible barrier which existed in the average priest's mind. This was the common pre-Vatican II outlook.

What can also happen is that lay people may be mixing and working with Muslims and even having religious discussions with them while their clergy restrict themselves to working with their Christian parishioners. Such priests often continue to carry their own prejudices around with them and are scarcely in a position to encourage their parishioners by word and example to interact with Muslims.

These examples underline the urgent need for courses on Islam for all priests and religious in formation. The person who conducts such a course should ideally be able to impart accurate information as well as encourage the students by drawing on his or her own experience of interacting with Muslims. As indicated above, such courses are greatly enhanced by some form of interaction with Muslims, no matter how simple it may seem. Courses which are in fact based on the principle of setting up a situation where such interaction can occur for about a week can prove to be very potent in breaking down prejudices and fostering mutual knowledge and respect. An experienced person is needed to organize and prepare the students for such courses[11].

It should be noted that this whole approach is quite lacking in glamour. Interacting with Muslims, conducting courses on Islam, arranging exposure programmes and en-

---

[11] Such courses are a regular feature of the programme of the first-year students of Theology at the Regional Theological Centre, Danapur, near Patna, India.

couraging young people to interact with Muslims are all basically relational in nature. They are aimed at helping young Christians to enter into relationships with Muslims and thus, from their own personal experience, grow in knowledge of them as persons. This is a far cry from any grand design, any attempt to control or manipulate others for one's own designs. It does not produce quick, easily verifiable results. Students, for example, pass on and it is not possible to follow them up. It would seem that nothing much is happening. Certainly there is nothing to get excited about. It would be a grave mistake, however, to belittle this process. For example, even finding such models and guides here in India is very difficult. They are extremely rare. Many factors of a religious, cultural, linguistic, political, social and personal nature combine to make this so. Similar factors are probably operative in other countries as well. Even getting one such dedicated person is itself like a quantum jump. Hence the circle of influence exercised by such a person is precious. As more and more such circles appear and begin to spread tangible changes will become visible. For the moment, however, it is very much like the turning of the tide. When low tide has been reached there seems to be little or even no change at all for a while. Later on, when the tide is running strongly, it is evident to one and all. If that barely perceptible event which we call the turning of the tide had not taken place, however, there would be no strongly running tide later on. Hence the great significance of any effort to reach out in friendship and understanding towards Muslims.

There have been several books written in recent years with titles like Attar Chand's *Islam and the New World Order*[12] and John Esposito's *The Islamic Threat: Myth or Reality*[13]? In a nutshell, both books look at Islam globally in the aftermath of the break up of the Soviet Union and ask if Islam is the new enemy of the West. It seems that such writings, which paint a monolithic picture of a powerful, transnational Islam flexing its muscles in preparation to taking on

---

[12] ATTAR CHAND, *Islam and the New World Order*, Akashdeep Publishing House, New Delhi, 1992.

[13] JOHN L. ESPOSITO, *The Islamic Threat: Myth or Reality?* Oxford University Press, New York, 1992.

the West, are meant to inspire fear and thus justify huge expenses on armaments. They also turn people in on themselves and make it psychologically impossible to even want to reach out towards Muslims. It will be noticed that such writings bring name and fame, as well as financial benefits, to their authors, but do they tend to encourage Christians and Muslims to come together? The net effect is diametrically opposite to that of those people mentioned above who, with the express blessing of the Church, strive to promote interaction and understanding between Christians and Muslims.

This is not to say that there is no need for careful analysis of the situation. There most certainly is. Such writings are characterized by the understanding they generate, not by the fears that they arouse. They give the lie to many generalizations and shatter numerous cherished stereotypes. An example of a creative, scholarly and stereotype-free work is Renard's *Seven Doors to Islam*[14]. To be sure violence and acts of terrorism have to be condemned, but they also have to be understood. Some are simply brutally repressive while others are misguided reactions stemming from a grave sense of injustice.

Another point to be noticed is that writings like those of Chand and Esposito barely mention the spiritual treasures of Islam. In addition to the Quran and other foundational writings of Islam there is an enormous treasure trove of literature reflecting the deep and intimate experience of God enjoyed by countless Muslim saints, known as Sufis, down the centuries. Their writings offer a rich fare of guidance and inspiration for those who hunger after God[15].

Collaboration

The document on "Dialogue and proclamation" speaks of four forms of dialogue:

"42. There exist different forms of interreligious dialogue. It may be useful to recall those mentioned by the 1984

---

[14] John Renard, *Seven Doors to Islam: Spirituality and the Religious Life of Muslims*, University of California Press, Los Angeles, 1996.
[15] The reader has a dozen works to choose from in the Series "The Classics of Western Spirituality" produced by the Paulist Press.

document of the Pontifical Council for Interreligious Dialogue (cf. D&M 28-35); It spoke of four forms, without claiming to establish among them any order of priority:

a. The *dialogue of life*, where people strive to live in an open and neighborly spirit, sharing their joys and sorrows, their human problems and preoccupations.

b. The *dialogue of action*, in which Christians and others collaborate for the integral development and liberation of people.

c. The *dialogue of theological exchange*, where specialists seek to deepen their understanding of their respective religious heritages, and to appreciate each other's spiritual values.

d. The *dialogue of religious experience*, where persons, rooted in their own religious traditions, share their spiritual riches, for instance with regard to prayer and contemplation, faith and ways of searching for God or the Absolute".

Let us now turn to the second of the four aspects of dialogue recommended by the Church: "The *dialogue of action*, in which Christians and others collaborate for the integral development and liberation of people".

We are now at the heart of our topic. This *dialogue of action* is a slightly more elaborate expression of the topic of this article. It has taken us a long time to reach this point. From what has been said it should be clear that collaboration, although so desirable, is not as easy as it sounds. In the Catholic Church the original impulse came from the following teaching of Vatican II promulgated in 1965.

"Over the centuries many quarrels and dissensions have arisen between Christians and Muslims. The sacred council now pleads with all to forget the past, and urges that a sincere effort be made to achieve mutual understanding; for the benefit of all men, let them together preserve and promote peace, liberty, social justice and moral values"[16].

It is clear that collaboration can take place at a variety of levels. The Pontifical Council for Interreligious Dialogue has

---

[16] *Nostra aetate*, 1965, n. 3.

been particularly active in a wide variety of meetings and programmes with Muslims. This has the added function of acting as an encouraging example for people in the field.

If we were to ask whether collaboration with Muslims was a hallmark of most Christian communities the answer would clearly be in the negative. The reasons for this have been outlined in this article. The first step is meeting, interacting and getting to know one another. The second step is joint action. Collaboration implies working together at all stages of a project right from the decision-making process to its execution. Such activity is possible only when a climate of mutual trust has been created. When this has taken place the time is ripe for collaboration. It all takes time, however. People looking for a "fast track" should stay with their computers.

The golden rule for collaboration is that the project has to be considered worthwhile by both parties. There is no question of getting involved in something we do not really value simply in order to please someone else. The second rule is that "small is beautiful". If you are thinking in terms of some grand project you are deceiving yourself. Probably nothing will ever materialize. Begin with something small and definite. It is not at all necessary that collaboration means an exact fifty-fifty input. It means deciding to summon up whatever is needed for a particular project. So long as each party freely agrees to a particular contribution the proportion does not really matter. The first category of project that comes to mind covers immediate social needs, particularly where Christians and Muslims are living together. There is really no restriction, however, on any form of collaboration in a project which is intrinsically good. It could be cultural, educational, or concerned with health or legal matters. The important thing is to begin.

One group which is doing good work in the field of collaboration is the Silsilah Dialogue Movement in Zamboanga City, Mindanao, Philippines. Regular readers of their *Silsilah Bulletin*[17] can keep abreast of their activities. In India efforts made by the Islamic Studies Association to promote mutual

---

[17] *Silsilah Bulletin*, published from Silsilah Center, Joval Building, 137 Governor Alvarez Street, 7000 Zamboanga City, Philippines.

understanding find an echo in the Association's quarterly, *Salaam*[18].

As well as the normal personality and other problems faced by people who try to collaborate together Muslims and Christians have different theological perspectives. The supreme value for Muslims is that God's Will be obeyed in all spheres of life. Islam means "submission to the Will of God", and a Muslim is a person who so submits himself or herself. In the Lord's Prayer Christians pray: "Thy kingdom come. Thy will be done on earth as it is in heaven". In the past many thought that the specific way this was accomplished was by conversion. Some people still think this way. Vatican II and recent Popes, however, have taken a wider view. Any increase in goodness, justice, active concern for others, mutual understanding or assisting those in need redounds to the praise and glory of God, for such things are certainly desired by Him. Hence collaboration in such enterprises deepens and extends God's reign. People who try to help others to the praise and glory of God experience the joy of participating in His creative process. This is a far cry from what happens to those people who are really intent on building their own empires, no matter what language they employ to cloak their real motives. God cannot be deceived. One instinctively thinks of the hypocrisy of the Pharisees which Jesus so often and so unerringly exposed. Collaboration is possible only among people of good will.

One other inestimable benefit from collaboration is that it provides the most fruitful matrix for dialogue. This begins at the level of the work being undertaken but easily and naturally moves on to deeper levels. Both parties will be able to clarify misconceptions and grow in knowledge of the lived reality of the faith of the other party. This can provide moments of astonishment. People who are deeply committed to the Living God can teach and inspire us in unexpected ways.

Would it not be better, however, if Christians and Muslims were to prescind from the faith dimension and simply work on projects for human development in the secular un-

---

[18] *Salaam*, published by the Islamic Studies Association, R-1/302, Hauz Khas, New Delhi 110 016, India.

derstanding previously enunciated? This is not really possible for a committed Muslim, for everything is seen as under God's sway. It is true that many discuss whether it is necessary for God to rule as well as reign, i.e. to have a theocratic form of government. The fact that there are many different forms of government in Muslim countries answers this question. For devout Muslims, however, every effort, *jihad*, is meant to further God's reign in ourselves and in our world. Whatever activity is beneficial for others is to the praise and glory of God. There is no dichotomy here or question of pretending otherwise.

Not all Christians think the same on this particular issue. Many, in view of negative aspects of religion as seen in countries like India, advocate that we prescind from the religious dimension and simply work for human development. Forget about transcendence! Tackle real human needs! Many members of the Society of Jesus have been struggling with this dilemma in an effort to find the best way to work for genuine human development. The Society has finally spelled out it attitude in these prophetic words:

Today we realize clearly:

No service of faith without
    promotion of justice
    entry into cultures
    openness to other religious experiences.
No promotion of justice without
    communicating faith
    transforming cultures
    collaboration with other traditions.
No inculturation without
    communicating faith with others
    dialogue with other traditions
    commitment to justice.
No dialogue without
    sharing faith with others
    evaluating cultures
    concern for justice[19].

---

[19] *34th General Congregation of the Society of Jesus*, 1995, Servants of Christ's Mission, n. 19.

Experienced people immediately sense the wholesomeness of this perspective. It addresses the whole man in the entirety of his needs and relationships. It places Christian-Muslim collaboration in its proper setting, for it enunciates clearly the multi-dimensional nature, as has been outlined in this article, of what can be mistakenly assumed to be a simple affair. Questions of faith, of religion, of culture and of justice are involved in collaborative effort. They have to be faced and discussed. What might otherwise be seen as a project *for* human development is now seen in its full complexity and richness as an enterprise in human development, for no aspect of a human being is consciously omitted.

Conclusion

Christian-Muslim collaboration in human development is not achieved easily. It has many obstacles to overcome, as indicated in this article, and many challenges to face. We stand, in fact, at the turn of a crucial tide in the history of the human race. Christian-Muslim collaboration, no matter how halting it may be, can eventually bring untold benefits and blessings to countless millions of people. Each step taken in this direction is a step towards God, for it is a step towards that form of human unity which mirrors the divine.

Christian-Muslim Dialogue for Justice and Solidarity

FABC - FEISA 1996

1. INTRODUCTION

1.1. As the Church in Asia approaches the Third Millennium, we are being called to respond with a new ardour to bring to a greater consciousness the need to be *"A New Way of Being Church"*. We began this journey of faith in a significant way with the Second Vatican Council and the Bishops of Asia through a process of dialogue, discovery and discernment. The inaugural assembly of the Asian Bishops that began in 1970, is our response to the call of the universal Church to become a *"sign and instrument of God's salvation in the world"* and to be at the service of humanity. To become "A Communion of Communities" in the context of Asia is to become a credible sign and instrument of God's salvation among our people and nations. We are at the same time invited to look at new areas of life that need to be transformed in order to be more credible witnesses of the Gospel in the context of Asia. It is for this reason that the Bishops called for a new thrust and orientation, one of renewal and reconciliation: "On this 25th anniversary of FABC, we have to confess humbly that the goal of conscientizing the local Church and building a communion of our Asian Churches is still far from being reached, despite the truly remarkable advances already made in this regard."

1.2. With this in mind, the FABC Office for Human Development and the Office for Interreligious and Ecumenical Affairs seek to make this a reality through the *"Faith Encounters in Social Action"* (FEISA) Series. We therefore gathered together to listen to the Lord, especially in our dialogue with our Muslim sisters and brothers. This was our attempts to become a "A New Way of Being Church". We affirm the call of the Church to *Journey together towards the Third Millennium so that we can be at the Service of Life.*

1.3. The forty-five participants made up of Bishops, Clergy, religious and laity from Bangladesh, India, Indonesia, Korea, Malaysia, Pakistan, Philippines, Sri Lanka, and Thailand in our ten days together attempted not only to understand better the world of religious dialogue but also to look at new ways of responding to the demands of the Gospel in the context of our nations and in our time of rapid change and uncertainty. We believe that this for us means a journeying with the Spirit of Jesus in the context of our lives.

2. NEW INSIGHTS INTO DIALOGUE THROUGH EXPOSURE-IMMERSION

2.1. In keeping with our methodology of the Pastoral Spiral that evolved from our Bishops' Institute for Social Action (BISA) and Asian Institute for Social Action (AISA), we began our exposure-immersion experiences with our Muslim sisters and brothers in Malaysia and Indonesia. This brought us closer to experience the various facets of inter-religious dialogue. These experiences were a source of new insights and learnings for most of us. The visits to "Pesantrens" (Religious Schools), community development workers, the contact with ordinary labourers, the interviews with committed university teachers and ordinary Muslim families gave us new perspectives of the human and spiritual qualities of Muslims and Christians working together for the development of the poor. We were particularly struck by the dedication and high degree of ethics that so many people manifested. We were edified and inspired by the way the people lived out their beliefs. We realised that the use of consultation and consensus in decision-making was an effective way of empowering people to plan their own lives. The personal encounters made us re-examine our own way of living and the deep compassionate approach needed to be at the service of the poor and marginalised.

2.2. We were touched by the common humanity we shared with those whom we met. Christians and Muslims are affected by human events in a similar way. It was so affirming to share the sadness, joy, fear and sufferings of the poor. Their warmth, openness, friendship, humility and hospitality bonded us together in a new way. Some of our prejudices were wiped out by our encounters with human goodness. Their openness enabled us to enter into a new level of relationships with them. We were convinced that the sharing of our own humanity with those of other religions is a good starting point for any genuine dialogue. We were led to go beyond human encounters to the meaning and spirituality behind so much profound human goodness.

2.3. We also realised at the same time that some of our experiences were not possible in other situations and countries due to various reasons. Our common sharing of experiences enabled us to look for more creative ways of introducing such processes in our respective countries. It was so affirming to be supported and challenged by the other participants. The exposure-immersion experiences showed us that interreligious dialogue must focus on our commonalties rather than our differences. We were led to look beyond our prejudices and to commit ourselves to the call of the Church in Asia to make inter-religious dialogue an integral dimension of the living out of our faith.

2.4. Our journey with our Muslim sisters and brothers was not only the meeting of persons but also an encounter with their deep religiosity and firmly founded cultural roots. The way in which they attempted to live out their faith in the exercise of their daily responsibilities and a concern for the young and children was a source of inspiration. We were able to see genuine yearning for harmony and a return to spiritual values in the midst of poverty and suffering. Simplicity and self-reliance were their way of giving importance to God in their lives and relationships. Their communication in parables accentuate our desire to inculturate our lives in our own traditions.

3. Our Re-Discovery of the Meaning of Dialogue through Discernment

3.1. Our varied Exposure-Immersion Experiences and reflections upon them served as the starting point to attain a common understanding of both the world of the followers of Islam and our own Christian faith. We began to discover gradually the presence and action of God among our Muslim sisters and brothers. "A New Way of Being Church" meant discerning the promptings of the Spirit as a Community in the Church, and responding to the invitation to a sincere dialogue among ourselves. The ensuing days of study and prayer enabled us to see more clearly that our vocation to be followers of Christ in the context of Asia moves us to be at the "service of the world and promote life in all its fullness".

3.2. *We became aware* of our commitment to rediscover the essential message of the Gospel not only among ourselves but for people of all faiths in Asia. This faith-imperative inspired us to look for new expressions of solidarity with our Muslim sisters and brothers who like us are confronted by iniquities which prevent us from attaining the fullness and sacredness of life. We firmly believe that in the sharing of these tangible signs of hope the foundation for a continued and authentic dialogue with our Muslim sisters and brothers can be effectively built.

3.3. *We were able to see* clearly that the relationship between Muslims and Christians is marked by an atmosphere of peaceful coexistence, tolerance and respect for each other. There are serious efforts to understand each other's religious practices and cultural dimensions of life. Collaborative efforts in advocacy action and in the implementation of development programmes have proven that both Muslims and Christians can work together in addressing pressing issues and problems that confront them in their respective areas.

3.4. *We also realised* that these hopes are dimmed by tensions and dilemmas that persist in areas where Muslims and Christians remain fearful and are engulfed in their mutual feelings of distrust and prejudices of each other. In predominantly Christian areas, Muslims are generally alienated and suffer discrimination, so are Christians in some predominantly Muslim regions. Religion has been manipulated by governments and/or unscrupulous politicians for their political ends. Efforts to enter into genuine dialogue and solidarity is blocked by the lack of openness and fundamentalist tendencies on both sides. Christians are anxious lest their actions be construed as acts of proselytising.

3.5. *We recalled sadly* that it cannot be denied that in our brokenness we have failed to fully express our sense of unity and oneness with other faiths particularly with our Muslim sisters and brothers. Our efforts at reconciliation seem inadequate. We need to overcome our brokenness and strive unceasingly to rectify our shortcomings and relentlessly bring about the essence of what it is to be a true Christian today.

4. A Critical Review of our Lives in the light of our Discernment

4.1. *Esteem for Muslims*

4.1.1. In the light of our experiences we find many facets of Islamic life which we regard with esteem. Their loyalty to their religion, the seriousness and discipline with which they conduct their prayer, fasting, and other religious duties, their trust in God and desire to surrender to His will, and their frequent awareness of God in daily life are all religious values which we as Christians revere. In social life, we respect their sense of community and solidarity, the concern for justice, and the principle of *musyawarah* — consultation and consensus — in human development and community building. In our personal encounters, we appreciate the faithfulness in friendship, the warm hospitality and simplicity of life, the caring for the needs of the poor and respect for the elderly.

4.2. *Difficulties in living together*

4.2.1. At the same time, we confess that we often encounter difficulties living together in society. Although personal relationships are frequently good on the day-to-day level, Christians in minority situations often feel that they are not accepted as full and equal citizens and that in some places are victims of discrimination.

Political issues can be a source of tension just as concessions granted by Muslim governments to the majority group can make local Christians feel marginalised and alienated. The politicisation of religion not only obscures the purity of Islamic faith but can result in hardship and suffering for Christian minorities. However, we admit that where Christians are in the majority and in control of political processes, we frequently fail to implement Christian principles of justice, equality, and solidarity in regard to Muslim minorities.

4.3. *Obstacles to dialogue between Christians and Muslims*

4.3.1. Fear, prejudice, and suspicion on both sides are prominent obstacles to dialogue and co-operation. Most Christians know little about the religion of Islam, and our understanding is often distorted by half-truths and superficial judgements, and shaped by the negative image of Islam presented in the media. Exclusivist tendencies among both Christians and Muslims that regard one's own religion as the only way to salvation do not permit real dialogue or sharing of religious experience. Sometimes, Christians seemingly exude some superiority complex, regarding themselves as better off and more advanced than Muslims, whereas on some occasions, Muslims appear to look down on Christians and treat them with disdain.

4.4. *The burdens of history*

4.4.1. The burdens of history are still with us and cause difficulties in relating. Muslims still regard Christianity as a "European religion" identified with the colonial powers and the mutual violence of the past and present. Muslims do not consider them to be truly patriotic and committed to the development and well-being of their countries. It also happens that in objecting to the geopolitical activities of Western powers, Muslims sometimes take out their anger on Christian co-nationals.

4.5 *Christian failures to dialogue*

4.5.1. In noting these failings among Muslims, we must also confess our own failures. We often show a lack of sensitivity to the plight of Muslims in situations of oppression and poverty. Our witness to be the "church of the poor" is inadequate. Our efforts at dialogue are too often fragmented, half-hearted, and sporadic. We are frequently guilty of passing on rumours and undocumented information that raise fears and tensions in society. The Church is often shortsighted in looking at issues, addressing symptoms but neglecting to confront root causes. Christian leadership is often more interested in championing causes that only affect Christians rather than in concretely working to build reconciliation, peace, and harmony.

4.6. *Common grounds for action*

4.6.1. Despite the obstacles and failures on both sides, the prospects for Christian-Muslim dialogue are not gloomy. In every part of Asia, we discover groups of Christians and Muslims actively involved in working as partners for the betterment of their peoples. Despite the real differences between the two religions, Christians see in Islamic faith potentials for mutual esteem and cooperation. The holistic nature of Islam, which combines ritual, family life, and community uplift in a seamless commitment to God's will, enables Muslims to consider human development, the struggle for peace, and the defence of moral values as sacred activities.

5. OUR REFLECTIONS IN FAITH EXPRESSED IN SOLIDARITY

5.1. "The history of salvation tells us that God is continually dialoguing with people" (FABC Congress on Mission, Manila, 1979). In faith encounters with people of different religions, we can participate mutually in that divine dialogue that is in the heart of each one of us, and we are able to recognise and live our common communion in God and with God. This communion of faith, then, enables us to accept each other joyfully as sisters and brothers and to encounter each other trustfully in the joyful and painful events and realities that are mutual to us and to all other brothers and sisters.

5.2. This encounter in faith is truly a gift of the Holy Spirit, the spirit of communion, providing us with the divine power to approach and accept each other in forgiveness and reconciliation and in gratitude and love.

5.3. Encounter in faith among Muslims and Christians has special importance and urgency in our times. The often turbulent relations among Christians and Muslims throughout past centuries are the cause of much conflict and disharmony among a large portion of the world population professing Christianity and Islam. This must give place to life-giving encounters in faith toward the building up of the Reign of God on earth.

5.4. While faith encounter may be profitable at various levels, among individuals at the personal level and in groups of different kinds, the more practical and profitable encounter can happen at grass-roots communities. In these basic communities of Muslims and Christians, faith encounter can be more tangibly appreciated, the work of charity more easily carried out, and communion and community living more lovingly celebrated.

6. The Demands of Interreligious Dialogue in the context of Asia

6.1. We realise that we live in a new era of the spiritual evolution of humanity, in a moment of grace. The whole world is shrinking into a global village, and the Divine Spirit is bringing believers of different religions to a common pursuit of truth and justice, peace and harmony. We Christians of Asia perceive in this redemptive work of the Spirit in our continent a threefold demand placed on us:

6.2. *An Invitation to Reconciliation*

6.2.1. To forgive the hurts of the past, overcome prejudices and walk with sisters and brothers of other religions on a 'common pilgrimage in view of finding God in the hearts of the human person' (Paul VI, 1964). We who have fought in the name of God, need to return to this same God to ask for forgiveness and become signs of reconciliation. There can be no peace without reconciliation, with God calling us to find unity within the human family.

6.3. *A Concern for Human Dignity and Rights*

6.3.1. To collaborate with believers of other religions has to mean a commitment to the promotion of justice and peace, social harmony and environmental integration in solidarity with the weaker sections and marginalised sectors of Asia. There are so many facets of life on which Christians and Muslims should be co-operating. Both must face new issues in society resulting from the globalization of economies and a cultural invasion of values that are alien to our Asian way of life. Both are concerned about the effects that the values transmitted by the "new media culture" are likely to have on future generations of Asians. Both must face various threats to society, such as the destruction of environment, the plight of migrant workers, the exploitation and harassment of women and abuse of children in industry and tourism, the drugs menace, and the pandemic of AIDS. These are areas where we must pool our resources, share insights, and take common stands.

6.4. *A Return to Authentic Spirituality*

6.4.1. We must delve deeper into the spiritual wellsprings of Asia, in order to make religion an effective instrument for the integral formation of life. But dialogue must not be limited to co-operation on social issues. Muslims and Christians are two communities of faith who seek to do God's will. We must work towards the mutual sharing of spiritual experience to inspire one another and to be enriched by the other. We believe that when a Christian and Muslim come together in sincerity and good-will God will guide their pilgrimage towards a greater appreciation of the Truth that is beyond all understanding. This dialogue of spiritual sharing is not easy. It demands a conversion leading to trust, and trust demands friendship. This is perhaps the first task in dialogue required of the Christian and Muslim in Asia today: to make friends with each other in order to open themselves to the divine.

7. Our Commitment to a Spirituality of Dialogue

7.1. The liberative response to the erosion of moral and religious values consists in strengthening ethical values through an honest and open dialogue among believers of various religions. We realise that only a humanising spirituality that evolves through a culture of dialogue can forestall the danger of this erosion. Hence we Asian Christians commit ourselves to a new way of being Church today, that is, to the promotion of a 'spirituality of dialogue' in all realms of life.

This for us would mean:

7.2. *Dialogue in the Spirit - Peace the Fruit of the Spirit*

Recognising this centrality of spirituality in interreligious relationships. We commit ourselves therefore:

— *To dialogue in the Spirit, giver of peace. In a world torn apart by strife, violence and war it is God alone who can restore peace through renewed minds and hearts converted to the Will of God.*

— *To act in a spirit of forgiveness in order to find peace in our hearts and bring peace to others.*

— *To a new pilgrimage from noise and hectic activities to silence and contemplation, that will enable us to move with compassion to all of humanity and to live in harmony with nature. This putting on the compassionate heart of the Creator is also one that prompts to courage, that will strengthen our will to speak the truth amidst fear and hopelessness, to become the voice of the voiceless and those unable to live with dignity.*

— To place God at the center of our lives in the midst of the dominant culture of worshipping money and power and glorifying the individual at the expense of the community.
— To return to the Will of God the sound foundation for realisation of a genuine interreligious dialogue as we move towards the Third Millennium.

We give thanks to God who has called us to be followers of Jesus Christ, our Master and Saviour. We ask God to bless all Christians and Muslims with the gifts of understanding and love so that we live together in peace, co-operation, and mutual enrichment. May Mary, whom the Holy Qur'an calls "a model for all humankind" accompany Muslims and Christians in our common desire to do God's will.

Human Development and Evangelization
(The first to the sixth plenary assembly of the federation of Asian bishops' conferences)

PETER C. PHAN

The burden of this essay is to examine the relationship between human development and the church's evangelizing mission as understood in recent Asian theology. One way to carry out this task is to review and evaluate the statements and declarations of the Federation of Asian Bishops' Conferences (FABC) and their various committees and institutes[1].

The FABC was founded in the wake of the Asian Bishops' meeting in Manila, Philippines, in 1970[2]. Its influence on the Asian churches has been deemed to be positive[3].

---

[1] For a convenient collection of these documents, see GAUDENCIO B. ROSALES and C.G. ARÉVALO (eds.), *For All the Peoples of Asia: Federation of Asian Bishops' Conferences Documents from 1970 to 1991* (Maryknoll: Orbis Books, 1992). Henceforth, *For All*. Citations of these texts will be referred to by the number of the page(s) of this volume and the number of the paragraph(s) in parentheses in which they occur, except the final statement of the sixth assembly which is not included in this volume and which was published by the FABC, 16 Caine Road, Hong Kong. An assessment of the FABC's theology of inculturation has been given by Stephen Bevans in "Inculturation of Theology in Asia: The Federation of Asian Bishops' Conferences, 1970-1995", *Studia Missionalia* 45 (1996): 1-23.

[2] For a brief history of the FABC, see C.G. AREVALO, "The Time of the Heirs", *For All*, xv-xxii. For Arevalo, the founding of the FABC represented "an increasing communion among the local Asian churches" and marked "the decisive 'turning to history', a movement toward realizing a Church in Asia" (xvi).

[3] For an overview and assessment of the impact of the FABC on the Asian churches, see FELIX WILFRED, "The Federation of Asian Bishops' Conferences (FABC): Orientations, Challenge and Impact", *For All*, xxiii-xxx. Wilfred notes that "the FABC has created horizontal communication between the bishops and the bishops' conferences; it has fostered a spirit of collegiality, community and cooperation among them" (xxix). However, he also points out that because the Asian churches, despite real similarities among themselves, are not homogeneous "the FABC can speak only in general terms and cannot address itself specifically to

So far the FABC has hold six plenary assemblies which issued final statements[4]. Besides these plenary assemblies, the FABC also has standing institutes, which published statements of their meetings,[5] as well as occasional colloquia, congresses, and consultations[6]. The Bishops' Institute for Social Action (BISA) has held seven meetings, from 1974 to 1986, and has issued statements at the end of each meeting.

Though the present essay focuses on the FABC's six plenary assemblies and the BISA's seven meetings, it is of great importance to note that for the Asian bishops it would be a serious theological error to separate social action for human development from the other two areas of the Asian churches' mission, namely, interreligious dialogue and inculturation[7]. Indeed, documents on interreligious dialogue and inculturation very often discuss at length the role of the church in promoting human development. Hence, due attention must be given to these two fields of the church's ministry as well.

Furthermore, since collective and official declarations are often the work of compromise to achieve a common viewpoint, I will highlight some of their diversities by drawing on the writings of contemporary, especially Asian, theologians.

Human Development and Evangelization

It is very significant that the FABC's first plenary assembly held in Taipei, Taiwan, in 1974 chose as its theme "evangelization in modern day Asia". It affirms that "the

---

concrete situations" and that because the resources at the disposal of Asian bishops are so limited, "they feel helpless in implementing the grand vision of FABC" (xxx).

[4] The locations and dates of the six plenary assemblies are: Taipei (April 1974), Calcutta (November 1978), Bangkok (October 1982), Tokyo (September 1986), Bandung (July 1990), and Manila (January 1995).

[5] The bishops' institutes include those for Missionary Apostolate (BIMA), for Interreligious Affairs on the Theology of Dialogue (BIRA), for Lay Apostolate (BILA), and most significantly for our essay, for Social Action (BISA).

[6] There have been a consultation on Christian presence among Muslims in Asia (1983), an international congress on mission (1979), and two colloquia, one on ministries in the church (1977), and the other on the church in Asia and global transformation (1997).

[7] There have been twelve meetings of the BIRA, from 1984 to 1991. For the FABC's theology of inculturation, see the article of Stephen Bevans cited in note 1 above.

preaching of Jesus Christ and His Gospel to our peoples in Asia becomes a task which today assumes an urgency, a necessity and magnitude unmatched in the history of our Faith in this part of the world"[8].

However, in the "new age of mission," says the FABC, evangelization can no longer be understood as a "one-way movement from the 'older churches' to the 'younger churches,' from the churches of the old Christendom to the churches of the colonial lands"[9]. Rather "every local church *is* and cannot be but missionary. Every local church is 'sent' by Christ and the Father to bring the Gospel to its surrounding milieux, and to bear it also into all the world. For every local church this is a *primary task*"[10]. Furthermore, evangelization cannot be conceived as simply a unidirectional proclamation of the Good News to a particular culture, a sort of monologue in which only the church speaks and the people simply listen. Rather, according to the FABC, the "essential mode" in which evangelization is carried out in Asia today must be "dialogue," more precisely, "through a more resolute, more creative and yet truly discerning and responsible inculturation; through inter-religious dialogue undertaken in all seriousness; through solidarity and sharing with the poor and the advocacy of human rights..."[11].

With regard to the third form of dialogue, namely, dialogue with the people, especially the poor, its goal is "total human development" or "integral human development"[12]. The BISA III affirms: "We need to strive for a new society, so that all men may reach full human development. Our work has to be for the development of the whole man and every man. This wholeness of man includes not only the in-

---

[8] *For All*, 13 (no. 8). The BIMA III also affirms that the proclamation of Jesus Christ to those who do not yet believe in him remains a priority: "*The necessity of first proclamation has lost none of its urgency in Asia*, where Christians constitute a very small minority" (*For All*, 104 [no. 9]).

[9] *For All*, 130 (no. 14).

[10] *For All*, 130 (no. 14).

[11] *For All*, 131 (no. 19).

[12] These two expressions are often used by the FABC to characterize the kind of human progress that the church seeks to promote.

dividual personal fulfillment, but the growth and blossoming of the whole reality on earth"[13].

It is clear then that for the FABC, human development (1) is an *essential* dimension of the evangelizing mission of the church and (2) must aim at the *total* person.

Human Development as a Constitutive Dimension of Evangelization

One point repeatedly stressed by the FABC is that human development and progress in all its aspects — political, social, economic, technological, and cultural — is an intrinsic and constitutive dimension of the church's evangelizing mission. One text frequently invoked by the Asian bishops is the 1971 Synod of Bishops' *Justice in the World* which affirms that "action in behalf of justice and participation in the transformation of the world fully appear to us as a constitutive dimension of the preaching of the Gospel, that is, of the mission of the Church for the redemption of the human race and its liberation from every oppressive situation"[14]. "Human Development," says the BISA V, "is the profound concept that translates sharply for our time the simple and fundamental command of the Gospel that we love one another"[15].

If the link between evangelization and work for human development is not adventitious but essential, it is made more crucial and urgent for the Asian churches, the FABC consistently argues, by the situation of massive poverty and pervasive oppression in all Asian countries. In its first plenary assembly, the FABC declares: "It is our belief that it is from the material deprivation of our poor people, as well as their tremendous human potential, and from their aspirations for a more fully human and brotherly world, that Christ is calling the churches of Asia"[16]. Again: "Since mil-

---

[13] *For All*, 208 (no. 5).
[14] *For All*, 15-16 (no. 22); 20, (no. 5); 21 (no. 9); 23 (no. 18); 208 (no. 4).
[15] *For All*, 218 (no. 6).
[16] *For All*, 16 (no. 22). The second plenary assembly, whose theme is prayer as the life of the church of Asia, affirms: "Far from alienating us from sharing in man's responsibility for the world and for the establishment of just and loving relationships among men and groups in society, prayer commits us to the true liberation of persons. It binds us to solidarity with the poor and the powerless, the mar-

lions in Asia are poor, the Church in Asia must be the Church of the poor. One element in holiness, here, is the practice of justice. Evangelization and development are not opposed. In Asia today they are integral parts of preaching the Gospel"[17].

Integral, Total Development

Another idea consistently developed by the FABC is that the human development which the church seeks to pro-

---

ginalized and oppressed in our societies". See *For All*, 33 (no. 23). The third plenary assembly, whose theme is the church as a community of faith in Asia, again stresses this urgency: "Our theological vision must be turned ever more resolutely to the Church's responsibility in the world, in the public spheres, in the construction of a more fully human future for Asian peoples. We must go beyond merely seconding Pope John Paul 's words, that 'the preference for the poor is a Christian preference,' and that 'it expresses the concern of Christ who came to proclaim a message of salvation to the poor,...the poor who are indeed loved by (the) God ... who guarantees their rights.' We must now make them the real pattern of our daily praxis". See *For All*, 60 (no. 17.1). The fourth plenary assembly, whose theme is the vocation and mission of the laity in the church and in the world of Asia, asserts: "Deep in the heart of Asia, the Paschal Mystery of Jesus is being remembered, becomes present and is relived. The immersion into the darkness of suffering, pain, death and despair brings the light of the Resurrection — its hope, justice, love and peace, integral liberation. This we believe is the promise of the Father". See *For All*, 178 (no. 1.4). The fifth plenary assembly, whose theme is journeying together toward the third millennium, recognizes the challenge of continuing injustice for the church's evangelizing mission: "... We evangelize because the Gospel is *leaven* for liberation and for the transformation of society. Our Asian world needs the values of the Kingdom and of Christ in order to bring about the human development, justice, peace and harmony with God, among peoples and with all creation that the peoples of Asia long for". See *For All*, 281 (no. 3.2.5). Finally, the sixth assembly, whose theme is Christian discipleship in Asia today in service to life, asserts: "Like Jesus, we have to 'pitch our tents' in the midst of all humanity building a better world, but especially among the suffering and the poor, the marginalized and the downtrodden of Asia. In profound 'solidarity with suffering humanity' and led by the Spirit of life, we need to immerse ourselves in Asia's cultures of poverty and deprivation, from whose depths the aspirations for love and life are most poignant and compelling. Serving life demands communion with every woman and man seeking and struggling for life, in the way of Jesus' solidarity with humanity" (*Christian Discipleship in Asia Today: Service to Life*, no. 14.2; henceforth, *Christian Discipleship*).

[17] *For All*, 23 (no. 18). The BIMA II in 1980 noted: "Among the forms of evangelization called for in our South Asian context our attention was first drawn to the need to promote integral human development and to witness to justice in our societies .... We stressed the need for our Churches to stand in protest wherever human rights are denied, irrespective of creed and caste, and to denounce structures of society which perpetuate an unjust social order". See *For All*, 100 (no. 12).

mote must be total or integral. It was forcefully expressed at the 1970 historic meeting of one hundred eighty Asian bishops in Manila on the occasion of Paul VI's visit to the Philippines. Their message, which has served as the theological manifesto for the FABC's subsequent plenary assemblies, states: "Resolutely we commit ourselves to the concern for the *total development* of our peoples. We believe that man's humanity is God's gift and making, and its promotion a task and duty laid on all of us by Him"[18]. The sixth plenary assembly expresses this integral development in terms of "holistic life": "Ours is a vision of *holistic life*, life that is achieved and entrusted to every person and every community of persons, regardless of gender, creed or culture, class or color. It is the fruit of integral development, the authentic development of the whole person and of every person"[19].

This total or integral nature of human development is understood in four senses. First, human development must embrace all the dimensions of the human person as a unity of body-psyche-spirit. The FABC explicitly rejects the reduction of human development to economic and technological progress. As will be seen below, it is precisely this reductionism that, according to the FABC, is causing havoc to the Asian peoples. In particular, with regard to the process of modernization, the FABC, while recognizing its benefits for the future of Asia, is aware that "modernization often leads to social and cultural dislocation. Traditional values and attitudes are called into question. Traditional symbols lose their power. The beneficiaries of modernization are too often infected with secularism, materialism and consumerism. In some countries there has arisen a new middle class which is highly consumeristic and competitive, and in general insensitive and indifferent to the overwhelming majority of poor and marginalized people"[20].

Secondly, total human development means that all resources and means, hence not only technological and material ones, should be pressed into service. In particular, the

---

[18] *For All*, 6 (no. 21). Emphasis added.
[19] *Christian Discipleship*, no. 10.
[20] *For All*, 276 (no. 2-1 6).

FABC singles out prayer as an effective means to achieve "integral human development": "Christian prayer is necessary for genuine human liberation and development, and to bring man to his full stature as a son of God"[21].

Thirdly, in order to be total and integral, the church's efforts for human development must go hand in hand with the other two components of its mission, namely, inculturation and interreligious dialogue. Indeed, it is part of the originality and depth of the FABC's theology of human development is that it is not conceived as an activity the church undertakes in parallel to dialogue with other religions and inculturation, but as intimately intertwined with these two activities whose success conditions the full development of the human person in Asia. The FABC repeatedly links the three ministries together: "These are the elements of crucial importance in the task of preaching the Gospel in Asia today:

— *Inculturation*, which renders the local church truly present within the life of our people.

— *Dialogue* with the great Asian religions, which brings them into contact with the Gospel, so that the Word in them may come to full flower.

— *Service of the poor*, uniting with them in the struggle for a more human world"[22].

Fourthly, human development, to be total and integral, must go beyond the human family and be extended to the cosmos as such. The BISA VII underlines the ecological motif of the FABC's understanding of human development: "A new spirituality that will suffuse evangelization and embrace the plan of God for the whole creation is imperative. Mere individual salvation is not enough; salvation must be for the whole person, all people and even for the cosmos. This spirituality must not be inward looking but must place the Church at the service of the whole human race"[23].

---

[21] *For All*, 41 (no. 16). Note that the two terms 'development' and 'liberation' are often used together, given the fact that in Asia lack of full human development is the result of oppressive structures. The FABC notes that these two terms are to be understood in the sense given them by *Populorum Progressio* and *Evangelii Nuntiandi*. See *For All*, 58, footnote.

[22] *For All*, 23 (no. 20).

[23] *For All*, 230 (no. 5). The BISA VII is here echoing and expanding a statement of the BISA VI: "The task of evangelization in the field of human develop-

In sum, for the FABC, human development is not merely an ethical injunction but a strict imperative and a constitutive dimension of the church's evangelizing mission. Furthermore, it must aim at the total and integral perfection of the human person as a unity of body, soul, and spirit, of the human community, and of the cosmos. It must avail itself of all the means and resources available, and must be carried out in tandem with inculturation and interreligious dialogue.

The Method of Social Action for Human Development

The FABC is deeply aware that though human development is an essential part of the proclamation of the Gospel, the Gospel itself does not provide ready-made solutions for the social, political, economic, and cultural of contemporary Asia: "The need has been felt to analyse critically and technically the problems we are faced with. We cannot jump from our faith experience to the concrete decisions of social action without due technical investigations and due account of the ideologies under whose influence we are living"[24].

To help persons engaged in programs of human development arrive at appropriate policies and effective courses of action, the BISA VII has outlined a methodology called the "pastoral cycle." It is composed of four steps. The first (*exposure-immersion*) exposes the agents of human development to and immerse them in the concrete situation of the poor with whom and for whom they work: "Exposure is like a doctor's visit for diagnosis; immersion is like the visit of a genuine friend entering into the dialogue-of-life. Exposure-Immersion ... follows the basic principle of the Incarnation..."[25].

---

ment is not worthy of the name unless it is suffused with spirituality. This spirituality embraces the plan of God for the whole creation. It is a spirituality that cannot be reduced to merely individual salvation but embraces the whole man and all men and the rest of creation". See *For All*, 226 (no. 18).

[24] *For All*, 204 (no 9).

[25] *For All*, 131 (no. 8). This exposure-immersion should not be seen merely as a temporary phase, though often it takes place in a short period of time. The FABC repeatedly insists that the church must share the lives and the poverty of the people to whom it proclaims the Good News: "Quite clearly, then, there is a definite path along which the Spirit has been leading the discernment of the Asian Church: the Church of Asia must become the Church of the poor" (*For All*, 145

The second step is *social analysis*. The objects to be investigated include the social, economic, political, cultural and religious systems in society as well as the signs of the times, the events of history, and the needs and aspirations of the people. Indeed, without this technical analysis, the International Congress on Mission points out, "the naivete of all too many Christians regarding the structural causes of poverty and injustice often leads them to the adoption of ineffective measures in their attempts to promote justice and human rights"[26]. The FABC does not specify which method of social analysis to be employed. However, it warns of the danger of "deception either by ideology or self-interest" and of incompleteness[27].

This brings us to the third step, namely, "integration of social analysis with the religio-cultural reality, discerning not only its negative and enslaving aspects but also its positive, prophetic aspects that can inspire genuine spirituality"[28]. This step requires *contemplation* in order to discover God's active presence in the society and preferential love for the poor. This contemplative dimension of human development brings the agents of social development into a sympathetic and respectful dialogue with Asia's great religions and the religiosity of the poor. Through this double dialogue, the authentic values of the Gospel are discovered and appreciated such as "simplicity of life, genuine openness and generous sharing, community consciousness and family loyalty"[29].

The fourth step is *pastoral planning*, which seeks to complete the first three steps by formulating practical and

---

[no. 6]). This phase corresponds to *praxis* which Latin American liberation theology insists as the methodological presupposition for doing theology.

[26] *For All*, 145 (no. 9). Indeed, almost all documents issued by the FABC and its various institutes invariably begin with a careful analysis of the social, political, economic, cultural, and religious condition of Asia or parts of Asia as appropriate.

[27] *For All*, 231 (no. 9). Implicitly, the FABC considers Marxist social analysis, which was favored by early Latin American liberation theology, insufficient for the Asian situation.

[28] *For All*, 231 (no. 10). The FABC's sixth plenary assembly suggests that "social analysis be integrated with cultural analysis, and both subjected to faith-discernment". See *For All*, 285 (no. 7.3.2.1.1).

[29] *For All*, 232 (no. 11). Aloysius Pieris calls this step "introspection": He argues that "a 'liberation-theopraxis' in Asia that uses only the Marxist tools of *social analysis will* remain un-Asian and ineffective until it integrates the psychological tools of *introspection* which our sages have discovered" (*An Asian Theology of Liberation* [Maryknoll, New York: Orbis Books, 1988], 80).

realistic policies, strategies, and plans of action in favor of integral human development. As these policies, strategies and plans of action are implemented, they are continuously submitted to evaluation by a renewal of the first three steps of the pastoral cycle[30].

HUMAN DEVELOPMENT IN ASIA:
CHALLENGES AND RESPONSES

On the basis of this pastoral cycle, what does the FABC propose for human development and progress in contemporary Asia? In other words, corresponding to the four steps of the pastoral cycle, it may be asked: (1) How does the FABC understand exposure to and immersion in the world of Asia as a part of evangelization? (2) Which problems and challenges facing the peoples of Asia and the church does it discern? (3) Which cultural and religious resources does it appeal to in formulating the church's responses to these problems and challenges? (4) Lastly, what policies, strategies, and concrete plans of action does it recommend for the church's ministry? It is of course impossible to answer these questions in full, given their complexity and extensive scope. I will single out only the most significant elements of the FABC's documents in answering these questions, keeping in mind the chronological progression of these documents, since their focus shifted according to the events and issues that arose during the FABC's quarter of the century existence.

The Asian Church's Preferential Option for the Poor

With humility and courage the Asian bishops have made the preferential option for the poor the fundamental direction of the church of Asia. Already at the 1970 historic meet-

---

[30] See *For All*, 232 (no. *12*). There is a parallel between the FABC's "pastoral cycle" and the method of Latin American liberation theology. Clodovis Boff describes the method of liberation theology as composed of three mediations: socio-analytic mediation (=social analysis), hermeneutic mediation (= contemplation), and practical mediation (= pastoral planning). These three mediations are preceded and accompanied by praxis in favor of justice and liberation (= exposure-immersion). See CLODOVIS BOFF, *Theology and Praxis: Epistemological Foundations*, trans. Robert R. Barr (Maryknoll, New York: Orbis Books, 1987).

ing in Manila, they declared: "It is our resolve, first of all, to be more truly 'the Church of the poor.' If we are to place ourselves at the side of the multitudes in our continent, we must in our way of life share something of their poverty. The Church cannot set up islands of affluence in a sea of want and misery; our own personal lives must give witness to evangelical simplicity, and no man, no matter how lowly or poor, should find it hard to come to us and find in us their brothers"[31]. The church of Asia as the "church of the poor" has become the *cantus firmus* of all the documents of the FABC and its various institutes. This option for the poor, according to the FABC, is mandated not only by Jesus and his message but also by the situation of Asia in which the teeming masses labor under crushing poverty.

In the midst of this dehumanizing poverty and oppression, however, there exists a gap, as the 1979 International Congress in Mission honestly confessed, between the words the Asian church preaches and its witness: "The Church in Asia is not known by the multitudes of the poor to be passionately concerned for their rights and dignity as human beings not selflessly committed to their total liberation from social injustice and oppression"[32].

Given the persistence of this situation, in its latest plenary assembly in 1995, the FABC felt compelled to urge again: "Like Jesus, we have to 'pitch our tents' in the midst of all humanity building a better world, but especially among the suffering and the poor, the marginalized and the down-

---

[31] *For All*, 5 (no. 19).

[32] *For All*, 145 (no. 8). In its third plenary assembly in 1982, the FABC is even harsher in its evaluation of the Asian churches: "How often too, our communities, especially among those more favored in life, have failed to grow in awareness of situations of social injustice, of the violation of human dignity and human rights massively present around them.... How indifferent and hesitant, only too often, has been our involvement in the concerns of human development and liberation; in issues where the rights of women, the poor and the powerless, are crushed; where the relationships and structures which perpetuate injustice and exploitation in society are extended and reinforced.... How little, in Asia, have we spoken or taken action against the oppression and degradation of women, especially among the poor and less educated, for the purposes and profits of various exploitative industries, tourism, the sex-trades, and the like" (*For All*, 58 [9.7-9.8]). One can hardly accuse the FABC of covering up its inadequacies and failings, a practice allegedly typical of Asians to " save one's face"!

trodden of Asia. In profound 'solidarity with suffering humanity' and led by the Spirit of life, we need to immerse ourselves in Asia's cultures of poverty and deprivation, from whose depths the aspirations of love and life are most poignant and compelling. Serving life demands communion with every woman and man seeking and struggling for life, in the way of Jesus' solidarity with humanity"[33].

The Changing Faces and Challenges of Asia

The FABC is aware that Asia is an extremely vast and variegated continent with two-thirds of the human population, and that therefore it is impossible to provide a common description of the social, political, economic, cultural, and religious situation of Asia. Nevertheless, in order to gauge the scope of the task of human development in Asian countries, it is important to examine how the FABC, in the light of its social analysis, envisions the challenges facing Asia and the church today. Given space constraints, it is only possible to list these challenges with the help of the successive summaries given by the FABC and their institutes.

In 1983, the BISA VI asked if there were "new or old and increasing obstacles and challenges to human development in Asia in the 1980s" and answered its own question as follows: "The new challenges that aggravate the old challenges to human development are the increasing militarization of the continent, the militant resurgence of traditional non-Christian religions like Islam, Buddhism and Hinduism and Asia's increased dependence on global economies .... Unjust trade and aid conditions, export-oriented industries and capital intensive technology, transnational corporations, agribusiness enterprises and tourism.... The global centers of economic power manipulate the mass media in Asian countries to create artificial needs that promote the production of luxury goods. This results in a consumerism which subtly undermines the deeply religious values of Asian cultures and erodes the moral fiber of the Asian peoples"[34].

---

[33] *Christian Discipleship*, no. 3.
[34] *For All*, 224 (no. 5).

Three years later, in 1986, the FABC's fourth plenary assembly enumerates the following problems affecting the workers: "... We likewise recognize that these dreams and efforts for integral liberation are being shattered by complex, mutually reinforcing powers that are often beyond the control of workers: the dominance of transnational corporations and large local companies in traditional indultries and their incursion in agribusiness, taking advantage of cheap labor or appropriating the land of small landowners; the banning of strikes and trade unions and so repressing legitimate protests; the exodus of rural workers into already overcrowded urban slums as the cities' cheap labor; the lack of supportive organizations among the vast majority of urban workers, small landowners and landless peasants; long hours of work, harassment, job insecurity and accident hazards; deterioration of health; unemployment and underemployment. Clearly, political, economic and agricultural structures have made both urban and rural workers cogs of an anonymous productive machine, their work a dispensable commodity depending only on the law of supply and demand"[35].

In particular, the fourth plenary assembly singles out the plight of Asian women: "International media have highlighted how tourism and the entertainment industries have exploied, degraded and dehumanized Asian women .... Many are the injustices heaped upon them because of the traditional societies which discriminate against them and because of the new economic and industrial situations. Dowry, forced marriages, wife-beating and destruction of female fetuses weigh heavily on them, driving many to desperation and even suicide. Modern industry exploits their work.... There is discrimination against them in the employment policies, and as domestic workers they are also abused. In general, Asian society views women as inferior"[36].

Finally, in 1995 the sixth plenary assembly gives another list of the grave threats to human development: "We were alarmed at how the global economy is ruled by market forces to the detriment of peoples' real needs. We considered the in-

---

[35] *For All*, 187-88 (no. 3.7.2).
[36] *For All*, 182-83 (no. 3.3.1).

security and vulnerability of migrants, refugees, the displaced ethnic and indigenous peoples, and the pain and agonies of exploited workers, especially the child laborers in our countries .... We recognized the growing violence, terrorism, conflicts and nuclear proliferation fueled by the arms race and greed for profit .... In the area of religious pluralism, we reflected on the growing fundamentalist extremism and fanaticism discriminating and excluding people who belong to other religious traditions .... As we reflected on these negative areas, we could not ignore the immense damage to the ecosystem of our planet which offends justice and the rights of people"[37].

These lists, though by no means exhaustive, of the challenges to human development in Asia seem endless and are overwhelming. What is significant is that in analyzing these challenges the Asian bishops look for their structural causes: "We bishops and our experts came to see the causes of this distressing situation. Because of colonialism and feudalism and the introduction of Western classical capitalism, the traditional texture of Asian society with its inbuilt balances has been disrupted. Often the economies of these countries are not geared primarily to satisfying the requirements of the nation but rather to responding to external markets, and within the nation, not to the basic needs of people (food, housing, education, jobs) but to the demands of a consumer society. The principal beneficiaries of this system are the foreign markets and investors and the local elites. The victims are the poor who are the majority of the people"[38].

---

[37] *Christian Discipleship*, no. 7.

[38] *For All*, 212 (nos. 4 and 5). In terms of the social mediation of the method of Latin American liberation theology, the Asian bishops go beyond the *empirical* explanation (e.g., poverty as vice) and *the functional* explanation (poverty as backwardness) to the *dialectical* explanation (poverty as a collective and conflictive phenomenon, as the result of exploitation and oppression). As the first plenary assembly in 1974 says about the Asian poor: "Poor, in that they are deprived of access to material goods and resources.... Deprived, because they live under oppression, that is, under social, economic, and political structures which have injustice built into them" (*For All*, 15 [no. 19]). Again, the BISA I affirms: "Our people are deprived of the goods and opportunities to which they have a right because they are *oppressed*. They live under economic, social, and political structures which have injustice built into them" (*For All*, 199 [no. 2]). For the three ways of understanding the cause of poverty, see LEONARDO BOFF and CLODOVIS BOFF, *Intro-*

As mentioned above, the Asian bishops are deeply ambivalent about modernity and the process of modernization in Asia. In particular, they strongly criticize the economic system associated with modernization, namely, capitalism or free enterprise. While recognizing that capitalism "proved its ability to organize labor for higher productivity and to unleash the modern technological imagination," and "has considerably liberated the entrepreneurial and managerial classes," the bishops note that "it has also degraded the working class to being a dispensable commodity"[39]. On the other hand, the FABC is also highly critical of centrally-planned economies or socialism. While recognizing that socialist economies "have rightly stressed that it is the workers who create the economy," the bishops point out that "they have mediated workers' control and solidarity exclusively through a centralized state. The workers are left with a new form of social domination, viz. the state"[40].

Cultural and Religious Resources

Despite the overwhelming challenges facing human development in Asia, the Asian bishops profess courage and hope. The basis for their optimistic attitude is rooted of course in the Christian faith, but it also springs from their

---

ducing Liberation Theology, trans. Paul Burns (Maryknoll, New York: Orbis Books, 1987), 25-27.

[39] *For All*, 189 (no. 3.8.2). In 1978, the BISA IV drew an interesting parallel between contemporary Asia and nineteenth-century Europe: "The Asian nations are now living through a cycle comparable to that of the 19th century Europe in which human beings and human values are sacrificed ruthlessly to maximum profits. The application of *laissez faire* economy to the already unbalanced systems of Asia, with little of the checks and balances that evolved in developed economies, demonstrates that it can be as pernicious now as it was then" *(For All*, 212 [no. 6]).

[40] *For All*, 189 (no. 3.8.3). In 1978, the BISA IV rejected both communism and classical capitalism: "Communism plays a very important role in Asia by the very fact that some 46% of all Asians live in communist states. We are aware that communism presents different faces throughout the world. But its Asian face makes us apprehensive, although we cannot deny that they also present some positive aspects. We have criticized classical capitalism because while professedly promoting economic growth, it has deprived man of the just fruits of his labor. We now criticize communism because, while professedly promoting liberation, it has deprived man of his just human rights. In their historical realization both have hindered true human development, the one creating poverty in the midst of affluence, the other destroying freedom in the pursuit of equality" (*For All*, 213 [no. 13]).

conviction that Asia possesses rich resources to respond to these challenges. As the BISA I puts it with justifiable pride: "The overwhelming majority of our people are poor, but let it be clearly understood what we mean by 'poor.' Our people are *not* poor as far as cultural tradition, human values, and religious insights are concerned. In these things of the spirit, they are immensely rich.... If, then, the Church in Southeast Asia is to be a Church of the people, it must be a Church that recognizes in what our people are rich: our Asian traditions, cultures, values"[41].

What are, concretely, the resources at the disposal of the church in its efforts for human development? Again, it is only possible to list them here without much commentary. They are the teeming masses of the poor themselves who are not only the object of evangelization but also its primary agents[42]; the Asian youth who form some 60% of the population with their idealism, energy, zeal and determination, and commitment[43]; Asian religions with their scriptures, rituals, spiritual and monastic traditions, their techniques of contemplation, and their commitment to social justice[44]; prayer itself[45]; and Asian philosophies of ontological complementarity (yin-yang) and cosmic harmony[46]. The bishops repeatedly recom-

---

[41] *For All*, 199 (nos. 2-3).

[42] The International Congress on Mission affirms: "... the poor are ultimately the privileged community and agents of salvation (as has always been the case in the history of salvation)" (*For All*, 144 [no. 4]).

[43] On Asian youth and their role in evangelization and human development, see *For All*, 181-82. The fourth plenary assembly says: "The youth of Asia are the Asia of today The compulsive struggle for liberation in Asia are reflected in the pains of growth among the youth and in their deepest longings for a new world and a meaning for life. The People of God In Asia must become in a certain sense a 'Church of the young'" (*For All*, 182 [no. 3.2.5]).

[44] The second plenary assembly says: "The spirituality characteristic of the religions of our continent stresses a deeper awareness of God and the whole self in recollection, silence and prayer, flowering in openness to others, in compassion, non-violence, generosity" (*For All*, 35 [no. 35]).

[45] On prayer as a means for social transformation, see the entire document of the second plenary assembly in *For All*, 29-44. One statement bears quoting: "Christian prayer is necessary for genuine human liberation and development, and to bring man to his full stature as a son of God" (*For All*, 41 [no. 16]).

[46] The BIRA IV/11 says: "When we look into our traditional cultures and heritages, we note that they are inspired by a vision of unity. The universe is perceived as an organic whole with a web of relations knitting together each and every part of it. The nature and the human are not viewed as antagonistic to each other, but as

mend that these abundant resources be harnessed to meet the challenges facing human development in Asia today.

Responses and Plans of Action for Integral Human Development

The issue under consideration here is not the Asian church's specific plans for the social, political, and economic progress of Asia. Indeed, as a community of faith, the church can only say with certainty which policies and concrete plans of action, from the moral standpoint, are acceptable in so far as they agree or conflict with the values of the Gospel. But the church is unable to judge apodictically which policy and course of action will lead to a greater degree of total human development in a particular location and at a specific time. In general, as pointed out above, the church insists that any concrete plan for human development must aim at the integral, total development and liberation of the whole person, each and every person, the human community, and the cosmos itself and ought to make use of all the resources available, and not only technological and material ones[47].

Within these parameters it is possible to enumerate some of the key recommendations put forward by the FABC for human development. First and foremost, the FABC again and again insists that the church of (and not only in) Asia must be "the church of the poor," with a conscious and effective preferential option for the poor.

Second, it also repeatedly insists that action for social, political, and economic development must be carried out in tandem with interreligious dialogue and inculturation. Without inculturation, social action is cut off from the deepest roots of the people for and with whom it is done; without interreligious dialogue, it is bereft of the transforming power of religious symbols and rituals.

---

chords in a universal symphony. The whole reality is maintained in unity through a universal rhyme (*Rta; Tao*)". See *For All*, 319 (no. 6). Obviously, this concept of harmony and balance is vital for developing an ecological theology.

[47] See *For All*, 213 (no. 12): "Our task, therefore, is not to propose specific blueprints for social, economic and political measure on existing situations and proposals against the values of the Gospel in order to point up directions which genuine humanization must take".

Third, in connection with interreligious dialogue, the FABC recommends that in order to be effective, action for human progress be performed in cooperation with the followers of other religions. This is demanded not only because of the minuscule number of Christians in Asia and their extremely limited resources, but also because certain social evils, e.g., discriminations based on the caste system and injustices caused by religious fundamentalism, cannot be eradicated without necessary changes in religious understanding and structures[48].

Fourth, since division among Christians is a scandal to Asians and constitutes a serious obstacle for evangelization, the FABC urges that "all Christian Churches should make a joint effort at evangelizing in the measure which the imperfect union already existing among them allows"[49]. It goes without saying that this joint effort should be extended to projects for human development as part of evangelization.

Fifth, the church cannot carry out its task of promotion of social transformation without enlarging significantly the role of the laity, especially women and youth[50].

Sixth, in connection with the role of the laity, the FABC recommends the establishment of more Basic Christian Communities: "The basic fact is that today in our Asian context we are in the process of re-discovering that the individual Christian can best survive, grow and develop as a Christian person in the midst of a self-nourishing, self-governing, self-ministering and self-propagating Christian community"[51].

---

[48] Thus, with regard to the dialogue between Christianity and Hinduism, the BIRA III says: "Christianity can stress the social and structural dimensions of religious commitment and encourage every value and attitude that would give a positive role to man and his creative effort in history to build up a new humanity of justice and brotherhood, while questioning in itself the tendency to privatize and ritualize religion and its easy acceptance of the evils of the caste system" (*For All*, 121 [no. 11]). With regard to religious revivalism and fundamentalism, the fourth plenary assembly says: "The negative aspect of the phenomenon, tending to religious dogmatism, fundamentalism and intolerance in precept and practice, has even led to violence and serious conflicts" (*For All*, 181 [no. 3.1.9]).

[49] *For All*, 98 (no. 6).

[50] On the role of the laity, see the entire document of the fourth plenary assembly on the vocation and mission of the laity in *For All*, 178-98.

[51] *For All*, 77 (no. 49). Though the language here is reminiscent of the Chinese Patriotic Church with its three "selfs", the intention of course is not to encour-

Seventh, the FABC urges that the various institutions of the church such as high schools, colleges and universities, health care facilities, and other social service agencies direct its activities primarily in the service of the poor[52].

Eighth, the use of mass media is strongly encouraged for evangelization and human development[53].

Ninth, with regard to economic models themselves, after criticizing both classical capitalism and socialism, the FABC argues that "the future, it would seem to us, lies in pioneering new forms of worker participation in industry — ranging from the renewal of the cooperative movement to worker cooperation in mixed or privately-held enterprises. This also means shaping an appropriate technology that prevents the concentration of power in the hands of a few, and supporting the use of technology in the service of labor and not the reverse. Such a model means developing small-scale technology that workers can own and control, at least as a cooperative"[54]. This is as concretely as the FABC has gone to recommend a particular economic system for human development appropriate for Asia which seems to negotiate a middle path between *laissez-faire* economy and centrally-controlled economic development.

Tenth, and lastly, the FABC is aware that the church's social action often encounters the reality of conflict. But it

---

age division and schism but co-responsibility and collegiality of the laity in forming truly local churches.

[52] On the education for justice and human development, see *For All*, 33-34, 156-59, 185-86, 214-15. In particular, with the role of Catholic universities, the FABC says: "The Catholic university is urgently asked to play a leading role in development education. Hence, the Catholic university should search for and formulate a model of human development, based on the social teachings of the Church" (158 [no. 16]). On health services, see *For All*, 190-91: "But even greater than the concern for the renewal of our traditional health institutions should be our concern for the great masses of the poor in rural areas who are very often deprived of the basic benefits of modern medicine due to their poverty and the lack of adequate medical services" (191 [3.9.6]).

[53] See *For All*, 162-63, 186-87, 291-92. The use of media in favor of the poor is incumbent especially on the laity, especially because the mass media in Asia are predominantly controlled by authoritarian governments or by a handful of economically and politically powerful persons: "This vision will require of the People of God, especially of its leadership, a supportive stance toward the systematic formation and training of the laity to assume even greater responsibilities in the media" (187 [no. 3.6.6]).

[54] *For All*, 189 [no. 3.8.4]).

takes care to stress two points: First, "conflict is not necessarily violence (which needs another process of discernment), nor is it necessarily opposed to Christian charity. Secondly, conflict is often a necessary means to attain true dialogue with people in authority. The poor do not achieve this until they have shown they are no longer servile and afraid"[55].

A NEW WAY OF BEING CHURCH

By way of evaluation, it may be said on the one hand that the FABC's theology of human development represents no significant departure from the current social teaching of the church, especially as this has been articulated by Popes Paul VI and John Paul II. Its insistence on human development and liberation as an intrinsic dimension of evangelization and on the necessity of aiming at total and integral development echoes the teaching of Paul VI. Its criticism of capitalism and socialism reflects much of John Paul's. And, of course, even if it has not cited the works of Latin American liberation theologians, it is heavily indebted to them for its insights on the preferential option for the poor, Christ as the liberator, the church as the "church of the poor," salvation as including social, economic, and political liberation, basic Christian communities, and social analysis as an intrinsic element of the theological method.

On the other hand, the FABC has also modified and significantly enriched the contributions of papal social teaching and Latin American liberation theology. Methodologically, in addition to social analysis, it has included "contemplation" or "introspection" into the way of doing theology[56]. Most importantly, it has made interreligious dialogue and inculturation necessary phases of the church's work for liberation to avoid possible distortions of a one-sided emphasis on the material and political aspects of salvation[57]. In so doing, it

---

[55] *For All*, 213 (no. 9).

[56] As mentioned above, the necessity of using contemplation has been repeatedly urged by Aloysius Pieris in his *An Asian Theology of Liberation* (Maryknoll: Orbis Books, 1988), 79-81.

[57] It may be argued that by combining these three aspects of the church's ministry together, the FABC has improved upon papal teachings on human development and most Western theologies of inculturation and interreligious dialogue.

can avail itself of richer and vaster resources for human development that are deeply rooted in the histories and lives of the peoples of Asia[58]. As a consequence, it has expanded and enriched basic Christian communities with "basic human communities"[59]. Furthermore, while adopting the dialectical analysis of poverty as the result of oppression and exploitation, the FABC is much less critical of the development model than Latin American theologians and has welcomed the assistance of various international organizations such as the United Nations, the World Council of Churches, Caritas Internationalis, Misereor, Sodepax and so on[60].

A complete evaluation of the FABC's theology of human progress, however, cannot limit itself to its theoretical aspects. Indeed, in all its declarations on human development in Asia, what the FABC has been doing is proposing a new way of being church, not in the sense of a novel abstract ecclesiology, but a new concrete praxis for all Christians . The FABC's sixth plenary assembly, reviewing its achievements during its twenty-five year existence, admits as much: "The overall thrust of activities in recent years has been to motivate the Churches of Asia towards 'a new way of being Church,' a Church that is committed to becoming 'a community of communities' and a credible sign of salvation and liberation"[61].

Despite the remarkable progress of the Asian churches in the last quarter of the century, as recently as 1991, the FABC Office of Evangelization admitted with candor: "The

---

[58] For a discussion of Asian resources for doing theology, see CHOAN SENG SONG, *Third-Eye Theology*, revised edition (Maryknoll: Orbis Books, 1990), 1-16; idem, *Theology from the Womb of Asia* (Maryknoll: Orbis, 1986); and *Doing Theology with Asian Resources*, ed. John C. England and Archie C. C. Lee (Auckland, New Zealand: Pace Publishing, 1993).

[59] On "basic human community", see ALOYSIUS PIERIS, *Fire & Water: Basic Issues in Asian Buddhism and Christianity* (Maryknoll: Orbis Books, 1996), 161: "What happens in the BHCs is a veritable *symbiosis* of religions. Each religion, challenged by the other religion's unique approach to the liberationist aspiration of the poor ... discovers and renames itself in its specificity in response to the other approaches".

[60] For a critique of the development model, see GUSTAVO GUTIÉRREZ, *A Theology of Liberation*, trans. Sister Caridad and John Eagleson (Maryknoll: Orbi Books, 1991), 13-25.

[61] *Christian Discipleship*, no. 3.

Church remains foreign in its lifestyle, in its institutional structures, in its worship, in its western-trained leadership and in its theology. Christian rituals often remain formal, neither spontaneous nor particularly Asian. There is a gap between leaders and ordinary believers in the Church, a *fortiori* with members of other faiths. The Church has created a powerful priestly class with little lay participation. Seminary formation often alienates the seminarian from the people. Biblical, systematic and historical theology as taught are often unpastoral and unAsian"[62]. Again: "... The Church is often giving a counter-witness to its evangelizing mission. This is most notable in its lack of practical identification with the poor, its lack of concrete involvement in interfaith dialogue and its lack of real interest in interculturation .... The Church is an institution planted in Asia rather than an evangelizing community of Asia"[63]. Words such as these would have sounded as an anti-Christian diatribe had they not come from an official organ of the FABC itself!

This FABC's harsh criticism of the Asian churches was not prompted by self-hatred but by a deep and lively sense of the church's critical role in the present situation of Asia, indeed of the possibility of its very survival. The 1977 colloquium on ecclesial ministries expressed this self-understanding of the church in dramatic terms: "We are fast approaching one of the most decisive turning points of world history and church history in Asia. Asia, with 60% of the planet's population, will at the turn of the century be the most populous, and probably the least Christian continent in terms of numbers. If Asian Christianity is not by then the leaven in the dough of the new Asia that is taking shape, it runs the risk of being wiped out in the dramatic events which might take place within the next few decades"[64]. Again: "The decisive new phenomenon for Christianity in Asia will be the emergence of genuine Christian communities in Asia — Asian in their way of thinking, praying, living, communicating their own Christ-experience to others .... If the Asian

---

[62] *For All*, 337 (no. 13).
[63] *For All*, 338 (no 15).
[64] *For All*, 69 (no. 13).

Churches do not discover their own identity, they will have no future"[65].

With the hindsight of more than twenty years, arguments pro and con the fulfilment of this prediction may be mounted from any quarter. One thing remains indisputable, however, and that is, if the Christian church does not become "a servant Church: servant of God, servant of Christ, servant of his plan of salvation; servant of the Asian peoples, of their deep hopes, longings and aspirations; servant of the followers of other religions, of all men and women, simply and totally for others"[66], it would cease to be the church of the gospel of Jesus Christ. And one way to become a "servant church" is for Christians fully to engage in efforts for the integral, total development and liberation of the Asian peoples.

---

[65] *For All*, 70 (no. 14, ii).
[66] *For All*, 340 (no. 23).

A Hindu Call to Humanism

Swami Rama

In this age of high technology, no community or race can maintain its existence without associating with other communities and races. So there must be better understanding among human beings. We have to share one another's losses and gains. We have to learn from each other's losses and gains. We have to learn from each other's experiences for our own growth. We have to promote the growth of others. rising above superiority and inferiority complexes, different groups of people must work together toward a common goal — that of peace and happiness. Different nations, religions, and cultures of the world must recognize their strength and weakness.

The contribution of science and technology cannot be undermined. Science has made the world quite small. Physical distances do not separate people the way they once did. Although people have begun sharing each other's material products, they do not share their thoughts and feelings. It appears that because material objects have brought them together, people have begun to regard each other as means for gaining material benefits. Because of a lack of spiritual awareness, human beings consider this world to be the sole reality. Consequently, they are busy in the race for material development. Their materialistic world view feeds their egos and creates inequality, discrimination, and odd complexes in our society.

The human race is suffering from its ego-born narrow-mindedness. Discrimination exists, based on religion, color, and nationality. In the same locality, people are being discriminated against just because they are European or Asian, black or white, Hindu or Moslem. As long as these man-made divisions exist in our society, there is no hope for peace and happiness. We must understand that we are born as humans and all other identifications are superimposed on us later.

Loving others and receiving love from others is our birthright. True freedom means loving all and hating none, including all and excluding none. For cultivating the true human within, we have to reach out to the hearts of our fellow beings. Political treaties and alliances are of little value. There has to be a desire in every human heart to overcome mutual differences that have been artificially imposed by selfish political, social, and religious leaders.

Removing differences and moving from diversity to unity are the essence of real spiritual practices. This process has to occur at every level of our individual and social lives. By realizing one Reality within all, we will be able to purify our hearts and minds. This purification can lead us to the experience of the Divine Light within.

Once we experience the Truth within, we will find ourselves to be a part of the universe, and vice versa. Upon such realization here and now, we will not need to imagine a heaven apart from this universe. By loving all and excluding none, by sharing everything and possessing nothing, we will attain freedom from the fear of hell and the desire for heaven. We can have our own heaven here on earth.

Our interpersonal relationships must be based on the philosophy of universal brotherhood. The power of science and technology must be guided by the higher principles of ethics, morality, and spirituality. Science and religion, technological discoveries and spiritual wisdom, have to come together. Today, there is no balance between science and spirituality, and as a result, science seems to be moving toward self-destruction. Instead of bringing peace, science has been creating fear in human hearts.

With the help of science, humanity has reached the nuclear age. Scientific discoveries have brought a great change in our standard of living. As far as physical comforts based on material objects are concerned, we are far better off than our ancestors, but peace of mind has declined many times more than the comforts and luxuries in the external world have increased.

No matter how many things we invent with the help of intellectual knowledge, we cannot free ourselves from inequality, fear, and doubt. True freedom comes from within. In order to know within, we have to withdraw our minds from the external world and make our minds inward. The solution to human problems can be found in the inner chamber of one's own heart. Unless one realizes the Divine Force, there is no way for a human being to attain eternal peace.

Mind and intellect are the finest tools for knowing the objects of the world or exploring the Truth within. However, they need to be trained so that they can discriminate right from wrong, and good from pleasant. We should also be aware of the limitations of mind and intellect. Intellect can lead us to the realization of the external world. It can come up with wonderful scientific discoveries, but it cannot fathom the absolute Truth. It cannot guide us beyond the domain of the material world since it does not have a light of its own.

Intellect functions under the guidance of a conscious force, Atman. The knowledge of Atman alone can reveal the totality and perfection of the Truth. Illumined by the light of Atman, intellect can change the course of its thinking and contemplation. Only then can it comprehend the higher Truth that lies behind all forces and matter of the world. Illumined by the knowledge of Atman, intellect can comprehend the principle of universal brotherhood. Such an intellect can practice and enjoy *samatva* yoga, the yoga of equality or harmony.

Training of the intellect begins with the transformation of one's attitude towards life and worldly objects. Mind should not be focused on running after worldly objects. We must employ our inner faculties to contemplate within. However, we must be aware of the fact that mind and intellect are not the greatest forces. They receive their inspiration from the higher force of the Atman.

Intellect must carry on its duties of thinking, contemplating and analyzing the multi-level manifest world. But, rather than becoming a victim of the ego, it must surrender itself to the Divine Force within. Such an intellect can help us become successful in the world, and at the same time, analyze our true nature within.

In Indian philosophy, intellect is described as a mirror that reflects the true nature of Atman. As long as that mirror is clean, the reflection is accurate. But when the mirror of intellect is clouded with thought constructs, it presents a distorted reality. Purification, concentration, and an inward-turning of the intellect are necessary if one is to attain eternal peace and happiness.

People of today's age of high technology certainly have more material objects than the people of a century ago, but they seem to be more dissatisfied and frustrated than their forefathers. They seem to be more manipulative, possessive, and self-centered. The richer and more resourceful a person is, the more he exploits the suppressed members of society. He has an unending desire for "more", and he does not hesitate to fulfill his desires at the cost of others' welfare.

Such an attitude cannot be cured by science. Without spiritual awareness, it is not possible to make the best use of scientific discoveries. By sharpening our intellects and training them for scientific discoveries, we bring more chaos to life. Purification and transformation is more important than sharpening and using the intellect for external achievements. A purified intellect can give one a better perspective of life. It can guide human destiny in the right direction.

Purification of intellect is not possible through the intellect itself. Intellect is clouded with the information it receives through sense-perception. Such an intellect cannot rise above the limitations of time and space. It is the light of divine illumination that can guide the intellect beyond the realm of the senses and the material world.

Human beings are still experimenting with the objects of the world. This experiment seems to be an unending process. So far humanity has not set up a definitive lifestyle to create happiness. Many people in the past have experienced the Reality within and have concluded that happiness lies within, not in the material world. However, their experience has not become the experience of all. Out of many, only a few follow the footsteps of the enlightened sages. They are the ones who attain happiness. They live in the world yet remain above it. By no means can their lifestyle and inner equilibrium be doubted.

Without that inner illumination, external life cannot be made pure and ideal. External life must be illuminated by the Divine Light within. Freedom from pain and misery can be achieved by unveiling the secret of inner life. Once the secret of inner life is unveiled, we receive the divine message. The moment the veil is lifted and ego is attuned to the higher Self, our thoughts, speech, and actions follow the will of the Divine.

Once there is balance between the will of the Divine and our worldly activities, we enjoy freedom here and now. One who has free access to the world within and without becomes a citizen of both worlds. He attains freedom, and eternal peace is his.

People want to live happy and peaceful lives, but in the absence of right means, their desires remain unfulfilled. Humanity is constantly striving to attain freedom from pain and misery. Many of the philosophers and thinkers in the past realized that human beings have infinite potential within, and that if they really want to achieve the state of freedom, it is possible for them to do it. Accomplished masters of yoga realized the power of will and with the help of that power have attained the highest goal of life.

If one person can attain freedom, then why can't others? All human beings are equally equipped with all potentials and resources. If one human being can become a yogi and attain enlightenment, then certainly others can do the same. Human beings are not born again and again for the sake of mere birth and death. Perfection is the goal that they are trying to attain through their perennial journey of life.

Human life is an opportunity. In this state, one has freedom either to move upward or downward. One can cast off his limitations, expand one's awareness, and become divine. On the other hand, out of laziness and inertia, one may slip to lower states of existence. There cannot be a greater loss than missing the opportunity of having a human birth and starting all over again.

Every human being knows that the goal of his life is to attain peace and happiness. He also knows that others have the same purpose. All of humanity is working toward one objective, eternal joy. An individual is part of creation, and by excluding the whole, he cannot survive. However, out of ego, he acts as though he has separated himself from the totality of existence, although he actually remains united. This dichotomy persists only because of his ignorance. Considering oneself to be separate from the perfect, all-pervading universal Truth is the main cause of all pain and misery.

On the one hand, the ignorance-born ego draws a wall around itself, while on the other hand, the force of inner unity pulls the sense of individuality toward its perpetual perfection. Even in nature, we can see the latter force in operation. Derivative parts are constantly being pulled toward the main body of their existence. Between individuals and creation, between external and internal phenomena, between manifest and unmanifest, there exists a force that always remains in perfect harmony and balance. That force inspires and sustains both parts of reality, the external and internal, the manifest and unmanifest. From the infinite existence of that force, this multifaceted universe receives its sustenance.

By drinking the nectar of that infinite Divine Force one attains immortality. In order to experience that immortal nectar, one has to penetrate the known and the unknown, the manifest and unmanifest. The path of yoga as described by the sages of the Upanishads is the way to penetrate the totality of the Truth.

Long ago, personal enlightenment was considered to be the highest goal of life. In those days, it was the proper goal because people could accomplish their tasks with a minimum of support from others. Because there was no modern communication media, the news related to the problems of a person or of a community did not spread very fast. Thus, people remained unaffected by the circumstances of others who lived at a distance.

But with the advances in communication technology today's situation has changed. News related to a particular person or society spreads rapidly. Furthermore, the present-day economy has made all human beings interdependent. The affliction of any part of our society affects the entire human race. At this stage of our evolution we must think of the welfare of the whole world.

Existing systems of religion can no longer guide humanity since they are confined to segments of society. We need a universal religion that can be equally applicable to all. In the light of a universal religion, we can strive toward equality, justice, and freedom. Adhering to a universal religion, we can take care of all personal and social duties. In order to climb to the next step of human civilization, we must transcend petty religious disputes.

All religions of the world believe in the incarnation of God as Messiah, Prophet, or Savior. Such a concept of God or godly manifestations confines our world view, and even forces us to divide humanity in the name of God. Identifying God as a person also prevents us from experiencing God in every human being. As a result, we do not respect our own brothers and sisters if they do not worship "our God". What ignorance, to consider God to be merely our God and not to be the God of all! Unfortunately, that has been the case with many of the followers of God. The destiny of mankind lies in experiencing the God beyond "my God", "your God", or "his God".

Before becoming divine, we have to become fully evolved human beings. Humanity as a whole requires us to love and care for all. That is the condition for becoming a true human being. All the great ideals, positive attitudes, and creative forces grow in the heart after becoming a true human being, and we naturally move forward on the path of transformation. And, one day, the Divine unfolds within us.

All the religions of the world have Truth as their main goal. The goal is one, but the paths are many. By following any of those paths, one can attain the goal, but no one can attain peace from the path itself. Peace lies in the experience of Truth. Out of ignorance, people have included hatred, jealousy, and discrimination based on race and color in religion. How can such attitudes be part of religion, and if they are, then how can such a religion be helpful for human growth?

The dharma of mankind inspires all human beings to live with one another in peace and harmony. In order to adhere to that dharma, the universal religion, an individual or society has to be free of selfishness and narrow-mindedness. Once human beings can expand their world view, establish a sense of equality, remove mutual differences, and search for the highest truth, they will find themselves to be more than just Hindus, Moslems, Christians, Jews or Buddhists.

The Ultimate Objectives of Nehru's Socialism

MADAN DEVANAYAKAM

Socialism is for me not merely an economic doctrine which I favour; it is a vital need which I hold with all my head and heart.

JAWAHARLAL NEHRU[1]

BERNARD SHAW is reported to have said after meeting Mahatma Gandhi, "He is not a man but a phenomenon"[2]; that is to say it is difficult to explain his astonishing personality. The same can be said without exaggeration of Gandhi's faithful disciple and political heir, Pandit Jawaharlal Nehru. Nehru's life more than his speeches and writings reveals him as an ardent patriot, an architect of modern India, a peace-loving internationalist and a militant opponent of dictatorship. But, above all these qualities, it is as a convinced socialist that his character is more accurately portrayed. He was, no doubt, a great hero of India's non-violent struggle for independence, for he suffered a great deal in the fight for freedom and was imprisoned nine times. And he was certainly an ambitious builder of his nation after independence and was fully concerned "with the physical targets of the National Plans and the urgent necessities of the Indian situation in so far as food and clothing and housing and education and work are concerned"[3]. But Nehru himself began to "feel that all this long list of physical targets, vitally important as they

---

[1] Cited by John Gunther, *Inside Asia*, New York, 1942 (3rd Ed.), p. 429.
[2] C.H. Philips: *India*, London, 1948, p. 115.
[3] Jawaharlal Nehru: 'Modern Problems Demand a Spiritual Approach', in *Bulletin of the Ramakrishna Mission Institute of Culture*, Vol. XIII, No. I, 1962, p. 15.

are and essential for his country, as for any other country, may not be quite enough if they stand by themselves, i.e. if there is nothing else to add to them"[4].

Nehru's personality would be less significant, were he to be only a freedom fighter and nation-builder: his achievement would be less lasting, were his life and policies based on nothing deeper than the goal of material prosperity. In fact, he had a philosophy of life which alone adequately explains his personality and achievements and this philosophy of life was none other than that of socialism which he held as a vital need with all his head and heart. True, often enough he made no secret of his preoccupation with the economic advancement of India and with the material prosperity of the millions of people in India. As a result, gigantic irrigation projects, power dams, steel mills and new industries which, in his own words, are the modern temples of India, were set up during his tenure of office as Prime Minister. This has led many of his admirers to think that Nehru never believed in or cared for anything beyond material welfare in national and international affairs, and that he was indifferent if not adverse to values, whether personal or religious. The object of this short essay is to show that he did believe in religious and personal values as the ultimate objective of his socialism and we shall analyse the nature of this ultimate objective as revealed in his writings, speeches and above all in his life itself.

I. Nehru's Socialism

The first question that presents itself to our inquiry is: what is socialism according to Nehru?

While Nehru was studying in Cambridge, he became attracted to socialism. He writes, "A study of Marx and Lenin produced a powerful effect on my mind and helped me to see history and current affairs in a new light"[5]. It is well known that for a time in the thirties he dallied with Marxism. When he arrived in India after his studies in England, his vague socialist leanings began to be entrenched. In his many

---

[4] *Ibid.*
[5] Jawaharlal Nehru: *The Discovery of India*, London, 1956 (4th Ed.), p. 15.

visits to the slums where he saw the poverty and suffering of the peasants and heard their grievances, he was deeply moved and wrote later:

> They (the peasants) showered their affection on us and looked on us with loving and hopeful eyes, as if we were the bearers of good tidings, the guides who were to lead them to the promised land. Looking at them and their misery and overflowing gratitude, I was filled with shame and sorrow, shame at my own easy-going and comfortable life and petty politics of the city which ignored this vast multitude of semi-naked sons and daughters of India, sorrow at the degradation and overwhelming poverty of India. A new picture of India seemed to rise before me, naked, starving, crushed, and utterly miserable[6].

His life in jail alone did not make him a socialist, but it gave him the time and opportunity for exhaustive political study and reflection. His ideas on socialism began to take concrete form and merged gradually with his nationalism. He saw the problem of India's independence not merely as a struggle between the Indian nationalists and the British colonizers but fundamentally as a struggle against capitalist imperialism. Imperialism for him meant capitalist profit-making and as such had to be fought against both on nationalist as well as on socialist grounds.

After independence the Congress party under Nehru's leadership, appalled by the contrasts between the poor and the wealthy to be seen everywhere in India and repelled by the patronage of bankers and industrialists, adopted socialism as the only means to solve the country's economic problems effectively. It is difficult to define socialism as Nehru conceived it. The first thing that comes to mind on hearing this word is a vague notion of something which does good to everybody and which aims at equality of wealth. But this does not take us very far. Socialism is not only a way of life but a certain scientific approach to social and economic

---

[6] Jawaharlal Nehru: *An Autobiography*, London, 1936, p. 52.

problems. It means that the general character of social, political and intellectual life in a society is governed by its productive resources. As these productive resources change and develop, so also does the life and thinking of the community. Without any alignment with certain privileged groups, it aims at self-sufficiency of the people and of villages. This kind of socialism should be considered as separate from the political elements of communism with the belief in the inevitability of violence.

Socialism and democracy

Nehru's socialism does not by any means involve totalitarian planning; it is democratic and therefore his concept of planning is entirely different from that of Marxist planning. The individual in society really matters and the freedom and welfare of individuals must be safeguarded in any scheme of planning. The Marxist planning, expounded in the U.S.S.R., stemming from dialectical materialism, is associated with state control of all means of production, even to the point of totalitarianism. Totalitarian planning is bound to curb or abolish the individual's rights and therefore cannot be conducive to general welfare. The Planning Commission was established in order to prepare plans for the most effective and balanced utilisation of the country's resources[7]. The main object of planning was defined as the initiation of a process of development which will raise living standards and open out to the people new opportunities for a richer and varied life[8].

Socialism and rural community

Since socialism has to be appropriate to India's vast rural areas if it is to be of profit to the majority of people, the villages have to be developed through community development projects. The panchayat, the co-operative and the school in

---

[7] 'Nehru's broadcast to the nation', quoted by Frank Moraes, in *Jawaharlal Nehru*, New York, 1956, p. 423.
[8] *Ibid.*, p. 422.

every village should be the three main basic units at the rural level by means of which the community development projects are to be carried out. The part played by the panchayats consists in discussing and deciding the developmental programmes; the co-operatives should see to the effective realisation of production, marketing of the produce and provision of credit; and lastly, the schools must become the centre of educational, cultural and recreational activities.

Socialism and agrarian reform

The pattern of land ownership is very vital in the establishment of a welfare state; if social inequalities are to be eliminated, agrarian reforms have to be carried out. This is precisely what is aimed at in the abolition of the zamindary system; the tiller becomes the owner of the land. The tenant is given lawful protection and security on the land. At the same time an opportunity is given to the tenants to gain in social status and thus the reduction of inequality will lead to the establishment of cooperative societies for provision of credit, co-operative farming and co-operative marketing.

Socialist pattern of society

The long-term objective of Nehru's planning and economic policies is the achievement of "a socialist pattern of society" in which the basic criterion for determining the lines of advance would not be private profit but social gain, and the pattern of development would be so planned that it would result not only in a rise in national income but also in closer equality in incomes and wealth. Thus the benefits of economies would accrue more and more to the relatively less privileged classes and concentration of incomes, wealth and economic powers would be progressively reduced. The goal of a socialist pattern of society is not based on any fixed doctrine or dogma nor is it a fixed or rigid pattern. The principles underlying it are supposed to serve merely as guidelines which may be altered on the basis of new experience. In essence the policy of socialism includes abolition of landlordism, extension of the role of the State in industry, trade and commerce, and development of rural economy through community projects.

II. THE ULTIMATE OBJECTIVE OF SOCIALISM

In Nehru's opinion, nation-building in accordance with socialistic policies had to be based on something spiritual. Nehru had in the past deliberately avoided the use of words of religious connotation such as spiritual, not because he did not attach value to them, as some tend to think, but because of the amount of bogus spirituality. Even some of those who were genuinely spiritual, wanted to escape from the problems of the day and their talk of spirituality was escapism according to him[9]. India is a hungry nation, a nation that needs many of the common necessities of life, which come almost automatically to the affluent nations of the West. India in such a condition has to solve these material problems and it is no use running away from them in the name of spirituality. On the other hand, economic well-being is not everything in life. Socialism for Nehru also included the spiritual values of man; these are essential for human life itself. In other words, the ultimate objective of socialism is the spiritual betterment of the individual within the society. This leads us to inquire into the philosophy of Nehru's socialism.

The fundamental rights

Marxist socialism is not the answer to man's ultimate aspirations; it even fails to explain adequately the meaning of human life itself. The Marxist ideal of socialism is an utopian goal which it is impossible to realise. Nehru observes: "Often I disliked or did not understand some development there (in Russia) and it seemed to me to be too closely concerned with the opportunism of the moment of the power politics of the day"[10]. "I am too much of an individualist and believer in personal freedom to like overmuch regimentation. Yet it

---

[9] Jawaharlal Nehru: 'Modern problems demand a spiritual approach', *loc. cit.*, p. 15.

[10] Jawaharlal Nehru: *The Discovery of India, op. cit.*, p. 15.

seemed to be obvious that in a complex social structure individual freedom had to be limited and perhaps the only way to real personal freedom was through some such limitation in the social sphere"[11]. Again he saw the failure of communism very clearly when he remarked:

> In spite of its apparent success, communism fails, partly because of its rigidity, but, even more so because it ignores certain essential needs of human nature... We see the growing contradictions within the rigid framework of communism itself. Its suppression of individual freedom brings about powerful reactions. Its contempt for what might be called the moral and spiritual side of life not only ignores something that is basic in man, but also deprives human behaviour of standards and values[12].

There is not the slightest doubt that the Indian Constitution safeguards the fundamental rights of every man quite explicitly. The State has "to promote the welfare of the people by securing and protecting... a social order in which justice, social, economic and political, shall inform all the institutions of the national life". These principles further require the State to direct its policies in such a manner as to secure the right of all men and women to an adequate means of livelihood, equal pay for equal work, and within the limits of its economic capacity and development, to make effective provision for securing the right to work, education and public assistance in the event of unemployment, old age, sickness and disablement or other cases of un-deserved want. The State has also to secure for workers humane conditions of work, a decent standard of living, and full enjoyment of leisure and social and cultural opportunities. The Indian Constitution enumerates seven broad categories of "fundamental rights", including the right of equality; prohibition of

---

[11] *Ibid.*
[12] 'The basic approach', in *Nehru, The Years of Power*, Vincent Sheean, London, 1960, p. 291. This document was written by Nehru himself for private circulation for the guidance of his friends and followers; but the All-India Congress Committee obtained permission to reprint it later in its fortnightly publication, *The Economic Review*.

discrimination on grounds of religion, race, caste, sex or place of birth; and equality of opportunity in matters of public employment... etc.

Now, the principle of socialism does not in any way go against the fundamental rights guaranteed by the Indian Constitution. Nehru says:

> I do not see why under socialism there should not be a great deal of freedom for the individual; indeed far greater freedom than the present system gives. He can have freedom of conscience and mind, freedom of enterprise, and even the possession of private property on a restricted scale. Above all, he will have the freedom which comes from economic security, which only a small number possess today[13].

The individual should not be sacrificed to socialism and indeed the real social progress will come only when opportunity is given to the individual to develop, provided this does not apply just to a selected group, but to the whole community. The touchstone therefore should be how far any political or social theory enables the individual to rise above his petty self and thus think in terms of the good of all[14].

Nehru saw in his own lifetime that the much needed social reform was being enforced in Hindu society itself. "Freedom is not a mere matter of political decision or new Constitution, not even a matter of what is more important, i.e. economic policy. It is of the mind and heart and if the mind narrows itself and is befogged and the heart is full of bitterness and hatred, then freedom is absent"[15]. Nehru was convinced of the fact that there is no such thing as abstract freedom and that freedom is always accompanied by responsibility; freedom always entails an obligation, whether it is a

---

[13] *The Unity of India*, p. 118; cf. *The Quintessence of Nehru*, edited by K. J. Narasimhachar, London, 1961, p. 142, which is a collection of texts selected from Nehru's writings and speeches.

[14] Jawaharlal Nehru: 'The basic approach', *loc. cit.*, p. 294.

[15] Jawaharlal Nehru: *Independence and After*, p. 10, cf. *The Quintessence of Nehru, op. cit.*, p. 146.

nation's or an individual's freedom[16]. Accordingly, he made strenuous efforts to eradicate the anomalies in Indian society. Untouchability was declared to be abolished by the Constitution (section 17) and caste restrictions lost their legal force. The two laws of the Hindu Code Bill, mainly drafted by Dr. Ambedkar, dealing with Hindu marriage and Hindu succession were passed in 1955 and 1956 respectively. The Hindu Marriage Act by making bigamy and polygamy criminal offences provides a legal basis for monogamy. The Hindu Succession Act in general gives equal rights to men and women (including widows) in the matter of inheritance and the holding of property.

Non-violence

While considering the economic aspects of India's problems (socialism, national planning etc.), Nehru strongly reminds us that the basic approach to all these problems must be through peaceful means[17]. "What I admired was the moral and ethical side of our movement and of *satyagraha*... The spiritualization of politics, using the word not in its narrow religious sense, seemed to me a fine idea. A worthy end should have worthy means leading up to it. That seemed not only a good ethical doctrine, but sound, practical politics[18]. "Violence does not lead to peace"[19]. Communist association with violence encourages a certain evil tendency in human beings. Any philosophy of life that advocates violence cannot possibly lead to a solution of any major problem because it is based on hatred. An atmosphere of mental conflict, hatred, distrust and suspicion leads to destruction and ruin. Besides, such a doctrine and practice of violence is contrary to India's spiritual heritage. India has a message, a message of tolerance, of co-existence. Gandhi's message of non-violence

---

[16] Jawaharlal Nehru: *Speeches (1953-57)*, p. 158, cf. *The Quintessence of Nehru*, op. cit., p. 148.
[17] 'The basic approach', *loc. cit.*, p. 298.
[18] Jawaharlal Nehru: *An Autobiography*, p. 73; cf. *The Quintessence of Nehru*, op. cit., p. 68.
[19] Jawaharlal Nehru: *Independence and After*, p. 319, cf. *The Quintessence of Nehru*, op. cit., p. 69.

should be made the guiding principle in all national and international affairs.

Truth

Peace achieved through non-violence for the building up of a socialist pattern of society should go hand in hand with adherence to truth. The true path of man is the path of truth and peace[20]. Nehru exhorts his countrymen to tread the path of truth and *dharma*[21], because the foundations of a lasting victory can only be laid on the rock of truth[22]. He says that as a human being he finds himself often struggling for some light, for a vision of what one should do, for a glimpse of the truth and of the pathway to the truth[23].

Religion

The path of truth and *dharma* which Nehru proposes for moral living leads to the question of his idea of religion. Religion according to him not only gave man a certain moral and spiritual discipline; it also tried to perpetuate superstition and social usage. Disillusion came and communism followed[24]. "It (religion) seemed to be closely associated with superstitious practices and dogmatic beliefs, and behind it lay a method of approach to life's problems which was certainly not that of science. There was an element of magic about it, an uncritical credulousness, a reliance on the supernatural"[25].

What then is religion? He thinks that probably it consists of the inner development of the individual, the evolution of his consciousness in a certain direction which is considered good. He understands religion as a way of life which lays stress on this inner development. Although a man who is the victim of economic circumstances and who is preoccupied

---

[20] Jawaharlal Nehru: *Speeches (1949-53)*, p. 122; cf. *The Quintessence of Nehru, op. cit.*, p. 61.
[21] *Independence and After*, p. 27; cf. *The Quintessence of Nehru, op. cit.*, p. 61.
[22] *Ibid.*, p. 28; cf. *The Quintessence of Nehru, op. cit.*, p. 62.
[23] *Speeches (1949-53)*, p. 370-1; cf. *The Quintessence of Nehru, op. cit.*, p. 62.
[24] 'The basic approach', *loc. cit.*, p. 291.
[25] Jawaharlal Nehru, *The Discovery of India, op. cit.*, p. 12.

with the struggle to live can rarely achieve the inner consciousness of a high degree, still no man can do without religion[26]. Religion for Nehru does not imply any belief in a personal God for the idea of a personal God seems very odd to him. "I do not call it the mysterious God, because God has come to mean much that I do not believe in. I find myself incapable of thinking of a deity or of any unknown supreme power in anthropomorphic terms"[27]. He felt attracted in a certain way towards the conception of monism which seemed to satisfy him intellectually. He appreciated to some extent the *advaita* (non-dualist) philosophy of the Vedanta[28]. He was thus inclined to think that "everything, whether sentient or non-sentient, finds a place in the organic whole; that everything has a spark of what might be called the Divine impulse or the basic energy of life force which pervades the universe"[29]. But he personally did not want to get involved in what he called metaphysical religions which would tend to take him away from the problems of life facing India. He did see however the practical aspect of the Vedantic monism for he says: "If we really believed in this all-pervading concept of the principle of life, it might help us to get rid of some of our narrowness of race, caste or class and make us more tolerant and understanding in our approaches to life's problems"[30].

In an appeal to his countrymen, he observed: "We have laid down in our Constitution that India is a secular State. That does not mean irreligion. It means equal respect for all faiths and equal opportunities for those who profess any faith. We have therefore always to keep in mind this vital aspect of our culture which is also of the highest importance in the India of today"[31].

Rationalism, the greatest enemy of religion, with all its virtues, appears to him to deal with the surface of things, without uncovering the inner core of human life. If there is

---

[26] Jawaharlal Nehru, *An Autobiography*, p. 379; cf. *The Quintessence of Nehru, op. cit.*, p. 179.
[27] *The Discovery of India, op. cit.*, p. 14.
[28] *Ibid.*
[29] 'The basic approach', *loc. cit.*, p. 294.
[30] *Ibid.*
[31] Citation from *The Church in Independent India*, T. Pothacamury, p. 4.

a sense of frustration and depression in India and in the world at large, it is due to a lack of a sound philosophy of life[32]. "In order to give the nation and the individual a sense of purpose, something to live for and, if necessary, to die for, we have to pay attention to the spiritual element in human nature and give in a wider sense of the word, a spiritual background to our thinking"[33]. Nehru remarks: "We talk of the welfare state and of democracy and socialism. They are good concepts but they hardly convey a clear and unambiguous meaning. What should be our ultimate objective? Democracy and socialism are means to an end, not the end itself. We talk of the good of society. Is this something apart from and transcending the good of the individuals composing it?"[34]

III. Nehru's Personality

So far we have been analysing Nehru's idea of socialism and explaining in its light the significance of his economic policies in their ultimate nature for human life and prosperity. Now let us briefly outline how this philosophy of life shaped his own personality. He was a sincere and honest man and practised what he believed. His life and work was permeated with the spiritual outlook of his socialism.

Professor Toynbee truly evaluates the essence of his personality when he writes: "I was in the presence of a human being who could fight and fight with might and main—without hating his human opponents. Fighting without hating was one of Mahatma Gandhi's principles. Here in one of his chief companions could be seen something out of the Sermon on the Mount being practised in real life, and this without any smugness and without any apparent effort"[35]. This lovable and loving human being was true to his philosophy of socialism which demands recognition of fundamental rights of every human being even though he be his enemy.

---

[32] Jawaharlal Nehru: 'The basic approach', *loc. cit.*, p. 293.
[33] *Ibid.*
[34] *Ibid.*, p. 294.
[35] Jawaharlal Nehru, in *Encounter*, August 1964, Vol. XXIII, No. 2, p. 3.

His political career for him was a means of serving his fellowmen not only in India but throughout the whole world. As an internationalist and socialist he did care intensely for mankind's welfare and destiny, and his vision of this will be the thing in him for which he will be remembered by posterity.

As a socialist he preferred to act and deal with his colleagues in the government and with other people in India and abroad in a democratic way; he abhorred dictatorial methods and, when he was accused of trying to be a dictator by his enemies in India, he sincerely offered to resign his office as Prime Minister of India. He was persuaded by the Congress High Command to continue in his responsible office. He valued personal dignity and individual freedom as more important and the mass persuasion as more effective than compulsion.

If he seemed to care less for religion in his life, it is because he was against priestcraft, communalism and intolerance fostered in the name of religion. He regarded the Brahmanical caste System as a major cause of India's decline and was as stern a critic of untouchability as Gandhi himself. He was convinced of the futility of mere spiritualism in the context of his country's most crushing economic and social problems. However, he never lost sight of the spiritual aspect of his service; it was in the background of his all-absorbing duties of daily life, sometimes coming into the limelight, sometimes obliquely referred to, but never completely abandoned.

Socialism for Nehru was not a mere economic theory that he adopted because of circumstances, but a vital principle governing his whole thought and action. He was, in fact, the apostle of socialism, a socialism all his own, showing the way for his countrymen to interpret India's religious and cultural heritage in the light of modern problems and preaching the socialist creed in order to give a new impetus to the Hindu society to develop itself in the upheaval of the twentieth century.

Human Progress According to Buddhism

ALEX WAYMAN

INTRODUCTION

This topic will be treated in accordance with three important Buddhist terms for 'training' (*śikṣā*), their tentative renditions: higher morality (*adhiśīla*), higher thinking (*adhicitta*), and higher insight (*adhiprajñā*), in relation to the Eightfold Noble Path. One of the texts to be employed is Buddhaghosa's *Visuddhimagga* ('path of purification'), whose three main parts present those three terms (in their Pāli language equivalents) as representing the path in that order[1]. I shall also use citations in the early part of Tsong-kha-pa's *Lam rim chen mo*, as well as his Bodhisattva section and 'Calming the Mind'.

I start though by referring to Nyanatiloka's *Buddhist Dictionary*[2], entry under 'M' of the path (Pāli, *magga*), where he shows that the Buddhist Eightfold Noble path is subsumed under those three categories, substituting *samādhi* for the *adhicitta*, although my translations of the terms, herein used, differ somewhat from Nyanatiloka's: 1. Right Views (P. *sammā-diṭṭhi*; S. samyak-dṛṣṭi) and 2. Right Understanding (P. *sammā-samkappa*; S. samyak-saṃkalpa) go with 'insight' (P. *paññā*; S. *prajñā*). 3. Right Speech (P. *sammā-vācā*; S. samyag-vāk). 4. Right Bodily Action (P. *sammā-kammanta*; S. samyak-karmānta), and 5. Right Livelihood (P. *sammā-ājīva*; samyag-ājīva) go with 'morality' (P. *sīla*; S. *śīla*). 6.

---

[1] *Visuddhimagga of Buddhaghosācariya*, edt. by Henry Clarke Warren, revised by Dharmananda Kosambi (Cambridge, Mass.: Harvard University Press, 1950); *The Path of Purification* (*Visuddhimagga*) of *Bhadantācariya Buddhaghosa*, Translated from the Pāli by the Bhikkdu Ñāṇamoli (Colombo, Ceylon: R. Semage, 1956).

[2] Nyanatiloka, *Buddhist Dictionary*; Manual of Buddhist Terms and Doctrines (Colombo: Frewin & Co., 1950).

Right Effort (P. *sammā-vāyāma*; S. samyag-vyāyāma), 7. Right Mindfulness (P. *sammā-sati*; P. samyak-smṛti), and 8. Right Mental Concentration (P. *sammā-samādhi*; S. samyak-samādhi) go with 'concentration' (P. *samādhi*; S. samādhi = *adhicitta*)³. Nyanatiloka labelled the first group of two, "III. Wisdom (*paññā*)", because, as he explained in that same entry of 'magga', meaning 'path', he does not accept the Eightfold Noble Path as really being a path, since 'Wisdom' comes first, which does not really happen in a 'path'. It is clear that he was convinced that Buddhaghosa was correct in having the three 'trainings' in his given order. But, if I were to choose between having the ancient Eightfold Noble path as the 'path' or having Buddhaghosa's *Visuddhimagga* as the 'path', I would choose the Eightfold Noble path, while acknowledging that the *Visudhimagga* still contains valuable material in all its three parts. Supporting my choice is the first scripture of the Buddha: Setting in Motion the Wheel of the Law, for which I use the version in the Pāli canon called Saṃyutta-Nikāya, Part V, 420ff. Here he announced to his initial five disciples that there is a Middle Path, avoiding the extremes of addiction to sense pleasures, or addiction to self mortification called the Noble Eightfold Path, which I presented above; and the Buddha continues in this version to stress that this Path leads to Enlightenment or to Nibbāna (= S. Nirvāṇa).

So I shall now present the Eightfold Noble Path — constituting the ancient Buddhist theory of human progress — as subsumed under the three 'trainings' (*śikṣā*), with the inclusion of the first two members under the training, no. I (not no. III, as Nyanatiloka insists), namely, *adhiprajñā*.

The training called Adhiprajñā

First, we must face the rendition of *adhiprajñā*, where I always render *prainā* ad 'insight', while those who follow Conze in his translation of part of the *Prajñāpāramitā* scrip-

---

³ I used the Sanskrit-Tibetan Buddhist dictionary called *Mahāvyutpatti* for determining the Sanskrit equivalents, namely, the 2-vol. Sakaki edn. published in Japan, the set 996 for the Eightfold Noble Path, and I was influenced by the Tibetan equivalent to no. 2 of the eight for my English rendition.

tures, agree with his rendition 'Perfection of Wisdom', and use the rendition 'wisdom' for *prajñā*[4]. We notice how acceptance of this rendition fooled Nyanatiloka, who therefore thought *prajñā* could not come first. But neither Conze, nor anyone else who accepts 'wisdom' for *prajñā* (or its Pāli equivalent *paññā*), can explain how 'wisdom' can be perfected, since 'wisdom' is itself a final stage. The prefix *adhi* appears here to connote 'improving', since it prefixes each of the three 'trainings'; hence, using my rendition 'improving insight', I shall explain how this choice of a translation works for the first two of the Eightfold Noble Path. One notices that my rendition 'insight' — because a mental function suggesting 'sight' and 'non-sight' — goes with no. 1, Right Views (*samyak-dṛṣṭi*) for the 'sight' suggestion of 'insight'; and with no. 2. Right Understanding (*samyak-saṃkalpa*), for the 'non-sight' suggestion of 'insight'.

Now, for the theory that this comes at the beginning of the path, as I claim, I am indebted to an article by Bhikkhu Thanavuddho[5] calling my attention to a Pāli scripture called *Mahācattārīsaka-sutta*, which discriminates between two kinds of each of the eight members, the defiled (*āsava*; S. āsrava) and the undefiled or transcendental (*anāsava*; S. anāsrava) kind; but he does not point out — as I read in this scripture — that the Buddha is here discriminating between what is called the 'Noble' (*ārya*) Eightfold Path, which starts with the Four Noble Truths, and the 'non-Noble' one which does not start with the Four Noble Truths. Besides, this particular scripture repeats over and over again that Right View comes first. My acceptance of this position agrees with the topics found in Buddhaghosa's *Visuddhimagga*, the last third part. Here, for the set 'Right Views', we find the Four Noble Truths of Buddhism, which are Suffering, its Cause, its Cessation, the Path (i.e. 8-fold) leading to its Cessation; the five aggregates (*skandha*) making up the human person, which

---

[4] *Aṣṭasāhasrikā Prajñāpāramitā*, Translated into English by Edward Conze (Calcutta: The Asiatic Society, 1958), with inside page message: "The Perfection of Wisdom in Eight thousand Ślokas, Translated by Edward Conze, Ph.D.".

[5] His essay called "The Practical Methodology of the Eightfold Path and Threefold Training", *Studies in Indian Philosophy and Buddhism*; Tokyo University, issue 4 (Dec. 1996), English summary, pp. 94-5.

are in two groups — the *rūpa-sk.* the formal and material elements: and the four 'formless' ones — *vedanā-sk.* (feelings), *saṃjñā-sk.* (ideas), *saṃskāra-sk.* (motivations), *vijñāna-sk.* (perceptions); the three worlds, which are the realm of desire, the realm of form, and the formless realm; the six elements, which are fire, wind, water, earth, plus perceptions (*vijñāna*) and space (*ākāśa*). Then, for the set 'Right Understanding' we find the 12-membered Dependent Origination (*pratītyasamutpāda*); the 37 states prefatory to enlightenment; what is and what is not a path; and what removes doubt. Thus, if these topics go with the beginning of the path, we find first under 'Right Views' the basic statement of one's religion (in Buddhism, the Four Noble Truths), the make-up of the person, the realms in which one lives and could possibly live; classification of the elements. Then for 'Right understanding' we are introduced to the theory of arising of natures by Dependent Origination; introduced to the theory of getting enlightened by 37 states; introduced to what is, and what is not something, in this case, the path; and learn what removes doubt. These first two, obviously contrasting, are the topics of some scriptural passages.

Now, I shall give my own translation from the Pālin namely, from the Book of Eights of the Aṅguttara-Nikāya[6]; here the 2d scripture which is devoted to *paññā* (insight). I present the first two paragraphs:

> (1) Here, O monks, a monk dwells near a teacher, or (near) some other fellow student who takes the place of the teacher, so that one is eagerly ready, with dictates of conscience, with affection and esteem. This is the first cause, the first condition, for obtaining the insight so far not possible; and which having been obtained is increased toward fullness; and having been made to become is brought to completion — for initial study of the Dharma. (2) That person dwells near a teacher or (near) some other fellow student who takes the place of the teacher, so that one is eagerly ready, with dictates of conscience, with af-

---

[6] I use the edition of the Aṅguttara-Nikāya published by the Bihar Govt., this Vol. 3, 1960, p. 271ff.

fection and esteem, and from time to time approaches (the teachers or substitute teachers) and puts questions: "Sirs, what is this?" "What does it mean?" To that person those venerable ones uncover what is veiled, clarify what is unclear, and dispel the doubt regarding numerous doubtful natures (*dharma*). This is the second cause, the second condition ... for initial study of the Dharma.

It appears a reasonable conclusion that these two paragraphs go respectively with Right View and Right Understanding.

1. Right View, and 2. Right Understanding

There are various other passages which could be cited. Tsong-kha-pa refers to the *Mahāyāna-Sūtrālaṃkāra*. I. 16: "Having first based (oneself) in hearing (*śruti*) (*śrutam. niśrityādau* ...)"[7]. And refers to the *Jātakamālā*, XVII, the story of the Jar: "But the offering to be made to the preceptor, is in seizing his wholesome words and turning them into one's self"[8]. Such passages seem to go with both Right View and Right Understanding.

Another feature that appears to go with Right View is Faith (*śraddha*), and Tsong-kha-pa cites a passage about it from the beginning of Śāntideva's *Śikṣāsamuccaya*:[9]

> For it is said in the *Ratnolka-dhāraṇī(-Mahāyānasūtra)*: "Faith is the guide, mother-generator, protection and expansion of all merits. Eliminator of craving, carrying across the stream, faith reveals the city of bliss. Faith is the calm of a non-soiled mind, expeller of pride and rooted in honor"[10]

---

[7] *Lam rim chen mo*, Tashilunpo edn., f. 41b-4.

[8] Tashilunpo edn., f. 29a-3; and Hendrik Kern, ed., *The Jātakamālā by Ārya Śūra* (Cambridge, Mass.: Harvard University Press, 1943). p. 105, verse 32cd: sampūjanīyas tu hitasya vaktā vākpragraheṇa pratipanmayena/.

[9] Tashilunpo edn., f. 25b-3f. and *Śikṣāsamuccaya of Śāntideva*, edt. by P.L. Vaidya (Darbhanga: The Mithila Institute, 1961), text, p. 4, line 24f.

[10] Śraddha purogata mātrjanetrī pālika vardhika sarvaguṇānām /
kāṅkṣavinodani oghapratāraṇi śraddha midarśani kṣamapurasya //
śraddha anāvilacittaprasādo mānavivarjitagauravamūlā /

Besides, Right View requires the acknowledgement of what is a Wrong View. So the *Mahā-cattārīsaka-sutta*, previously referred to, which I now cite[11]:

> "Monks, what is a Wrong View? There is no [actual] gift, no [actual] offering, no [actual] sacrifice, no [actual] result or ripening for deeds — whether well-done or badly done. This world is not [actually]; the world beyond is not [actually]. There is no [actual] mother; no [actual] father. Sentient beings do not [actually] arise. There are not [actually] in the world ascetics (P. *samaṇa*; S. śramaṇa) and brahmans proceeding rightly, succeeding rightly, who endorse this world and the world beyond, having realized them by their own occult talent (S. abhijñā).

The scripture goes on to mention the Right View that is defiled, i.e. not conducive to Nirvāṇa; and it turns out to state positively what the Wrong View had denied, i.e. there is an [actual] gift, (down to) there are [actual] ascetics and brahmans who realize in the manner mentioned. Then the scripture goes on to describe the Right View that is conducive to Nirvāṇa, and so is not defiled, and belongs to the Eightfold Noble Path:

> Whatever is insight (P. *paññā*; S. prajñā), the organ of insight, the power of insight; the component of enlightenment that analyzes the *dharmas*; i.e. the Right View as a member of the Path.

One may promptly notice that this emphasis on insight (prajñā) agrees with the position already emphasized above.

This sharpening of one's insight with both Right view and Right Understanding should be considered the proper introduction for the next 'training' — the improving morality (*adhiśīla*). Morality, as was noticed above, has three topics: 3. Right Speech, 4. Right Bodily Action, and 5. Right Livelihood. We start with 3. Right Speech.

---

[11] The Majjhima-Nikāya (edn. of Bihar Govt.), Part 3 (1958), pp. 135-6.

3. Right Speech

Since these topics first start with the wrong kind, I shall start with 3. Right Speech in terms of the Wrong Speech. First from the Tibetan Vinaya (disciplinary code): (When one should stand), (a monk) should not say that sitting is standing; should not say that lying down is sitting; should not say that sitting on a high seat is sitting on a low seat; nor that the bad is good; should not say that going in front is going outside; should not say that going along a road is going along the side of the road[12]. And then again the *Mahācattārīsaka-sutta*, on 3. Right Speech, presents first Wrong Speech, as "lying, slanderous speech, harsh speech, gossiping". Then goes on to mention that ordinary Right Speech is simply the abstaining from those four kinds of wrong speech. But the right Speech that also abstains from those four kinds and belongs to the Eightfold Noble Path has been prepared for by Right View: the first, followed by Right Understanding, the second, which are forms of developing insight (*prajñā*). Besides, a treatise called *Śatapañcāśatka-nāma-stotra*, which is ascribed to Mātṛceta, has a Chap. 7 (Vākstotra) [praise of speech], containing these verse 72-78[13]:

> 72. For from this mouth of yours, pleasing to the eye, this your most ear-entrancing speech drops like nectar flowing from the moon.
> 73. Your speech is as a rain could laying the dust of passion, as a Garuḍa-bird exterminating the snake of hatred.
> 74. It is like the sun again and again thrusting aside the darkness of ignorance.
> 75. Free of falsehood because based on knowledge, free of confusion because of the absence of impurity, easily understood because rightly applied, your speech is trebly excellent.

---

[12] Tashlinpo edn., f. 19a-1f.

[13] Two thirds of this work were reconstructed by W. Siegling from Turfan fragments. Also Pelliot and Stein fragments publ. by S. Levi (*JA*, 1910, 450f).; also Hoernle, *Manuscript Remains*, I, p. 58ff. And la Vallée Poussin in *JRAS*, 1911, with the help the Tibetan version, lists the thirteen chapters, from which is cited Chap. 7, Tashilunpo edn., f. 79a-1ff.; and I use the edition by D.R. Shackleton Bailey (Cambridge, 1951).

76. Just at first your words ravish the hearers' minds; then, being pondered, remove their passions and delusion.
77. Your words are adapted to all, cheering the afflicted, striking terror into the heedless, alarming the lovers of pleasure.
78. These words of yours are for all; they please the wise, strengthen the intelligence of the middle sort, and dispel the darkness of the slow-witted[14].

This should suffice for 3. Right Speech.

4. Right Bodily Action

We start with the wrong kind. There are basically three: onslaught on creatures, taking what was not given, and wrong enjoyment among the sense pleasures — the order in the *Mahācattārīsaka-sutta*. Again, the ordinary Right Bodily Action is simply abstaining from those three, while the right Bodily Action that is part of the Eightfold Noble Path is the abstaining from them preceded by the Right View and Right Understanding, then the Right Speech. But more can be stated about this right and wrong bodily action.

a. The onslaught on creatures. I cite the *Āryasatyaka-parivarta*[15]:

---

[14] 72. asmād dhi netrasubhagād idaṁ śrutimanoharam /
mukhāt kṣrata te vākyaṁ candrād dravam ivāmṛtam //
73. rāgareṇuṁ praśemayad vākyaṁ te jaladāyate /
vainateyāyate dveṣabhujaṅgoddharaṇaṁ prati //
74. divākarāyate bhūyo 'py ajñānatimiraṁ nutat /
śakrāyudhāyate mānagirīn abhividārayat //
75. dṛṣṭārthatvād avitathaṁ niṣkleśatvād anākulam /
gamakaṁ suprayuktatvāt trikalyāṇaṁ hi te vacaḥ //
76. manāṁsi tāvac chrotṝṇāṁ haranty ādau vacāṁsi te /
tato vimṛśyamānāni rajāṁsi ca tamāṁsi ca //
77. āśvāsanṁ vyasanināṁ trāsanaṁ ca pramādinām /
saṁvejanaṁ ca sukhināṁ yogavāhi vacas tava //
78. viduṣāṁ prītijananaṁ madhyānāṁ buddhivardhanam /
timiraghnaṁ ca mandānāṁ sārvajanyam idaṁ vacaḥ //
[15] Tashilunpo edn., f. 117a-2f.: / bden pa po'i leu' las / rgyal po khyod ni srog gcog ma mdzad cig / skye bo kun la srog ni rab tu phans / de bas yun riṅ tshe bsruṅ su 'dod pas / yid kyi dgu la'aṅ srog gcog mi bsam mo /.

Your majesty, do not destroy life! Life is important to all beings. Therefore, if you wish to protect and lengthen your own life, among your many thoughts, you should not think of taking another's life.

Of course, history shows that some rulers are intent on mass murder, but they cannot compete with the Lord of Death:

Mercilessly, the Lord of Death slays accomplished persons aimlessly. Aware of the impending arrival of that slayer, what wise man busies himself with cherishing vanities?[16]

b. Taking what was not given. I cite the verse immediately following the above one from the *Āryasatyakaparivarta*[17]:

O World Protector, you should abandon taking what is not given. Thereby you will gain steady possesions. When one painstakingly accumulates many things, taking the possessions of others, oneself becomes destitute.

c. Wrong enjoyment of sense pleasures. I cite the verse immediately following the foregoing one[18]:

Your Majesty should avoid the wives of others and be content with your own queen. She then becomes your beloved and shall be incomparable.

The *Visuddhimagga* in its early section on morality, has these verses, of which two are from the Buddhist classic *Dhammapada* (its verse 13-14) and two are from an unidentified source:

---

[16] Tashilunpo edn., f. 65a-2. This is from *Mahārājakaniṣkalekha* by Mātṛceta, tr. by F.W. Thomas in *Indian Antiquary*, 32 (1903), pp. 345ff.

[17] This verse comes from the doctoral dissertation of Lozang Jamspal, *The Range of the Bodhisattva: A Study of an Early Mahāyānasūtra, Āryasatyakaprivarta*, Columbia University, 1991. Jamspal has given permission to cite this verse from his work. That given title is given in the Tibetan and Chinese Buddhist canons as the *Āryabodhisattvagocara-upāyaviṣaya-vikurvaṇanirdeśa*, a Mahāyāna Sūtra.

[18] Jamspal has given permission to cite this verse from his work (cf. n. 17, above).

> As to the senses: formations, sounds, smells, tastes, and tangibles, when these doors are open and unguarded, thieves will raid as though it were a village. Even as rain penetrates an ill-thatched house, so does lust penetrate and untrained mind. (Dh. 13).
>
> As to the senses: formations, sounds, smells, tastes, and tangibles, when these doors are closed and guarded, thieves will not raid as though it were a village. Even as rain does not penetrate a well-thatched house, so does lust not penetrate a well trained mind. (Dh. 14)[19].

Besides, the *Visuddhimagga* (I, 42, p. 14) has a passage for each of the senses, increasing the list to six for the mental sense:

> Upon seeing a formation with the eye, (that person) grasps neither the exterior signs nor grasps their particulars, ... through which sinful, unvirtuous natures (P. *dhamma*; S. dharma), or covetous, distressing (natures) might invade (that person). Upon hearing a sound with the ear ...; upon smelling and odor with the nose ...; upon tasting a flavor with the tongue ...; upon touching a tangible with (a part of) the body ...; upon cognizing a (mental) nature with the mind (organ) ...

What is evidently meant by avoiding the entrance of sinful, etc. natures is illustrated above by my first citation in this subsection of the king who avoids being attracted to wives of others. This appears to mean that when the king does see those other wives he pays no attention to sexual features, etc.; and so sees only his own wife as a partner. We may conclude this section devoted to Right Bodily Action by emphasizing that when the Wrong Bodily Action is simply avoided, this is of course possible. But when this Right Bodily Action is part of the Eightfold Noble path, it is assured that one is properly trained to conduct this Right bodily Action because preceded by Right View, Right Understanding, and Right Speech.

---

[19] The *Visuddhimagga* (n. 1, above), p. 30.

5. Right Livelihood

The Pāli word for livelihood is *ājīva*. The *Mahācattārīsaka-sutta* mentions four kinds of Wrong Livelihood: a. deceitful talk (P. *kuhanā-lapanā*); b. prognostication (P. *nemittikatā*); c. trickery (P. *nippesikatā*); d. greed for gain upon gain[20].

a. The wrong livelihood base on deceitful talk is illustrated in the *Visuddhimagga*, I, 60. Here, an evil person lays a false claim to a higher than human state, hoping it will help his livelihood. A monk or nun pretends to be sick so he or she can get superior food to eat.

b. The wrong livelihood based on prognostication is illustrated in the *Visuddhimagga*, I, 83. Even some worthy ascetics are trying to earn a living by palmistry, fortune-telling, divining omens, interpreting dreams. These pursuits are not permitted.

c. The wrong livelihood based on trickery is illustrated in the *Visuddhimagga*, I, 61. In this case, some persons make faces, scheme, use indirect talk, in order to get ahead.

d. The wrong livelihood based on greed for gain upon gain is alluded to in *Visuddhimagga*, I, 84, mentioning the pursuit of gain with gain. Then, in I, 123, one should abandon greed for requisites, using only those requisites that have been obtained lawfully.

A book by Nārada mentions that Right Livelihood (P. *sammājīva*) is of two kinds, the right livelihood of both monks and laymen. The latter are prohibited from trading in arms, slaves, intoxicants, animals for slaughter, and poison[21].

Since the bulk of monks, nuns, and lay persons avoid trespassing in wrong livelihood, it is what is expected of them, so their practice of Right Livelihood does not ordinarily merit praise. The avoiding of such interdicted livelihood by some one following the Eightfold Noble Path is assured because preceded by Right View and Right Understanding among the Insights, and by Right Speech and Right Bodily

---

[20] The Pāli text (n. 11, above), p. 139 (near top, Para. 5).
[21] Nārada, *A Manual of Abhidhamma; An Outline of Buddhist Philosophy* (Kandy, Ceylon: Buddhist Publication Society, 1968), p. 345.

Action as varieties of improving morality. So Right Livelihood is included as a member of the Eightfold Noble path. This now concludes our treatment of Right Morality.

The next group of three are covered by 'improving mentality' (*adhicitta*) — 6. Right Effort, 7. Right Mindfulness, 8. right Mental Concentration.

6. Right Effort

Here, there are alternate names. The Pāli *sammāvāyāma* is equivalent to *sammappadhāna* (Right Endeavor). In Nārada's book, there are four supreme efforts: a. The effort to discard evils that have arisen. b. The effort to prevent the arising of unrisen evils. c. The effort to develop unrisen good. d. The effort to augment arisen good. I am also indebted to this Nārada book for the information that the Pāli term *viriya* is also an equivalent term[22]. Since the Sanskrit term is *viryā*, it is possible to get more information from the Bodhisattva theory of Mahāyāna Buddhism where it is the fourth of the six 'perfection' (*pāramitā*). To show the applicability of the Sanskrit *viryā*, we notice that the opponents to Right Effort stated in *Visuddhimagga*, IV, 55, as the idle (i.e. lazy) person as well as stiffness and torpor; that these are precisely the opponents to the *viryā* (which I translate 'striving')[23] as the fourth 'perfection' — e.g. the 'faults in torpor and sleepiness'; the 'lazy man's' failure[24]. The *Caryāvatāra* [VII, 3, by Śāntideva] is cited for the lazy person:

> Laziness arises because of the craving based on negligence, savoring of pleasure, and sleep, and from lack of unease amidst the sufferings of *saṃsāra*[25].

The same work (VII, 7) is cited for the languor:

---

[22] Nārada, p. 93.
[23] Cf. Alex Wayman, tr., *The Ethics of Tibet*; Bodhisattva Section of Tsong-kha-pa's Lam Rim Chen Mo (Albany, N.Y.: State University of New York Press, 1991), Perfection of Striving Chapter, pp. 170-195.
[24] Wayman tr. *Ethics of Tibet*, pp. 171, 172.
[25] *Ethics of Tibet*, p. 175.

> As when a serpent comes onto the lap, one would get up without delay, so also when sleepiness and languor occur, one should ward them off without delay[26].

And the *Sūtrālaṃkāra* [XVI. 70] is cited in favor of the striving:

> The striving person is not overcome by enjoyments, not overcome by defilement, not overcome by weariness, not overcome by [small] receipts[27].

This chapter in Tibetan presents three kinds of striving: a. armored striving, b. striving which amasses virtuous nature, and c. striving which serves the aim of sentient beings.

a. armored striving. To give the main idea here: The Bodhisattva has a preliminary resolve not to quit the striving through the eons, were it just to dispel the suffering of one person, and in pursuit of Enlightenment — such is 'armored striving'[28].

b. striving which amasses virtuous natures. The explanation here is: "Because one should rightly accomplish the six perfections, one operates in those". The six are perfections of Giving (*dāna*), of Morality (*śīla*), of Forbearance (*kṣānti*), of Striving (*viryā*), of Meditation (*dhyāna*), of Insight (*prajñā*).

c. striving which performs the aim of sentient beings. The explanation: "it is the striving which operates in the eleven (kinds of) helping". The eleven are: 1) helping those needing help; 2) helping those deluded as to the need; 3) helping those who have already helped (the performer); 4) giving refuge to those in fearful danger; 5) relieving the suffering of those afflicted with suffering; 6) helping those who are destitute; 7) meant for those who want a reliance in a place; 8) meant for those who want a mind in common; 9) helping those who have engaged rightly; 10) helping those who have engaged wrongly; 11) helping those who need to be frightened into right conduct[29].

---

[26] *Ethics of Tibet*, p. 192.
[27] *Ethics of Tibet*, p. 171.
[28] *Ethics of Tibet*, pp. 172-3.
[29] *Ethics of Tibet*, note section, pp. 231-2. Here are some further explanations, especially for Nos. 7 and 8.

While Buddhism usually criticizes the possession of pride, in fact certain kinds of pride are extolled here: The Tibetan text states, "Now the one who desires to bring one's vow to fulfillment should cultivate three prides (VII, 49a-b [of *Caryāvatāra*])":

> The action [to be done], the defilement [to be eliminated], and the capability [to succeed], about these three one should have pride.

The explanation of 'pride about action' is: "No matter who else is a companion while accomplishing one's own path, one does not depend on him, but accomplishes it entirely by one's self". Of 'pride about capability': "One thinks, 'Since the living beings are in the dominion of defilement, they are incapable of accomplishing even their own aim, how much less the aim of others! I am capable of accomplishing my own and others' aim!" Of 'pride against defilement': "Thinking, through deprecating all kinds of defilement, 'I am victorious over these; and these will never defeat me'; one creates constancy by generating the mental courage to defeat the opposing side (i.e. the defilements)[30].

The appears to be sufficient to explain Right Effort = Right Endeavor = Right Striving. The follower of the Eightfold Noble Path who started with Right View the first, has now finished No. 6.

7. MINDFULNESS (P. *SATI*; S. SMṚTI)

This section will be a condensation of a Pāli scripture entitled *Satipaṭṭhāna-sutta*. The version I employ is in the Majjhima-Nikāya, Vol. I, scripture no. 10. The English rendering by Horner is available, but because of my presenting only the main ideas I put more weight on the original Pāli[31].

This scripture sets forth four applications of Mindfulness. In each, the Mindfulness is said to control the craving

---

[30] *Ethics of Tibet*, pp. 184-5.
[31] *The Collection of the Middle Length Sayings*, Vol. I, tr. from the Pāli by I.B. Horner (London: Luzac & Company, 1967), "Discourse on the Applications of Mindfulness", pp. 70-82; Majjhima-Nikāya, I (Bihar Govt., 1958), pp. 76,ff.

and distress in the 'world' [of each of the four]. The four: a. Observing the body (*kāya*) in the body. b. Observing the feeling (*vedanā*) in the feeling. c. Observing the mind (*citta*) in the mind. d. Observing the (mental) natures (*dharma*) in the (mental) natures.

    a. Observing the body in the body. The advice to sit cross-legged (whether in the forest, base of a tree, or in any vacant space) is because the initial treatment involves the body from its base to top of head. Later the legs are also treated and so in that case are not 'cross-legged'. The Mindfulness begins with being mindful of the breaths: whether out or in, a long one or a short one. The person observes, "I am breathing in a long (breath)", and so on for breathing in or out. And after a while at this exercise of Mindfulness, the person thinks, "As I breath in, I shall experience the entire body"; and "As I breath out, I shall experience the entire body". Then, "As I breath in, will tranquillize the body's activity"; and "As I breath out, will tranquilize the body's activity". He observes origination-things in the body, or dissolution-things in the body. When walking, one observes "I am walking"; so also, when standing still, sitting, or lying down. So also, with any other activity, carrying something, eating something, obeying calls of nature, etc. one observes, "I am (doing that)". And this person (monk or layman) observes precisely this body, from the soles of the feet up and from the crown of the head down, as encased in skin, full of various impurities. And this person observes the body's elements, namely, of extension, of cohesion, of heat, and of motion. And when noticing a corpse thrown into a cemetary, being devoured by vultures, etc., the person observes one's own body as of the same nature. In all such cases, the mindfulness is just what is necessary for knowledge, for recollection, and conducted independently of the world as a whole.

    b. Observing the feeling in the feeling. When experiencing a pleasant feeling, one observes, "I am experiencing a pleasant feeling". Likewise, when experiencing a painful feeling, or a feeling that is neutral (neither pleasant nor painful). When experiencing a pleasant feeling toward material objects, one observes, "I am experiencing a pleasant feeling toward material objects". Likewise, when experiencing a painful feeling, or a neutral feeling toward them; or a pleasant feeling, a painful feeling, or a neutral feeling toward non-material objects, no two of which feelings can be experienced together. Then one observes in the feelings origination-things, dissolution-things, or origination-dissolution-things. In all such cases, the mindfulness is just what is necessary for knowledge, for recollection, and conducted independently of the world as a whole.

c. Observing the mind in the mind. Here a person recognizes a lusting mind as a lusting mind; a mind without lust as one without lust. A hating mind as a hating mind; also the one not so. A deluded mind as a deluded mind; also the one not so. Recognizes the mind that is attentive as attentive; and the mind that is distracted as distracted. The mind that is lofty as lofty; and the mind that is depressed as depressed. The mind with another superior to it, as superior to it; with no other superior to it, as so. Recognizes the mind that is (meditatively) calmed as calmed; the one not (meditatively) calmed, as so. Recognizes the mind that is freed as freed; the one not freed, as so. That person observes the mind in the mind within; the mind in the mind outside; the mind in the mind both within and outside. Observes origination-natures (*dharma*), or dissolution-natures, or both origination-dissolution-natures in the mind. In all such cases, the mindfulness is just what is necessary for knowledge, for recollection, and conducted independently of the world as a whole.

So does a person recognize and observe the mind in the mind.

d. Observing the mental natures in the mental natures. This is a rather long part in the Pāli; and so I shall have to summarize this section. First come the five 'hindrances' (P. *nīvaraṇa*). The person should recognize if attracted to 1) sensuality (P. *kāmacchanda*), or if not. Should recognize if addicted to 2) ill-will (P. [*abhijjhā-*]*vyāpāda*), or if not. Should recognize if subject to 3) sloth and torpor [of body and mind] (P. *thīna-middha*), or if not. Should recognize if overcome by 4) restlessness and worry (P. *uddhacca-kukkucca*), or if not. Should recognize if not free from 5) wavering or doubt (P. *vicikicchā*), or if free from that. In all such cases, the mindfulness is just what is necessary for knowledge, for recollection, and conducted independently of the world as a whole.

Then come the standard group of five groups of clinging (P. *upādānakkhandha*). In Sanskrit the five are: rūpa-skandha (set of material forms), vedanā-sk. (set of feelings), saṃjñā-sk. (set of ideas), saṃskāra-sk. (set of motivations), vijñāna-sk. (set of perceptions). The person should observe that, starting with the first of the five, such is the set of material forms, so do they arise and so pass away; and the same with the others of the five. And again the mindfulness is just what is necessary, and so on.

Then come the six internal and six external sense bases. The person observes the eye and its object of shapes and colors; and observes the fetter dependent on the pair. Observes the ear and its object of sounds; the nose and its smells; the tongue and its flavors; the body and its tactile objects; the mind and its object of mental natures; and observes the fetter dependent on each pair of sense bases. He also observes the getting rid of the fetters dependent on each pair, and the non-arising in the future of such fetters. Such is the mindfulness of these mental natures.

There comes the group called the "the seven Limbs of Enlightenment" (in Skt. saptabodhyaṅgāni). The standard seven in Sanskrit are: smṛti (mindfulness), dharmapravicaya (analysis of natures), viryā (striving), prīti (rapture), praśrabdhi (cathartic), samādhi (mental concentration), upekṣā (equanimity). A person should recognize whether or not possessing the member of Mindfulness. Likewise for the member Analysis of Natures, for Striving, for Rapture, for the Cathartic, for the Mental Concentration, and for the Equanimity. In each case, the person should recognize whether or not possessing the member. Such recognitions suggest to the person what to improve of these mental natures. And this is all mindfulness.

The section then went to the Four Noble Truths; but I shall postpone treating them. This in effect concludes the four Applications of Mindfulness.

Then the text discussed the length of time needed to develop these four Applications of Mindfulness. Apparently seven years is the outer limit. Fewer years are mentioned, finally just one year. And then there is mention of seven months. And then even lesser periods, down to half a month, and then just seven days. The implication is that the period of time depends on the individual. Presumably someone like Gautama Buddha would only need seven days.

8. Right Mental Concentration = Samādhi

For this section I shall select a few remarks from a translation I made years ago-namely, the part entitled "Calming the Mind"[32]. That Tibetan author mentions six essentials for newly producing a good *samādhi*: 1) Residence in a favorable place; 2) Meager desire; 3) Contentment; 4) Elimination of multiple activities; 5) Purity of morality; 6) Elimination of discursive thinking of craving, and so on. "In particular, purity of morality, seeing the disadvantages in cravings, and residence in a favorable place are the chief ones"[33].

The text gives the reason for crossed legs (or just one leg drawn in), because the upright straightness of the body prevents torpor or sleepiness[34]. "The merits of the *samādhi* to be cultivated are as follows: If calming is accomplished, there are both ample rapture in the mind and pleasure in the body, so that one dwells pleasantly in the nature (*dharma*) that is seen"[35]. "The Lord stated four meditative objects of the yogin, namely, the universal meditative object, the meditative object for purification of addiction, the meditative object for skill, and the meditative object for purification of defilement... there are four kinds of universal meditative object, reflected image with discursive thought, reflected image without discursive thought, limits of the entity, and fulfillment of the requirement"[36]. By 'limits of the entity' is meant the phenomenal limit and the noumenal limit. The text explains all four meditative objects, and which persons go with each of them.

---

[32] Alex Wayman, translator, *Calming the Mind and Discerning the Real; Buddhist Meditation and the Middle View*, from the *lam rim chen mo* of Tsoṇ-kha-pa (New York: Columbia University Press, 1978), the part "Calming the Mind" goes pp. 98-172. Motilal Banarsidass, my Delhi publishers, have put out several printings of the Indian edition.
[33] *Calming the Mind*, pp. 98-99.
[34] *Calming the Mind*, p. 101.
[35] *Calming the Mind*, p. 104.
[36] *Calming the Mind*, p. 105.

There is considerable emphasis on Mindfulness, supporting the position of Mindfulness as no. 7 of the Eightfold Noble Path; also, its list of the seven Limbs of Enlightenment provides seven terms that are frequently mentioned in this Calming section. "Hence mindfulness is the basis for the non-slipping-away of the meditative object"[37]. There are two chief faults of staying on the mediative object: fading (of the object) and scattering (to other objects), which have an extended discussion[38]. There are later emphases on the importance of Mindfulness. Having got rid of those two chief faults, there are six forces for accomplishing the path of calming: 1) By the *force of hearing*; 2) By the *force of pondering*; 3) By the *force of mindfulness*; 4) By the *force of awareness*; 5) By the *force of striving*; 6) By the *force of intimacy*[39].

Since Tsong-kha-pa treats both 'Calming the Mind' and 'Discerning the Real', he shows that the successful *samādhi* must deal with both[40], and that it does lead to Nirvāṇa. This large section on 'Calming the Mind' has rich materials on this *samādhi*. This now concludes the three parts for 'improving mind' (*adhicitta*). And this ends our treatment of the Eightfold Noble Path to show human progress.

Then just briefly on the Four Noble Truths. There is a scripture dealing with the topic in the Majjhima-Nikāya, Vol. III, no. 141, the *Saccavibhaṅgasutta*. The first Noble Truth: There is Suffering, explained with varieties of suffering, such as birth (the acquiring of sense bases), old age and dying; and grief over various calamities, as well as misery in general. The second Noble Truth: There is the Cause (or Source) of Suffering is especially in craving — for sense pleasures, for becoming, even for annihilation. The third Noble Truth of cessation is the complete stopping of that craving, with none of it left. The fourth Noble Truth is the Eightfold Noble path to that cessation; and the present essay has expanded upon the eight members. We may observe that the Buddhist theory of human progress is to become aware of the suffering in man's present situation, then how to rise above it.

---

[37] *Calming the Mind*, p. 118.
[38] *Calming the Mind*, pp. 121f.
[39] *Calming the Mind*, pp. 143-144.
[40] *Calming the Mind*, p. 159 (bottom).

Le Bouddhisme et le Bien-Être des Autres

YVES RAGUIN

Bien que le Bouddhisme insiste sur ce qu'il appelle «l'irrealité» de toutes choses, et de «la personne», cela ne l'empêche pas de vouloir donner aux hommes le bonheur. Ce bonheur ne peut pas se limiter aux conditions présentes de la condition humaine, puisque l'idéal est finalement de s'en libérer.

Ceci apparaît très clairement dans la présentation que le *Risshô Kôsei-kai* fait de lui-même. Il se présente comme un mouvement bouddhique de laïcs qui se propose de conduire les hommes au bonheur. Cet état final est entrevu comme «un état de parfaite quiétude dans lequel toutes les souffrances humaines seront éteintes»[1].

Le concile Vatican II a rappelé aux chrétiens la valeur du «monde» dans le plan de la Rédemption, et la grandeur de l'humain est rendu plus évidente encore par l'Incarnation. Toute la philosophie chrétienne de l'histoire est là pour nous faire comprendre que le développement humain est une «révélation» de l'action divine dans le monde.

Le Bouddhisme s'est lui-même trouvé en face de ce problème, il y a longtemps. L'idéal du Bouddhisme Therevâda, qui fait du moine le «vrai» bouddhiste, car lui seul a l'espoir d'arriver au nirvâna, ne trouve rien pour justifier théologiquement l'engagement dans les tâches terrestres. Jusqu'à récemment, en Thaïlande, les moines vivaient dans un monde à part, coupés de toute vie sociale et intellectuelle. Les choses changent rapidement, et l'organisation du Sangha Bouddhiste (la communauté des moines) cherche vraiment à ouvrir

---

[1] RISSHÔ KÔSSEI-KAI, *A New Buddhist Movement in Japan*. An Introduction, Tokyo, p. 8.

l'esprit des jeunes bonzes aux sciences modernes et aux problèmes du monde[2].

En Thaïlande, la réorganisation de la hiérarchie et des structures de l'Eglise bouddhique s'est inspirée des Eglises chrétiennes. Mais, bien plus important encore, c'est que l'on propose comme modèle d'activité pour les bonzes, les activités qui sont courantes parmi les prêtes catholiques. Durant le *Seminar on Buddhism and Present Thai Society*, l'un des conférenciers a demandé que les moines soient plus engagés dans les œuvres d'éducation et de jeunesse. Il leur revient d'enseigner le Bouddhisme, mais ils devraient aussi s'engager dans l'enseignement de la philosophie et, dans leurs œuvres d'éducation, mettre l'accent sur l'aspect moral et religieux[3].

On trouvera les mêmes tendances dans les autres pays où le Bouddhisme est en train de se moderniser, à Ceylan où il tient une place prépondérante, au Vietnam où il est sorti d'une longue léthargie et s'est affirmé sur le plan politique et social, à Taïwan où il crée continuellement des instituts pour l'étude du Bouddhisme; ces tendances se manifestent d'une manière toute particulière dans la fondation de ce qu'on appelle les nouvelles religions.

Dans ces nouvelles religions comme le *Risshô Kôsei-Kai*, dont il a déjà été question, le *Sôka Gakkai*, le *Reiyû-Kai*, etc. on trouve une forte proposition de traditions bouddhiques. On peut donc considérer ces nouvelles religions comme une réponse du Bouddhisme japonais à des besoins religieux, sociaux et humains, du Japon moderne. Le grand moyen d'action du *Risshô Kôsei-Kai* est la discussion en commun des problèmes personnels, sous la forme de «group counselling». On sait combien le *Sokâ Gakkai* fomente en ses membres un sens étonnant de l'entraide. Dans beaucoup des ces nouvelles

---

[2] *Buddhism and Present Thai Society*. Content of the Seminar Report on *Buddhism and present Thai Society* organized by the Siam Society. By Alfonso DE JUSAN, s.j., 1970. La tendance à l'ouverture au monde moderne est mentionnée en plusieurs endroits de ce rapport. Il existe deux résumés de ce rapport faits par le Père Paul O'BRIEN, s.j., l'un en anglais et l'autre en français. — *Renouveau bouddhiste en Thaïlande*, Chine-Madagascar, n. 130, décembre 1970-janvier 1971, p. 107. Ce texte est extrait d'un texte plus long du Père O'Brien publié dans *Asian Report* (Manila), 15 août 1970, Year II, n. 5, page 1, sous le titre: *Buddhist Revival in Thailand?*

[3] *Buddhism and Present Thai Society*, p. 18 et suiv.

religions, on pratique la guérison des maladies par la prière. Tous ces éléments contribuent à leur succès. Mais elles n'auraient pas un tel succès au Japon si elles n'étaient pas spirituellement enracinées dans les traditions les plus profondes de la culture japonaise.

Ce phénomène des nouvelles religions, toutes plus ou moins syncrétistes, n'existe pas dans tous les pays. On le retrouve au Vietnam qui a vu naître, depuis le début du siècle, deux grandes sectes qui se disent bouddhiques, mais qui sont très syncrétistes, le Caodaïsme et la secte des Hoa-Hoa[4].

Ce qui frappe dans ces nouvelles religions, c'est leur caractère pratique. Elles offrent à leurs fidèles une religion réduite à l'essentiel, et des institutions sociales.

Ici se pose pour le Bouddhisme le problème fondamental de l'engagement ou du non-engagement dans le monde. Les bouddhistes chinois s'insurgent quand on leur dit que le Bouddhisme est opposé à l'engagement dans le monde. Ils disent que le retrait du monde est une des caractéristiques du *Hinâyâna* ou Petit Véhicule, mais que la doctrine fondamentale du *Mahâyâna*, ou grand Véhicule est un souci constant des autres. C'est d'ailleurs, disent-il, l'essentiel de la doctrine du Bouddha.

Tous les bouddhistes de renom interrogés lors d'une enquête faite il y a quelques années au Japon sont d'accord pour dire que le Bouddhisme n'est pas seulement une doctrine pour l'individu et que sa nature sociale est évidente[5].

Malgré les protestations des bouddhistes du Grand Véhicule, il faut bien admettre que, même en Chine, le Bouddhisme s'était retiré dans une solitude contemplative et trop souvent oisive. Il en était de même dans les autres pays d'Asie Orientale.

Une des caractéristiques des différents renouveaux bouddhiques est précisément un retour au monde et une volonté de travailler au bien-être des hommes par l'éducation, les œuvres sociales, les hôpitaux, etc. Ce renouveau n'aboutit pas nécessairement à la fondation de «nouvelles religions»,

---

[4] Pour la situation du Bouddhisme dans les différents pays, voir *Buddhismus der Gevenwart*, publié sous la direction de H. Dumoulin, s.j., Herder, Freiburg, 1970.

[5] *Living Buddhism in Japan*. prepared by Yoshiro Tamura, Tokyo, International Institute for the Study of Religions, 1965, p. 75.

comme au Japon, mais c'est un renouveau chrétien dans lequel nous sommes engagés.

Le Bouddhisme de Corée a parfaitement conscience de la nécessité d'une modernisation, mais, comme le fait remarquer un article de la revue «Korean Buddhism», le Bouddhisme coréen est très chargé de traditions du passé. Il y a beaucoup de traditions à éliminer pour en faire un Bouddhisme des temps modernes. Mais «un effort radical de modernisation pourrait faire commettre à nouveau l'erreur de le séculariser»[6].

L'auteur de l'article cité, un jeune bonze dans la trentaine, propose un mouvement de modernisation du Bouddhisme, qui se ferait par la réalisation de trois projets: établissement d'un système moderne d'éducation pour les bonzes, travail missionnaire intensifié grâce à des méthodes modernes, et traduction en coréen moderne des ouvrages bouddhiques qui ont été composés en chinois[7].

Les difficultés ne manquent pas, continue l'auteur de l'article, mais le Bouddhisme coréen ne doit pas manquer à sa mission historique qui est «une réforme conduite avec sagesse et résolument vouée à la modernisation sur la base de la vraie tradition»[8].

C'est aussi un des aspects essentiels du Bouddhisme «Won», fondé en Corée en 1916. Le but du fondateur était d'avoir un Bouddhisme «qui marcherait au même pas que le temps et que la vie pratique»[9]. le nom «won» de cette secte veut dire «cercle». Ce cercle représente la nature du Bouddha ou l'Esprit originel de toutes les créatures. Le but du Bouddhisme est de construire un monde de bienfaisance et de gratitude[10].

Un des articles fondamentaux de cette religion dit expressément que «L'idéal du Bouddhisme Won est la construction d'un monde dans lequel la civilisation matérielle et la civilisation spirituelle seront bien harmonisées»[11].

---

[6] Citations de la revue *Han-guk Pulkyo* (Korean Buddhism) dans un article de So Kyong-su: *The Present Situation of Korean Buddhism*, dans *Korean Journal*, Vol. 11, n. 5, May 1971, p. 15.

[7] *Ibid.*

[8] *Ibid.*

[9] *Manual of Won Buddhism.* Headquarters of Won Buddhism, Iri City, Chollopukto, Rep. of Korea, p. 2.

[10] *Ibid.* p. 3.

[11] *Ibid.* p. 4.

Autrefois, dit le *Manual of Won Buddhism*, «la vie des moines bouddhistes en Corée pouvait être décrite comme une vie monastique dans les montagnes écartées, sans relation avec l'existence humaine dans le concret. Pour cette raison nous prétendons que le Bouddhisme doit marcher de pair avec notre vie quotidienne»[12].

On trouverait les mêmes affirmations dans la plupart des autres manifestes des bouddhistes en quête de renouveau, que ce soit à Hong Kong, à Taïwan, au Vietnam, en Indonésie, ou ailleurs.

Tandis que les théoriciens du Bouddhisme essaient de faire prendre conscience aux fidèles que leur doctrine implique un constant souci des autres et qu'elle doit être une lumière pour la société humaine, les organisations bouddhiques s'engagent dans des œuvres caritatives de toutes sortes. Il suffit de suivre les nouvelles du monde bouddhique dans les revues pour voir surgir des hôpitaux bouddhiques, des orphelinats bouddhiques, des asiles pour les vieillards, des dispensaires, etc. Après les typhons ou autres calamités, les Associations bouddhiques de Taïwan organisent des collectes pour le sinistrés et des équipes de secours. Chaque année, les Bouddhistes organisent une grande quête dans les rues de Taipei, pour ce qu'on appelle le «secours d'hiver».

Les Associations bouddhiques de Hong Kong ont, en 1970, ajouté un grand hôpital à leurs autres entreprises.

Il est certain qu'en cela le Bouddhisme a subi l'influence du Christianisme. Souvent, dans leurs revues, les bouddhistes font remarquer que dans ce domaine ils désirent imiter les chrétiens.

Ces œuvres de charité influent sur leur conception même de l'existence. Les réalités de la vie humaine prennent un sens beaucoup plus profond. Il ne suffit pas de prêcher la libération de cette existence. Il faut aider cette existence à devenir meilleure. On est étonné, en lisant certains articles destinés aux classes instruites, de voir combien les textes rappellent, par le ton et par le contenu, les textes de Vatican II sur l'Eglise dans le monde. Le détachement fait place à un réel engagement, et la compassion détachée à un véritable amour.

---

[12] *Ibid.* p. 7.

Un changement d'attitude du Bouddhisme en général se fait sentir très fort depuis la fin de la dernière guerre. Les Bouddhistes adoptent déjà en bien des endroits un nouveau style de vie. «Les études sur le terrain faites par de anthropologues durant les dix dernières années nous permettent, écrit Jacobson, d'être vraiment spécifiques pour ce qui est du rôle du Bouddhisme dans la modernisation. Des moines, dans les pays du Theravâda, écrivent des tracts sur le problèmes du développement, proposant des normes d'épargne, de diligence, et de travail ardu, qui auraient contraint Max Weber lui-même à corriger son image de l'éthique bouddhique et de l'ordre établi en Asie. Des personnes «orientées-vers-le-nirvâna» (*nibbâna-oriented*) semblent avoir la réelle discipline intérieure, aussi bien que l'expérience en matière d'organisation sociale, qui est demandée pour que la modernisation soit facilitée. Elles son souvent orientées vers de réalisations, développant de nouveaux programmes d'action sociale, d'éducation moderne, de santé publique, d'action politique domestique et internationale. Leur position de guides en matières plus spécifiquement spirituelles n'est nullement compromise par tout ce «mouvement révolutionnaire moderne», comme un livre appelle la renaissance du Bouddhisme dans le Sud-Est asiatique. Les Bouddhistes sont de plus en plus nombreux qui savent, comme le roi Asoka, qu'il «n'y a pas de plus grande devoir que le bien-être du monde entier»[13].

Il y a bien, continue Jacobson, des oppositions à la modernisation, mais, par exemple, en Inde la Maha Bodhi Society a depuis un demi-siècle joué un rôle de premier plan pour obtenir un changement dans l'ordre social. Si à Ceylan les moines qui tirent leurs revenus de larges terres sont souvent opposés à la modernisation, dans ce même pays les dirigeants du Bouddhisme ont depuis plus d'un siècle été dans le domaine social militants et, par moments, révolutionnaires[14].

Pour conclure cette section, il faut en revenir à cette remarque faite par les Bouddhistes qui comprennent la portée

---

[13] Nolan Pliny JACOBSON, *Buddhism, modernization, and science.* In *Philosophy East and West*, April 1970, p. 160. Le livre cité plus haut est de Ernst BENZ, *Buddhism or Communism: Which holds the Future of Asia?* Garden City, N.Y., Doubleday and C° 1965, p. 133.

[14] JACOBSON, *Art. cité*, p. 161.

du vrai *dharma*. Si un bouddhiste est délivré de tout attachement à un moi qui n'a pas de réalité, il est naturellement ouvert aux autres et aux problèmes du monde moderne. L'idéal du bouddhiste et la totale libération de l'idée de «soi» et donc de tout désir de possession. Ce qu'il cherche, c'est la liberté à l'égard de lui-même, à l'égard de la loi du *karma*, à l'égard de tout ce qui actualise le *karma* dans des formes historiques et sociales. La révolution que le Bouddhisme tend à réaliser, s'il est fidèle à lui-même, ne peut se concrétiser dans les buts d'une révolution socio-politique. «Les buts que le Bouddhisme se propose d'atteindre, lit-on dans une étude sur le Bouddhisme et la Révolution, sont hors de tout contexte social ou politique; aussi la source ultime de l'esprit révolutionnaire du Bouddhisme se trouve par-delà tout contexte historique et social: il ne commence ni ne s'achève jamais dans aucune forme d'ordre social. Paradoxalement, alors, c'est précisément cette vue fondamentalement asociale et négative du Bouddhisme sur la société qui en fait une philosophie de la révolution perpétuelle»[15]. Et c'est ce qui fait que l'engagement social du Bouddhiste n'aura jamais le caractère théologiquement essentiel qu'à l'engagement chrétien fondé sur la valeur d'expression du divin que le chrétien reconnaît à la personne humaine, à l'histoire et à la création entière.

Les grands maîtres du Bouddhisme actuel répètent que le Bouddhisme est la seule religion qui puisse apporter un remède aux maux dont souffre l'Occident, tout particulièrement à son activisme. A cette fin il offre les méthodes de contemplation élaborées par les différentes écoles du Zen. Si paradoxal que cela puisse paraître, en offrant le Zen et ses méthodes, le Bouddhisme moderne répond effectivement à un des grands problèmes du monde actuel. Le Zen est en effet une méthode de découverte de l'intériorité, donc une voie de libération des contraintes de la société et de la vie moderne.

Mais, pour être juste, il faut dire que si l'attrait pour le Zen est très grand aux Etats-Unis d'Amérique et en Europe, il l'est certainement moins au Japon ou dans les autres pays d'Asie orientale. Ce serait donc une erreur de croire que le

---

[15] R. PULIGANDHA et K. PUHAKKA, *Buddhism and revolution*. Dans *Philosophy East and West*, Oct. 1970, p. 354.

Zen est très répandu dans les pays bouddhiques. La manière dont les nouvelles religions du Japon répondent aux besoins du monde moderne n'est pas le Zen.

Il reste cependant que le Zen est ce qui, dans le Bouddhisme, offre le plus d'attrait pour les non bouddhistes d'Europe ou d'Amérique. Les bouddhistes qui réfléchissent aux problèmes de l'Occident voient bien que la sécularisation, le progrès matériel, l'engagement trop violent dans les tâches extérieures, tout cela laisse dans l'âme une insatisfaction qui ne peut être comblée que par un retour à l'intériorité. Il offre donc une «intériorité» qui reste humaine et s'épanouit dans la saisie directe de soi. Le Zen permet de pousser la découverte de l'intériorité aux limites de l'humain, sans pourtant l'ouvrir sur le divin. La richesse du Zen est donc finalement sa limitation. Dans le Zen l'ultime expérience, que l'on peut définir comme saisie directe de notre être, ne peut être perçue comme «saisie» de Dieu.

Le problème du Zen dans le monde moderne est tellement particulier que je me contente d'y faire allusion ici. D'ailleurs il semble aller à l'encontre des efforts faits par le Bouddhisme pour s'engager dans les tâches humaines. En fait, il n'en est rien. Mais comme je viens de le dire, ce problème est trop complexe pour pouvoir être étudié ici.

Alla Ricerca della Giustizia:
La Chiesa in dialogo con la società
in Sud-Est Asia

FABC

Riportiamo la «riflessione pastorale», esito del Colloquio dei vescovi del Sud-Est asiatico a cui hanno partecipato vescovi della Thailandia, Filippine, Malaysia, Singapore; c'erano anche, come invitati, vescovi del Giappone, Bangladesh e Sri Lanka. Svoltosi in Thailandia dal 9 al 12 novembre 1987 sul tema del dialogo tra Chiesa e società, il Colloquio è stato promosso dalla Federazione delle Conferenze episcopali dell'Asia (FABC).

Introduzione

Dal 9 al 12 novembre 1987 alcuni di noi, vescovi del Sud-Est asiatico, impegnati nelle nostre rispettive nazioni nel lavoro per la Pace e la Giustizia, ci siamo incontrati in Thailandia per riflettere sul ruolo della Chiesa nella società. Questo nostro incontro di riflessione ha avuto come occasione il XX anniversario della enciclica di Paolo VI, Populorum Progressio. Stesa due anni dopo la fine del Concilio Vaticano II, la lettera enciclica era in linea con la «Gaudium et Spes» (la Chiesa nel mondo moderno) e spiegava il significato di «sviluppo». Esso deve essere autentico e integrale, non limitato alla sola crescita economica: deve cioè promuovere il bene di ogni uomo e di tutto l'uomo. Quattro anni dopo la Populorum Progressio, il Sinodo dei Vescovi affermava con tutta forza e chiarezza che l'azione per la giustizia e la partecipazione alla trasformazione del mondo sono dimensioni costitutive dell'annuncio del Vangelo, che è la missione della Chiesa (Vedi «Giustizia nel Mondo» - Introduzione). Il nostro incontro si è proposto uno scambio di vedute sulla nostra comune missione nelle società del Sud-Est asiatico, una verifica dei nostri orientamenti per la scelta preferenziale per i poveri, di unire le nostre forze nella comunione e sollecitare una più efficace responsabilità collegiale.

A. Situazione del Sud-Est asiatico

Nella nostra analisi delle realtà del Sud-Est asiatico, a cominciare da quella delle nostre rispettive nazioni, abbiamo notato alcuni punti in comune, tra cui i seguenti:

1. Tutte le nostre nazioni sono impegnate seriamente in programmi di sviluppo. Tali programmi, tuttavia, sono orientati soprattutto verso l'aspetto economico a spese, spesso, di uno sviluppo integrale.

2. I profitti non sono condivisi con giustizia con i lavoratori.

3. Quanto viene prodotto, in generale, non è per i bisogni fondamentali della gente, ma per soddisfare i bisogni del mercato internazionale. Ciò fa aumentare i prezzi dei prodotti basilari, e la povertà cresce.

4. I Governi tendono a salvaguardare gli interessi degli investitori invece che i bisogni dei lavoratori. Le leggi o i vari emendamenti alle leggi vengono effettuati per salvaguardare maggiormente gli interessi dei primi.

5. Chi alza la voce per difendere e promuovere i diritti dei lavoratori, viene facilmente etichettato come sovversivo, marxista o comunista.

6. Quasi tutte le nostre nazioni hanno leggi che permettono di incarcerare cittadini senza processo per ragioni di sicurezza nazionale.

7. L'educazione alla giustizia, alla libertà e alla collaborazione, è spesso vista come minaccia alla sicurezza nazionale.

Questi non sono, in verità, problemi nuovi e continueranno a tormentarci ancora per lungo tempo. Essi sono parte integrante dei problemi della povertà e del sottosviluppo, dello sfruttamento e dell'oppressione. L'averli riportati alla nostra attenzione ci ha aiutati a capire in profondità le parole pronunciate da Gesù per definire l'area in cui la Chiesa deve lottare: «Voi siete nel mondo». Come durante altre nostre discussioni, siamo stati colpiti dalle divergenze esistenti nelle varie nazioni e, di conseguenza, dalle varie posizioni: la Chiesa è una piccola minoranza che lotta e che non può assumere un preminente ruolo profetico nella società, come è invece avvenuto nella recente storia della Chiesa filippina. Questa posizione minoritaria della Chiesa ha provocato in noi il bisogno di tenere in considerazione le divergenze culturali nella lotta per la giustizia. Il concetto stesso di giustizia non sembra abbia un significato univoco per tutte le culture. Inoltre ci rendiamo conto che i problemi del Sud-Est asiatico hanno una rilevanza mondiale, basata sulla natura storica dello sviluppo socio-politico della nostra area e sulla natura del sistema economico mondiale, che rende più ricche le nazioni già ricche, e più povere quelle povere. Questo fatto ci fa riflettere sulle enormi possibilità che ci si aprono se solo prendessimo seriamente in considerazione il carattere «mondiale» della Chiesa. Cosa potrebbe accadere se le preoccupazioni dei vescovi asiatici (p.e., le ingiustizie nel sistema commerciale mondiale e lo sfruttamento economico) venissero affrontate dalle Conferenze episcopali del Primo Mondo per farne oggetto di pressione sui rispettivi governi?

Questa riflessione è diventata ancora più urgente in seguito alle crisi in atto — con gravi ripercussioni sulle Chiese locali — in Singapore e Malaysia, dove numerose persone sono state arrestate ed imprigionate senza processo in nome della sicurezza nazionale; o nelle Filippine, dove una democrazia ancora in fasce sta lottando per la sopravvivenza. Abbiamo anche riflettuto sulla situazione in altre nazioni dell'Asia, come le pressioni verso la liberalizzazione a Taiwan, in Cina, a Hong Kong e Corea del Sud, e il conflitto razziale nello Sri Lanka, da dove proprio oggi ci è giunta la notizia, che ci riempie di costernazione e tristezza, della tragica uccisione di un sacerdote religioso.

B. LA VIA VERSO LO SVILUPPO

Scambiandoci le nostre esperienze, abbiamo espresso le nostre ansie e speranze di sviluppo, di giustizia e pace nelle nostre rispettive nazioni e nella nostra regione asiatica.

B.1 *Il bisogno di un nuovo modello: dare potere alla gente*

Lo sviluppo nella nostra regione ha sempre cercato di scimmiottare l'industrializzazione dei paesi del Primo Mondo con una forte dipendenza sulle esportazioni e sull'alta tecnologia. Ciò ha portato ad un neocolonialismo ed a pesanti deficit ed indebitamenti. Noi siamo convinti che le nazioni abbiano bisogno di cercare un modello di sviluppo che, pur non chiudendosi alle richieste del sistema mondiale di mercato, sia capace di portare all'auto-sufficienza e di prendere atto delle storie culturali dei nostri popoli. Tale macro-concetto ci porta a guardare allo sviluppo della nostra gente a livello di villaggio. Notiamo così i numerosi contributi positivi delle Chiese locali nella formazione e nella coscientizzazione della nostra gente, specialmente i poveri, verso la propria realizzazione, la coscienza della propria dignità e del proprio valore, delle realtà socio-economiche e politiche in cui essi lottano, e del loro potere. Questo richiederà uno sforzo sistematico teso all'organizzazione e guida delle comunità, compito urgente nelle nostre culture in qualche maniera condizionate da tradizionali atteggiamenti di dipendenza e rispetto per processi autoritari piuttosto che democratici e liberali. Per cui abbiamo ritenuto necessario riflettere sulla lotta per i diritti umani, data la presente situazione di repressione in certe nazioni, questione rilevante nelle preoccupazioni pastorali delle nostre Chiese sorelle in quelle nazioni. Siamo convinti che non può avvenire un'autentica liberazione dove i diritti alla libertà non sono rispettati (Libertà cristiana e liberazione, ç 13).

B.2 *Solidarietà*

Il Sinodo dei vescovi del 1971 ha già fatto rilevare la infrastruttura di dominio a livello mondiale che indica la subdola natura di numerose strutture e relazioni sociali. Riteniamo che la lotta contro il male richieda la collaborazione di ogni settore della società, anche a livello mondiale (Giustizia nel mondo, ç 26). Perciò notiamo con gioia che la rete di solidarietà sui temi della pace e della giustizia cresce all'interno delle differenti fedi religiose e tra persone di buona volontà.

La profondità e la portata di tale solidarietà nel Sud-Est asiatico e in altre regioni non è ancora adeguata come dovrebbe. Vari fattori, tra cui gli strumenti di comunicazione e i valori culturali, ci impediscono di realizzare una solidarietà totale. Ma la solidarietà è uno dei principi basilari enunciati con chiarezza dagli insegnamenti sociali della Chiesa. Essa è fondata sulla fratellanza umana e la dignità della persona umana (cfr. Libertà cristiana e Liberazione, ç 73 e ç 17). La solidarietà è espressione di amore evangelico.

B.3 *Il ruolo della fede e dell'ideologia*

L'amore evangelico è alla radice di ogni nostro sforzo verso un giusto sviluppo. Ecco perché abbiamo dovuto riflettere sulla fede e sull'ideologia. Le ideologie sono necessarie per lo sviluppo. Senza di esse non vi sarebbe un piano possibile e razionale per l'ordine nazionale. Con esse si delinea una direzione e viene dato un impulso. Tuttavia, nella prospettiva di fede attraverso cui noi dobbiamo sempre vedere le realtà terrene, le ideologie sono relative. Esse vanno giudicate in relazione ai valori del Regno di Dio: la giustizia, la pace, la verità e l'amore. Quando una ideologia viene assolutizzata, essa diventa un sostitutivo della fede stessa e giustificazione di ogni decisione nelle vicende umane. Grazie al primato della fede noi vediamo la repressione dei diritti umani in nome della sicurezza nazionale in alcune nazioni della nostra regione, ed il sistematico ricorso alla violenza in nome della liberazione nazionale in altre. Crediamo che ogni passo verso un'autentica liberazione deve essere segnato dalla giustizia e i fini non giustificano i mezzi. C'è una moralità dei «fini» così come una moralità dei «mezzi». Tale è il rapporto fede-giustizia.

B.4 *Gesù il liberatore*

Per questa ragione noi guardiamo a Gesù che si presenta come liberatore. Lui è il modello della prassi cristiana. La radicalità della sua vita e del suo messaggio emerge nell'apparente assurdità del cammino che egli ha intrapreso per la nostra liberazione integrale. Il Mistero Pasquale, come altri misteri di salvezza, sfida ogni analisi sociale scientifica, essendo forza e sapienza di Dio. Nessuna meraviglia perciò se la via del dialogo e della non violenza attiva è sempre per il cristiano la via più adeguata alle esigenze dell'amore evangelico (cfr. Libertà cristiana e liberazione, çç 77 e 80), così come efficacemente rappresentato dalla autodonazione e dalla totale vulnerabilità di Gesù in Croce. Tale via ci richiama alla mente le altre parole del Signore: «Voi non siete di questo mondo».

C. LA NECESSARIA SPIRITUALITÀ

La Chiesa è nel mondo ma non è di questo mondo. Questa oggettiva natura storica della Chiesa ci indica anche quale tipo di spiritualità è richiesto dalla comunità dei credenti nella via verso la realizzazione del Regno. Gli elementi di questa spiritualità sono comuni a tutti i membri della comunità dei credenti in Gesù. Essi danno la definizione della persona spirituale, come pure del cammino di autentica liberazione in Cristo, verso la giustizia e la pace. Nella nostra riflessione, abbiamo messo in evidenza alcuni elementi di questa spiritualità.

C.1 *La convocazione al Regno*

Innanzitutto non possiamo mai presupporre che l'Utopia sia da realizzare entro un tempo storico. Questo elemento della nostra fede dovrebbe spingerci a rifiutare perentoriamente le pretese delle messianiche ideologie temporali che promettono il cielo in terra. La chiamata del Signore è sempre verso un «essere di più», un processo dinamico che non è raggiunto mai completamente in nessun dato momento. D'altra parte, il Regno che deve venire, come un seme, ci chiama ora a coinvolgerci nelle vicende di questo mondo, ad immergerci nella lotta della gente, a «cercare di fare di più, di conoscere di più, ad avere di più per essere di più» (PP, ç 66).

C.2 *L'opzione preferenziale per i poveri*

La vera persona spirituale è quella che si identifica con i poveri, come ha fatto Gesù il Liberatore. Egli non solo ha fatto delle azioni per loro. Egli ha camminato con loro, è diventato «povero per amor nostro, così che noi potessimo diventare ricchi». Egli li ha chiamati ai misteri più profondi delle loro esistenze vissute come dono di Dio, dalla fame di pane deperibile alla comunione di vita con Dio. Il suo amore e il suo servizio hanno abbracciato tutti coloro che mettevano a nudo la propria totale povertà davanti al Padre, e solo gli arroganti e i superbi si sono chiusi alla libertà e alla liberazione che egli offriva. Così deve essere la persona spirituale: in solidarietà d'amore con i poveri di questo mondo. La misura della sua liberazione dipenderà dalla misura della sua vita e del suo servizio all'ultimo dei fratelli di Dio (Mt 25).

C.3 *La dimensione comunitaria della spiritualità*

Il movimento dall'individualismo al senso comunitario è uno dei segni luminosi che vediamo nella Chiesa. Percepiamo questo nelle Comunità Ecclesiali di Base e in altri movimenti laicali. In un mondo di conflitti e divisioni la persona spirituale percepisce la dimensione comunitaria dei Sacramenti che diventano per la comunità un condividere l'azione liberatrice di Gesù nel Mistero Pasquale. Tale persona metterà i bisogni e gli interessi della comunità al di sopra di quelli personali. Essere per gli altri diventerà l'impulso che guida la sua vita.

C.4 *Preghiera e contemplazione*

Oltre al modello di vita di Gesù, la persona spirituale integrerà le dimensioni attiva e contemplativa della vita umana, in modo tale che l'una motivi e generi l'altra. Notiamo con rammarico che molti delle nostre sorelle e dei nostri fratelli nella fede più dotati e preparati, cadono nei due estremi di totale ritiro o dalle vicende umane o dalla preghiera e contemplazione. Gesù era attivo per eccellenza, eppure si ritirava spesso nella solitudine in preghiera al Padre. Per questo noi crediamo che «i più alti valori dell'amore e dell'amicizia, della preghiera e della contemplazione, permetteranno la pienezza di un autentico sviluppo» (PP, ç 20).

D. Implicanze pastorali

Siamo consapevoli che le nostre riflessioni non hanno potuto coprire tutto l'ampio spazio che il rapporto tra Chiesa e società ricopre. Tuttavia nel breve periodo di tempo in cui abbiamo riflettuto insieme, abbiamo raggiunto alcune concrete indicazioni valevoli per noi nel nostro lavoro pastorale:

1. Il nostro lavoro di evangelizzazione e coscientizzazione deve continuare con sempre maggiore intensità, specialmente tra gli strati poveri della nostra società. Questo richiederà più ampi corsi per la formazione di leaders e per l'organizzazione delle comunità, in modo che il compito di rendere la gente capace di ottenere libertà, giustizia e pace diventi veramente una preoccupazione della gente stessa. Ciò richiederà il sostegno delle organizzazioni popolari.

2. Dobbiamo continuare a difendere e promuovere la dignità umana e diritti della gente nella nostra regione, prescindendo da razza, religione, classe e ideologia. Di fronte al Dio della storia ogni persona è uguale e deve, allo stesso modo, essere un buon Samaritano.

3. Abbiamo visto il bisogno di una più profonda e più estesa solidarietà tra le varie fedi religiose e tra persone di buona volontà. Alla luce della fede tale solidarietà è ancora più urgente e come imperativo di amore evangelico ci domanda maggiore attenzione. Dovremo esplorare vie più creative ed efficaci di mutua collaborazione per un giusto sviluppo e per la pace.

4. Perché l'impegno di costruire un mondo giusto e pacifico dia i suoi frutti, deve essere lo Spirito del Signore che lo inizia e che lo porta a compimento. La persona che cammina nello Spirito è l'agente-cooperatore nel lavoro di liberazione. Dobbiamo sostenere lo sviluppo di una tale persona chiarendo gli elementi di una spiritualità che sia adatta ai nostri tempi.

5. In modo più specifico il nostro suggerimento finale si rivolge alla nostra stessa Federazione delle Conferenze Episcopali dell'Asia (FABC). Abbiamo notato che nessun organismo della FABC è stato creato ufficialmente o demandato ad impegnarsi nei problemi della giustizia e della pace. Sebbene l'Ufficio per lo Sviluppo Umano abbia fatto e continui a fare una grande mole di lavoro in questo settore cruciale

della vita asiatica, tale compito è stato informale ed è solo uno dei suoi numerosi compiti. Chiediamo che la FABC chiarisca la situazione e prenda le misure appropriate richieste dalla lotta per la giustizia in Asia. Per facilitare il lavoro di coordinamento a livello di FABC, si deve maggiormente incoraggiare il coordinamento ai livelli diocesano, nazionale e regionale.

Finito di stampare l'8 maggio 1998
Tipografia Poliglotta della Pontificia Università Gregoriana
Piazza della Pilotta, 4 – 00187 Roma